THE MORALS OF MARKETS

AND RELATED ESSAYS

A Liberty Press Edition

Harry Burrows Acton was born in 1908. He was educated at Magdalen College, Oxford (1927–1931) and taught philosophy at University College, Swansea, and at Bedford College, London, from 1931 to 1940. He was with the Ministry of Supply and Board of Trade from 1940 to 1945. He was professor of philosophy at Bedford College from 1945 to 1965 and professor of moral philosophy at the University of Edinburgh until his death on 16 June 1974. He was a visiting professor of philosophy at the University of Chicago in 1949, was president of the Aristotelian Society in 1952–3, and was editor of *Philosophy* from October 1956 until July 1972.

H. B. ACTON

THE MORALS
OF MARKETS
AND RELATED
ESSAYS

EDITED BY DAVID GORDON

AND JEREMY SHEARMUR

LIBERTY FUND

Indianapolis

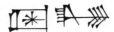

Foreword and other editorial additions © 1993 by Jeremy Shearmur and David Gordon. For permissions and other copyright information see page xxii. All rights reserved. All inquiries should be addressed to Liberty Fund, Inc., 8335 Allison Pointe Trail, Suite 300, Indianapolis, IN 46250-1687. This book was manufactured in the United States of America.

Frontispiece photo courtesy Mrs. Barbara Acton.

Library of Congress Cataloging-in-Publication Data

Acton, H. B. (Harry Burrows), 1908–1974
    The morals of markets and related essays / H.B. Acton ; edited by David Gordon and Jeremy Shearmur.
       p.   cm.
    Includes bibliographical references and index.
    ISBN 0-86597-106-4 (alk. paper). — ISBN 0-86597-107-2 (pbk. : alk. paper)
    1. Business ethics.   2. Capitalism—Moral and ethical aspects.
I. Gordon, David, 1948–   .   II. Shearmur, Jeremy, 1948–   .
III. Title
HF5387.A252   1993
174'.4—dc20   92-42151
                                                CIP

10   9   8   7   6   5   4   3   2   1

CONTENTS

FOREWORD

Harry Burrows Acton (1908–1974) was a prolific scholar with particularly wide-ranging interests in philosophy and its history. Although his earliest work was on metaphysics, his principal reputation rests on his writings in three fields: moral and political philosophy, the history of modern philosophy, and the critical study of Marxism. He served for many years as editor of the Royal Institute of Philosophy's journal, *Philosophy,* and he also had a long-standing interest in French philosophy.

Acton's approach to political philosophy in some ways resembles that of F. A. Hayek. Acton and Hayek both wrote in defense of a market-based society at a time when such ideas were unfashionable. Also, both writers often set out their own views through discussion of the history of ideas. Those who enjoy reading Hayek but do not know of Acton's work are in for a treat. However, as the reader will discover, there are some significant differences between them, both in points of philosophical argument and in their broader approach. Acton is more of a traditionalist than Hayek, and he is also more concerned with issues of morality.

The centerpiece of this collection is *The Morals of Markets.* This work is of lasting interest because Acton has wise things to say about so many of the questions that will occur to the thoughtful person concerning the morality of markets. It also addresses a central topic in political theory:

the constraints that morality imposes upon forms of social organization.

Republication today is timely. Marxism—like the poor—will always be with us. But the collapse of the Soviet Union and of "Marxist" regimes in Eastern Europe has served, for the time being, to dampen enthusiasm both for Marxism and for the centrally directed, state-run economies with which it became associated. In addition, there is now a widespread recognition of the practical effectiveness of market-based forms of economic organization. All this, in turn, makes it likely that the *moral* criticism of markets will come back into fashion. Marxism, while rooted in moral concerns, disavowed an explicitly moral approach to social issues. Instead, it emphasized political economy and the idea that a radical change from a market-based economic system to socialism was needed. For a long while, debate about these issues overshadowed other kinds of critical discussion of markets—notably the moral objections raised by such writers as Carlyle, Ruskin, and Tawney. The recent events are likely to focus critical attention once more upon moral issues raised by market economies. *The Morals of Markets* addresses just these issues.

Acton engages in a campaign on two fronts. He endeavors to refute claims that a free market economy is immoral, and he argues that a market-based economy best accords with ethical requirements and with prudence. The tasks are distinct. To show that arguments against the market fail does not by itself prove that moral reasons favor the market. Similarly, to adduce ethical advantages of a market economy leaves untouched the worth of arguments that challenge the market's legitimacy. A full defense of the free market requires attention to both sorts of argument. Acton meets this twofold task with a considerable measure of success.

He pays special attention to a line of criticism advanced against the market by John Ruskin in the nineteenth century and R. H. Tawney in the early twentieth century. They contrasted the craftsmen of the Middle Ages devoted to their art, and the conscientious professional dedicated to his clients, with the modern businessman who—it is claimed—ignores all else but profit.

These arguments are no mere museum pieces. Concerns like Ruskin's are expressed today at every turn: from discussions of popular culture and mass production in newspapers to the social criticism of the Frankfurt School. Two socialist critics of Reagan's America and Thatcher's Britain recently drew attention to the work of Tawney when seeking to identify a "central feature of the British political tradition that free-market conservatism has yet to displace."[1] Michael Walzer—and other "communitarian" political theorists—criticizes market-based societies for allowing the businessman to have too much influence, to the detriment of other social groups. And the recent influential work of philosopher Alistair MacIntyre displays a deep hostility to a market-based society, based in large part upon the supposed opposition between free markets and traditional conceptions of virtue.[2] *The Morals of Markets* poses a strong challenge to such views by arguing for the fundamental compatibility between market-based social arrangements and traditional ideas about morality and virtue.

Acton does not share the optimistic view of some eighteenth-century writers that markets will always lead us to

1. Kenneth Hoover and Raymond Plant. *Conservative Capitalism in Britain and the United States: A Critical Appraisal.* London and New York: Routledge, 1989, p. 280.

2. Michael Walzer. *Spheres of Justice.* New York: Basic Books, 1983, and Alistair MacIntyre. *After Virtue.* Notre Dame, IN: University of Notre Dame Press, 1981.

the best possible social conditions. But he endorses the view that, within markets, people provide for others while working for themselves. This furnishes him with a broad moral justification for the businessman's endeavor to make a profit—an activity, he insists, that should be seen as on a moral par with the activities of other participants in markets, including consumers and those working for a wage. He further argues that such activities do not amount to attempts to take advantage of others in a vicious sense.

Acton rebuts the idea that engagement in markets is at odds with a concern for the well-being of others. He also stresses that, within markets, there are opportunities for the practise of such virtues as justice, honesty, and reliability. But what of the Christian virtues of humility, charity, and self-sacrifice? Acton suggests that it is absurd to think that such virtues could properly be exercised by business firms (although he does point out that there may be room for such activity *within* them). However, Acton insists that markets are not coextensive with society. Those engaged in markets may do so because of their other concerns: for their family, for their religion, or for philanthropy. Not only do these other spheres of their lives allow for the exercise of other virtues, but it is the successful discharge of their activities in the marketplace that makes it possible for people to fulfil their responsibilities in these other areas.

Acton's argument is careful and, we think, telling not least because he draws attention to some of the concrete realities of our day-to-day lives which can easily be lost sight of in discussions of these issues.

Before turning to another criticism of the market, it is worthwhile to pause here, as the point just made brings out an important element in Acton's philosophy. He strongly emphasizes the importance of traditional virtues such as self-reliance, honesty, and thrift. A point that worried him about classical liberalism was that its constant emphasis on criticism might undermine the essential bedrock of morality—as he makes clear in "Tradition and Some Other Forms of Order." John Stuart Mill and other classical liberals emphasized the need to expose all ideas to debate. In this view, commonly accepted institutions should also be submitted to continuing reappraisal. Opponents of Mill feared that if people were to subject their institutions to such scrutiny, society might lack sufficient stability. Distinctively, Acton combined a classical liberal interest in discussion with a concern for tradition.

The problem with which Acton was engaged has been discussed at considerable length by the sociologist Daniel Bell in *The Cultural Contradictions of Capitalism*. As his title suggests, Bell is inclined to think that the freedom of decision upon which a market society is founded sits together uneasily with the emphasis upon tradition that he thinks necessary for its culture. Bell regards this as an unresolved tension in contemporary free societies. In this he has been seconded by Irving Kristol.[3] Acton's substantially more optimistic assessment of the prospects for overcoming this tension, in these essays, merits careful consideration. Acton is alive to the importance of cultural tradition, but he is far from thinking that a free market undermines it.

Acton's analysis thus responds in advance to Kristol's and Bell's concerns that a free economy is self-undermining—

---

3. Daniel Bell. *The Cultural Contradictions of Capitalism*. London: Heinemann, 1976. Irving Kristol. *Two Cheers for Capitalism*. New York: Basic Books, 1978; see the Epilogue, " 'When Virtue Loses All Her Loveliness'—Some Reflections on Capitalism and the 'Free Society,' " pp. 255–70.

that the very abundance that capitalism creates will be the source of its downfall. It has been claimed that people will become soft and interested primarily in luxury: that they will cease to have the virtues necessary to carry on the system. (This concern has more recently been explored by Fred Hirsch and by many commentators on his work.[4]) No doubt Acton would have agreed with these writers that, for its continuance, capitalism demands that the members of a society have certain virtues. But, in Acton's opinion, there is nothing inevitable about a lapse from thrift and moderation. Character is not *determined* by the economic system, which, as Acton notes, is but a part of people's lives.

Some critics of the market take a different tack. They do not reject it altogether as a mechanism for distribution. They contend, however, that some goods and services—food, housing, and medical care are most frequently mentioned— are too vital to be left to the vagaries of market supply. These goods are essential for survival: to ensure a decent life for all, everyone must have unimpeded access to them. This argument has become one of the most influential in current political theory. Bernard Williams, for instance, has claimed that there is a natural principle of distribution for goods such as medical care. Medicine should be distributed strictly on the basis of medical need.[5] Money should not be a factor in the allocation of care: why should rich people get better care than others? Michael Walzer has extended Williams's point and made of it a full-scale social theory, in *Spheres of Justice.*[6] From a somewhat different angle, the point features

4. Fred Hirsch. *Social Limits to Growth.* London: Routledge & Kegan Paul, 1977. A. Ellis and K. Kumar, eds. *Dilemmas of Liberal Democracy.* London and New York: Tavistock, 1983.

5. Bernard Williams. "The Idea of Equality." *Problems of the Self.* Cambridge: Cambridge University Press, 1973.

6. See note 2, above.

heavily in John Rawls's celebrated *A Theory of Justice*.[7]
Rawls thinks that everyone must possess certain "primary
goods": those things any rational person will require for a
decent life.

Acton does not directly challenge the concept of a natural
principle of distribution, as Robert Nozick does in *Anarchy,
State, and Utopia*,[8] although he does argue that poverty and
misfortune are evils but not injustices. He is not unsympa-
thetic to the idea that there should be public provision in
reserve, when people encounter problems that they cannot
meet from their own resources. But he argues strongly for
the desirability of people meeting their own needs to the
extent that they can. For instance, a system of private, for-
profit, medical provision would be better than a single system to which everyone belongs, within which all medical
needs are met without payment.

His argument against the latter system invites us to look at
how it would function in practical terms. After the manner
of "public choice" analysis,[9] Acton invites us to consider
what would happen if people were to pursue their interests
within such a system, acting on their own understanding of
their needs. In such a system, he argues, if a few individuals
make excessive claims, others will be induced to press their
claims, in self-defence. The outcome, Acton suggests, will be
that "some of the well-to-do are likely to be much more
effective in obtaining special benefits than the less articulate
among the poor"[10]—an argument that anticipates the results of empirical study of the working of the British Na-

7. John Rawls. *A Theory of Justice.* Cambridge, MA: Harvard University
Press, 1971.

8. Robert Nozick. *Anarchy, State, and Utopia.* New York: Basic Books, 1974.

9. For a useful introduction, see J. Buchanan. *The Economics of Politics.* London: Institute of Economic Affairs, 1970.

10. See below, page 116.

tional Health Service, undertaken many years after Acton wrote.[11]

The abiding value of *The Morals of Markets* is its endeavor to identify, and to meet, some of the most central among the moral objections to markets. Acton discusses whether the profit motive makes virtues out of the vices of selfishness and avarice. He considers the claim that the strife of competition should be replaced by cooperation, and he looks at whether a competitive market order is chaotic and unjust by comparison with a planned economy. He discusses the claim that competition must lead to monopoly and to tyranny and the criticism that justice and morality are inevitably lost sight of within the impersonalities of a market system.

It is difficult to think of another work by a writer sympathetic to markets that engages such a range of important issues. Acton's work is particularly valuable because so many of the leading proponents of markets have put more traditional moral concerns to one side and have argued in terms of freedom, well-being, and efficiency. These are important matters, of course, but Acton draws our attention to issues of morality, and to the importance of the *morals* of markets.

A number of Acton's shorter works supplement his full-scale analysis of the market, and several of these have been included here. *The Ethics of Capitalism* reviews briefly some of the issues discussed in *The Morals of Markets* and thus serves as a fitting introduction to the larger work. Acton also includes a brief account of Samuel Smiles, the noted Victorian advocate of self-help and hard work, with whom Acton shows obvious sympathy.

11. See Robert Goodin and Julian LeGrand. *Not Only the Poor*. London: Allen & Unwin, 1987.

In "Tradition and Some Other Forms of Order" Acton compares three forms of social organization: tradition, classical liberalism, and collectivism. He rejects collectivism and manifests almost no sympathy for its idea of a rational social order. Acton finds the choice between liberalism and tradition harder. He finds important similarities between them: both rely on the unintended consequences of human action. He carefully expounds the parallels between F. A. Hayek and Edmund Burke, both of whom emphasize the role of custom in social evolution, and his account includes useful characterizations of "tradition" and "unintended consequences." As mentioned earlier, Acton fears that continuing challenge to traditional institutions may undermine the "primary moral rules" on which social order rests, and he recognizes the difficulty of maintaining a traditional society once people have begun to question its customs. His own preference, in the end, is for a vision of classical liberalism that incorporates a strong dose of traditionalism.

Many opponents of a market economy criticize it because it fails to distribute wealth in what for the critics is a morally acceptable way. A person in a capitalist society may be vastly rich or on the brink of disaster largely owing to luck. Those fortunate enough to have had wealthy parents may live a life of ease while others must struggle to survive. Instead, the critics suggest, distributive justice must be instituted to moderate, if not replace altogether, this capitalist lottery.

Acton considers this argument in his "Distributive Justice, the Invisible Hand and the Cunning of Reason", a work that also demonstrates his remarkable erudition. Denying that distribution in a market economy occurs in a random way, Acton argues that, within it, one attains wealth by supplying consumers better than one's competitors. Acton demurs to the charge that the market deviates from the canons of distributive justice. He claims that a fixed rule of distribution can be applied only in exceptional circumstances. There can be no distributive justice for society as a whole, since there is no objective way to assess the weight of the various criteria that are relevant to "fair" distribution. Acton again uses his detailed command of the history of philosophy to great advantage. He shows that in Aristotle's usage distributive justice had a much narrower scope than its modern proponents give it. The essay also includes a detailed and illuminating comparison of Adam Smith's notion of the "invisible hand" with Hegel's "cunning of reason."

"Distributive Justice . . . " is highly compressed. The fact that Acton did not have the opportunity to develop this material in a more systematic manner is an indication of how much we lost through his early death.

We mentioned earlier that there are obvious parallels between Acton's work and that of F. A. Hayek. Acton's "Distributive Justice . . . " discusses issues in which Hayek had a strong interest, while "Tradition . . . " touches briefly on some of their differences. Acton's "Objectives . . . " was originally part of a collaborative assessment of Hayek's *Constitution of Liberty.* Although Acton greatly esteemed Hayek's work, this essay also shows him at work as a critic of Hayek. Acton gives a penetrating account of Hayek's contention that a complex, progressive society arises out of agreements freely made and that it cannot be planned. He is sympathetic to Hayek's conclusions, but finds problems about the way in which Hayek develops his argument. Careful study of Acton's essay and of his discussion of freedom, progress, and tradition cannot fail to enhance one's understanding of Hayek and of classical liberalism in general.

We hope that this reprinting of *The Morals of Markets* and the essays that supplement it will generate renewed interest in Acton as a social philosopher. The collection might usefully be read together with Norman Barry's *The Morality of Business Enterprise*[12] and Bertrand de Jouvenel's *The Ethics of Redistribution.*[13] Barry's book complements Acton's work particularly well. For while Acton deals with broader ethical issues, Barry's strength is in his more detailed discussion of such contemporary problems as insider trading, takeovers, and the morality of Wall Street. Jouvenel's slightly earlier book, which has recently been republished, emphasizes the moral problems posed by interference with the economic institutions of a free society. Acton, like de Jouvenel, Hayek, and a very few others, anticipated the thesis prevalent in contemporary moral philosophy that arguments for social institutions should not be based exclusively on economic considerations.

It is not sufficient for the defense of a market-based social order to point to the economic problems faced by socialism as an ideal, or to the collapse of experiments in socialism in the U.S.S.R. and Eastern Europe. It is important to understand the economic strengths of market-based regimes. But that is not enough. Though they agree on little else, Robert Nozick and John Rawls both insist on the need for a fullfledged moral defense of the form of society that one advocates. Anyone who seeks to defend a market-based society today *has* to engage issues of morality. Acton's combination of detailed historical knowledge, analytical ability, and devo-

---

12. Norman Barry. *The Morality of Business Enterprise.* Aberdeen, Scotland: Aberdeen University Press and The David Hume Institute, 1991.
13. Bertrand de Jouvenel. *The Ethics of Redistribution.* Indianapolis: Liberty Fund, 1990.

tion to a free society makes his work essential reading for anyone wishing to consider these issues themselves.

November 1991   David Gordon
                                                    Jeremy Shearmur

David Gordon is a Research Fellow of the Social Philosophy and Policy Center, Bowling Green State University, Bowling Green, Ohio.

Jeremy Shearmur teaches political theory in the Department of Political Science, Faculty of Arts, at the Australian National University, Canberra, Australia.

EDITORS' NOTE

In preparing this edition, we have practiced a division of labor. David Gordon has been largely responsible for the Foreword, Jeremy Shearmur for the textual editing; he would like to thank the reference librarians at the Library of Congress and at Georgetown University Library and the librarian at the Institute for Humane Studies, George Mason University, for their assistance, as well as the staff of the Institute for Humane Studies for their support and encouragement.

In editing the text, we have pursued a conservative policy. We have done our best to identify and provide references to quotations or to passages cited. We have done so by silently adding information to Acton's existing notes or by adding a new note of our own in brackets. During the course of our editorial work we discovered a few slips in references and quotations; these we have corrected without noting the fact that this has been done. Similarly, we have corrected a few typographical mistakes found in the original publications and regularized Acton's punctuation to British styling throughout. We have also provided a select bibliography of Acton's writings. In this, we have tried to include his main publications in English, but do not claim to have included everything that he wrote.

Acknowledgments

We would like thank the following organizations and individuals for permission to include copyrighted material and for their kind assistance in making this volume possible.

The Ethics of Capitalism was first published in 1972 by the Foundation for Business Responsibilities, London.

The Morals of Markets: An Ethical Exploration was first published in 1971 by the Institute of Economic Affairs in association with Longman Group Ltd., © 1971 by Longman Group Ltd. Copyright transferred by Longman Group Ltd. to the Institute of Economic Affairs and by the IEA to Mrs. Barbara Acton, 1991.

"Tradition and Some Other Forms of Order," Acton's presidential address to the Aristotelian Society in London on November 10, 1952, appeared in *Proceedings of the Aristotelian Society* 53, pp. 1–28, © 1952–1953. Reprinted courtesy of the Editor of the Aristotelian Society.

"Objectives: An Essay on Hayek's *The Constitution of Liberty*" first appeared as "Objectives" in Part I, "Principles of a Free Society," in *Agenda for a Free Society: Essays on Hayek's* The Constitution of Liberty, 1961, pp. 67–84, edited by Arthur Seldon, and published for the Institute of Economic Affairs by Hutchinson of London, © 1961 by The Institute of Economic Affairs. Reprinted courtesy of the Institute of Economic Affairs.

"Distributive Justice, the Invisible Hand and the Cunning of Reason" first appeared in *Political Studies* 20(4), 1972, pp. 421–31, © 1972 by Oxford University Press. Reprinted courtesy of Blackwell Publishers.

SELECTED BIBLIOGRAPHY

1932. "Phenomenology." *Aristotelian Society Supplementary* 11: 101–15.

1934–5. "The Correspondence Theory of Truth." *Proceedings of the Aristotelian Society* 35: 177–94.

1936a. "The Theory of Concrete Universals (I)." *Mind* 45: 417–31.

1936b. "The Expletive Theory of Morals." *Analysis* 4: 42–45.

1937. "The Theory of Concrete Universals (II)." *Mind* 46: 1–13.

1938a. "Man-Made Truth." *Mind* 47: 145–58.

1938b. "The Alleged Fascism of Plato." *Philosophy* 13: 302–12. [Reprinted in R. Bambrough, ed., *Plato, Popper and Politics*. Cambridge, England: Heffer, 1967.]

1938c. "Is Ethical Relativity Necessary?" *Aristotelian Society Supplementary* 17: 170–82.

1938d. "Moral Knowledge." *Analysis* 7: 25–29.

1939. "Philosophical Survey: Philosophy in France." *Philosophy* 14: 341–44.

1939–40. "The Philosophy of History." *Proceedings of the Aristotelian Society* 40: 75–88.

1947a. "The Marxist Outlook." *Philosophy* 22: 208–30.

1947b. "Philosophical Survey: Philosophy in France." *Philosophy* 22: 161–66.

1947c. Reviews of *Three Spheres of Society,* by Charles Waterman and *The Liberal Tradition,* by William A. Orton. *Philosophy* 22: 171–73.

1948a. "Moral Subjectivism." *Analysis* 9, no. 1: 1–8.

1948b. "Moral Ends and Means." In A. H. Hannay, ed., *Philosophical Studies: Essays in Memory of L. Susan Stebbing.* London: Allen & Unwin for The Aristotelian Society, 5–19.

1948c. Review of *The Analysis of Political Behaviour: An Empirical Approach,* by Harold Lasswell. *Mind* 57: 510–14.

1949a. "Man Without Conscience?" *The Hibbert Journal* 48: 33–40.

1949b. "Philosophical Survey: Philosophy in France." *Philosophy* 24: 77–81.

1949c. Reviews of *Maine de Biran,* by G. Funcke and *Les conversions de Maine de Biran,* by H. Gouhier. *Mind* 58: 107–9.

1950a. "Philosophical Survey: Philosophy in France." *Philosophy* 25: 271–74.

1950b. "Religion, Culture and Class." *Ethics* 60: 120–30.

1950c. "Rights." *Aristotelian Society Supplementary* 24: 94–110.

1950d. Review of *My Philosophy and Other Essays on the Moral and Political Problems of Our Time,* by B. Croce. *The Hibbert Journal* 48: 201–3.

1950e. Review of *Power and Morals,* by Martin Hillenbrand. *Philosophical Review* 59: 549–52.

1951a. Review of *Pascal's Pensées. With an English Translation, Brief Notes and Introduction,* by H. F. Stewart. *Philosophy* 25: 366–67.

1951b. Review of *The Foundations of Common Sense,* by N. Isaacs. *British Journal of Psychology* 42: 193.

1951–2. "The Materialist Conception of History." *Proceedings of the Aristotelian Society* 52: 207–24.

1952a. "Prejudice." *Revue Internationale de Philosophie* 6, no. 21, Fasicule 3: 323–36.

1952b. "Comte's Positivism and the Science of Society." *Philosophy* 26: 291–310.

1952c. "Philosophical Survey: Philosophy in France." *Philosophy* 27: 66–69.

1952d. Review of *In Defence of Philosophy Against Positivism and Pragmatism,* by Maurice Cornforth. *Mind* 61: 119–21.

1952–3. "Tradition and Some Other Forms of Order." *Proceedings of the Aristotelian Society* 53: 1–28.

1953a. Review of *The Discourses of Niccolo Machiavelli,* translated by L. J. Walker. *Mind* 62: 410–13.

1953b. Review of *An Introduction to the Philosophy of History,* by W. H. Walsh. *Mind* 62: 564-65.

1954a. Review of *Henri Comte de Saint-Simon: Selected Writings,* edited and translated by F. M. H. Markham. *Philosophy* 29: 381–82.

1954b. Review of *Human Society in Ethics and Politics,* by B. Russell. *The Hibbert Journal* 53: 301–2.

1954c. Review of *Von Montaigne zu Sartre*, by E. Callot. *Philosophical Quarterly* 4: 285–86.

1954d. Review of *The Taming of the Nations*, by F. C. S. Northrop. *Philosophical Review* 63: 289–92.

1955a. "The Ethical Importance of Sympathy." *Philosophy* 30: 62–66.

1955b. *The Illusion of the Epoch; Marxism-Leninism as a Philosophical Creed*. London: Cohen & West. [Second impression, 1962. Also published by Beacon Press, Boston, 1967, and by Routledge & Kegan Paul, London, 1973.]

1955c. Review of *Historical Inevitability*, by Isaiah Berlin. *British Journal for the Philosophy of Science* 6: 338–40.

1956a. "Political Justification." In H. D. Lewis, ed., *Contemporary British Philosophy*. Third series. London: Allen & Unwin, 23–44.

1956b. Review of *The Impasse in Ethics and a Way Out*, by B. Blanchard. *Philosophy* 31: 284.

1956c. Review of *The Emotive Theory of Ethics*, by A. Stroll. *Philosophy* 31: 284–85.

1956d. Review of *The True and the Valid*, by R. I. Aaron. *Philosophy* 31: 374–75.

1958a. "Karl Marx's Materialism." *Revue Internationale de Philosophie* 12, no. 45 and 46, Fasicule 3 and 4: 265–77.

1958b. "The Marxist-Leninist Theory of Religion." *Ratio* 1: 136–49.

1959a. "Marxism, Magic and the New Rationality." *Political Studies* 7: 181–83.

1959b. Review of *Actes du Congrès du Tricentaire de P. Gassendi*, *Erasmus* 12: 577–79.

1959c. Review of *Marxism and the Open Mind*, by John Lewis. *Philosophical Review* 68: 408–9.

1960. "The Philosophy of Language in Revolutionary France." *Proceedings of the British Academy* 45: 199–219. [Also published separately by Oxford University Press in 1960 and in J. N. Findlay, ed., *Studies in Philosophy*. Oxford: Oxford University Press, 1966.]

1960–1. "Animal Pleasures." *Massachusetts Review* 2: 541–48.

1961. "Principles of a Free Society: Objectives." In A. Seldon, ed., *Agenda for a Free Society: Essays on Hayek's* Constitution of Liberty. London: Hutchinson, 1961, 69–84.

1963a. "Negative Utilitarianism." *Aristotelian Society Supplementary* 37: 83–94.

1963b. "Lenin's The State and the Revolution." *The Listener* 70. October: 649–50.

1964. "Marx, Engels and Marxism." *Political Studies* 12: 235–37.

1965a. "The Marxist Outlook." In F. Baumer, ed., *Intellectual Movements in Modern European History*. New York: Macmillan, 102–17.

1965b. "Foreword" to *Is Metaphysics Possible?* by Pratima Bowes. London: Gollancz.

1965c. Review of *Philosophy and Ideology*, by Z. A. Jordan. *Philosophical Quarterly* 15: 90–92.

1966. Review of *La philosophie politique d'Hegel*, by E. Fleischmann. *Philosophical Quarterly* 16: 283.

1967a. *What Marx Really Said*. London: Macdonald; New York: Schocken.

1967b. "The Absolute," "G. Berkeley," "B. Bosanquet," "F. H. Bradley," "G. W. F. Hegel," "Dialectical Materialism," "Historical Materialism," and "Idealism." In P. Edwards, ed., *The Encyclopaedia of Philosophy*. New York: Macmillan.

1968. "Social and Political Philosophy." In R. J. Hirst, ed., *Philosophy: An Outline for the Intending Student*. London: Routledge & Kegan Paul.

Ed. 1969a. *The Philosophy of Punishment*. London: Macmillan; New York: St Martin's Press.

1969b. "Introduction: The Philosophy of Punishment." In 1969a: 9–38.

1970a. "On Some Criticisms of Historical Materialism." *Aristotelian Society Supplementary* 44: 143–56.

1970b. *Kant's Moral Philosophy*. London: Macmillan; New York: St Martin's Press. [Also published in H. D. Hudson, ed., *Modern Studies in Ethics*. London: Macmillan; New York: St Martin's Press, 1974. The work came out as part of the series *Modern Studies in Ethics*, and the series was also published under one cover as a volume. Additionally, each item in the series was published as a volume in its own right.]

1971. *The Morals of Markets: An Ethical Exploration*. London: Longman Group Limited, Institute of Economic Affairs.

1972a. "Distributive Justice, the Invisible Hand and the Cunning of Reason." *Political Studies* 20: 421–31.

1972b. *The Ethics of Capitalism.* London: Foundation for Business Responsibilities, 1–9.

1972c. "Strikes, Trades Unions and the State." In B. Parekh and R. N. Berki, eds., *The Morality of Politics.* London: Allen &. Unwin, 136–47.

1972d. "Punishment: For and Against." In H. H. Hart, ed., *Punishment: For and Against.* New York: Hart Publishing Company, 38–55.

1972e. *The Right to Work and the Right to Strike.* London: Aims of Industry.

1972f. J. S. Mill. *Utilitarianism, Liberty, Representative Government, Selections from Auguste Comte and Positivism.* Edited and Introduction by H. B. Acton. London: Dent.

1972g. "Herbert Spencer." *Encyclopaedia Britannica.* 14th ed. vol 21: 1–3. [Also appears in the *New Encyclopaedia Britannica* (Micropaedia), vol 11, 1974.]

1973a. "Bacon, Hobbes et les Platoniciens de Cambridge." In Yvon Belavel, ed., *Histoire de la philosophie II: De la Renaissance à la révolution kantienne.* Paris: Gallimard, 404–17.

1973b. "The Enlightenment et ses adversaires: Locke, Berkeley, Hume." Ibid: 621–71.

1973c. Review of *Die Marxsche Theorie,* by Klaus Hartman. *Archiv für Geschichte der Philosophie* 55: 343–48.

1973d. "Hegelian Political and Religious Ideas." In P. P. Wiener, ed., *Dictionary of the History of Ideas* 2. New York: Charles Scribner's Sons, 407–16.

1974a. *The Idea of a Spiritual Power.* London: Athlone Press, University of London.

1974b. "Empiricisme et évolutionisme," "La philosophie Anglo-Saxonne," and "Logique, pluralisme et empirisme." In Y. Belavel, ed., *Histoire de la philosophie III: Du XIXe siècle à nos jours.* Paris: Gallimard, 257–82, 357–91, and 501–25.

1974c. "Moral Futurism and the Ethics of Marxism." In P. A. Schilpp, ed., *The Philosophy of Karl Popper.* La Salle, IL: Open Court Publishing Co., 876–88.

1975. G. W. F. Hegel. *Natural Law,* translated by T. M. Knox. Introduction by H. B. Acton. Philadelphia: University of Pennsylvania Press.

THE MORALS OF MARKETS

AND RELATED ESSAYS

INTRODUCTION: THE ETHICS OF CAPITALISM

In order to have self-respect and what is today called a sense of identity, it is necessary to have a view of oneself, of one's links with the past and contributions to society, which is both reasonably coherent and morally acceptable. The entrepreneur or business man seems to be in increasing danger of being deprived of this. A hundred years ago he could look back to his emancipation from control by what he regarded as a mindless aristocracy, to the establishment not merely of new industries but of a new industrial civilisation within which free thought and democratic institutions were developing. At that time he would have looked forward, as Cobden[1] did, to the spread of free trade, the disappearance of war between nations, and its replacement by competition in the arts of civilisation, as exemplified in the International Exhibitions which were periodically assembled in great cities from London, Milan and Paris to New York and Chicago. For a time, civilisation itself appeared to be capitalist civilisation.

The popular moral teaching of this civilisation was spread by the celebrated Samuel Smiles, a man of humble origin

1. [Richard Cobden (1804–65). British entrepreneur and politician and a leading figure in the repeal of the Corn Laws.]

from Haddington in East Lothian [, Scotland]. His main work was *Self-Help* (1859), but he continued his moral exhortations in *Character* (1871), *Thrift* (1875) and *Duty* (1880). All of these books sold widely in many editions, but *Self-Help* was particularly successful, and was translated into Turkish, Arabic and Japanese as well as into the languages of Europe. In these books working men were urged to emulate the efforts, vividly described, of hundreds of self-made men who had overcome difficulties by hard work, enterprise and imagination.

Heroes, Success and Workers

To begin with I should like to call attention to three important aspects of Smiles' teaching.

In the first place his readers were being urged to follow in the footsteps of certain great heroes of endeavour and enterprise. Smiles gave examples from many walks of life, and encouraged his readers with reports of the careers of such men as Sir Walter Scott, Sir Robert Peel[2] (who was not a self-made man), Titian and George Stephenson.[3] The chapter on those he calls 'men of business' has as its epigraph two sentences from the *Book of Proverbs:* 'Seest thou a man diligent in his business? He shall stand before kings,' and in the course of it Smiles writes that 'Trade tries character perhaps more severely than any other pursuit in life.' But he goes on to sing the praises of 'the high-minded mercantile man trained in upright habits of business, and distinguished for justice, truthfulness and honesty of dealing in all things . . . '[4]

2. [There were, in fact, two Robert Peels, both of whom were discussed by Smiles. The father (1750–1830) was an industrialist; the son (1788–1850), British Prime Minister.]

3. [George Stephenson (1736–1819). British inventor and founder of railways.]

4. [Samuel Smiles, *Self-Help,* London: John Murray, 1859, pp. 210 and 212.]

In the second place, it appears from the Preface to the 1866 edition of *Self-Help* that Smiles had been accused of taking too much notice in the book of 'men who have succeeded in life by helping themselves, and too little of the multitude of men who have failed'. He repudiated this criticism with the remark that although at the close of life we may console ourselves for failure, 'there is reason to doubt whether it is an object that ought to be set before youth at the beginning of it.'[5] We may compare with this the whining self-pity that characterises so many of the songs that are written for the young today.

A third thing to notice about Samuel Smiles' *Self-Help* is that it is addressed to young working-men—indeed, it arose from a lecture which he had been asked by a group of them to give at a club which they had set up 'in a large dingy apartment . . . which had been used as a temporary Cholera Hospital'.[6] He was offering his own version of capitalist ethics, therefore, to members of the working class at their request. 1859, however, the year of its publication, was the year when Marx's *Critique of Political Economy, I,* appeared. Marx and Engels were soon to be busy in the foundation of The First International (1865), and the first volume of *Das Kapital* appeared in 1867. We can see, therefore, that at the very time when Smiles' books were having their great popular success the foundations of anticapitalism were being laid.

During the eighteen sixties, too, the first moves were being made to enable the trade unions to function without running into insuperable legal difficulties. Nowadays working men do not read books extolling individual enterprise,

5. [See S. Smiles, *Self-Help,* Centenary Edition, London: John Murray, 1958, pp. 33–4.]

6. [See *Self-Help,* 1859 edition, p. iv.]

hard work and self-help. The heroes their leaders present to them are not men like Stephenson and Watt,[7] but the Tolpuddle Martyrs,[8] Tom Mann,[9] Keir Hardie,[10] and perhaps Lenin. Their mythology is now likely to include Peterloo,[11] the Mur des Fédérés,[12] Black Friday,[13] the October Revolution, and the tales from China or Cuba. To what heroes, then, and to what myths can the business man appeal today? In France he may still think of the leaders of the Great Revolution, but it is frequently Marxist historians who write about them and pass the story on to the next generation.

Denigration of Great Men

In Britain many of the great men of nineteenth century society have been denigrated and abused. Lytton Strachey led the way in the nineteen twenties and thirties, and the literary slaughter of our recent ancestors has gone on apace since then. In France the term 'bourgeois' is a term of abuse in intellectual circles, and in this country the dress of many of our young men and women is intended to dissociate them from the world of business.

7. [James Watt (1736–1819). Scottish engineer.]

8. [A group of British agricultural labourers, members of Grand National Consolidated Trades Union; charged with unlawful administration of oaths and sentenced to transportation in 1834.]

9. [Tom Mann (1856–1941). British Trades Unionist and one of the founders of the British Communist Party.]

10. [Keir Hardie (1856–1914). British socialist and first Labour Party Member of Parliament.]

11. [Dispersal by cavalry of radical meeting held in St. Peter's Fields, Manchester, England, 16 August 1819.]

12. [Wall at Père-Lachaise Cemetery, Paris, where last defenders of the Paris Commune were shot in 1871.]

13. [British railway and transport unions decided on 15 April 1921 not to strike in sympathy with striking miners.]

These attitudes have been encouraged by works of economic and social history. Engels first, and after him Marx, made selective use of official reports of conditions in mines and factories during the first half of the nineteenth century. Their method of treating the writing of history as a sort of indictment has been continued in books by the Hammonds[14] and others that are still widely read, and university historians have interested themselves much more in trade unions and rebels than in firms and their directors. In 1905 the editor of Samuel Smiles' *Autobiography* wrote in his Preface to it that *Self-Help* was being increasingly ridiculed by socialists.[15] Nowadays, I imagine, it is only consulted by historians of ideas. We hear over and over again about the children forced (apparently by their parents) to work in mines and factories, but much less about the improvements in the standard of life which the growth of capitalist industry made possible.

Samuel Smiles' *Thrift* has now, of course, lost much or most of its relevance. Money put in the bank probably loses its value at a rate which makes a small man's savings nugatory except for short periods. Buying on 'the never-never',[16] as it used to be derisively called, becomes the sensible thing to do for rich and poor alike. But is *Self-Help* equally outdated? Has the system of production by competing firms to satisfy demand expressed in terms of money consumers have to spend lost its moral credentials? Let us briefly consider the criticisms it has to meet.

14. [John Lawrence Hammond (1872–1949) and Lucy Barbara Hammond (1879–1961). Collaborated on several works on labour history, which painted a grim picture of conditions in the Industrial Revolution.]

15. [See *The Autobiography of Samuel Smiles, LL.D.*, ed. Thomas McKay, New York: E. P. Dutton, 1905, pp. xi–xii.]

16. [Buying on the installment plan.]

Codes of Conduct

One criticism made over a long period from Carlyle and Ruskin to Tawney's *Acquisitive Society* (1921) is that business men, unlike professional men such as doctors, lawyers and soldiers, are concerned primarily with profit for themselves rather than with service to the community. This, it is suggested, becomes apparent when we consider the professional codes which stigmatise certain activities as 'unprofessional' or 'unethical', and provide for exclusion from the profession of those who practise them. In an attempt to meet this sort of criticism, codes of conduct have been devised over the past forty years or so for adoption by various types of business activity. Stockbrokers, estate agents and others agree to ban certain lucrative but dishonest practices and to penalise those who engage in them.

But of course, if these codes of conduct are to be more than mere recommendations, they must be enforced by organisations from which expulsion is a serious penalty, and this means that they must to some extent become monopolies. The monopolies of lawyers and doctors have often been criticised, however necessary they may be, but monopoly in the business sphere is the very antithesis of the system of competitive capitalism. Indeed, this system grew up in part as a reaction to the system of guilds which endeavoured to control standards of work and production and in so doing had interfered with trade in ways that aroused justified criticism. The abolition of these 'corporations', we are told, was one of the valuable achievements of the French Revolution.

Nowadays the system of competitive capitalism is often criticised on the ground that now demand neither originates in consumers nor exists to satisfy them. Large corporations, it is said, cannot afford to make mistakes in manufacturing for an extensive market, and hence they manipulate the demand by advertisement in order to secure the sales they need for their profits.

This view is put forward both by the 'liberal' J. K. Galbraith (*The New Industrial State,* 1967) and by the Marxist radical Herbert Marcuse (*One-Dimensional Man,* 1964).[17] Galbraith does not support his view with evidence, and the remedy he puts forward can fairly be described as the permeation of government by university professors so as to bring pressure on the great producing firms to improve and beautify their products. Marcuse offers no remedy except a revolution of 'the outcasts and outsiders, the exploited and persecuted of other races and other colours, the unemployed and the unemployable'. On his view the revolt of such people offers 'nothing but a chance'. Student revolutionaries in the United States and elsewhere have been attracted by this apocalyptic attack on what they call 'late capitalism'.

There is much to be said, it seems to me, for Adam Smith's view that in the system of competitive capitalism the function of production is to satisfy demand, that 'consumption is the sole end and purpose of all production.'[18] In this system it is understood that moral standards come into operation mainly at the level of demand, so that a drunken and profligate population will demand one type of thing and a sober and chaste population another. The nature of the demand itself will depend upon the upbringing of the population and will, in general, reflect it. What producers would think of producing would depend upon their own upbringing and

17. [J. K. Galbraith, *The New Industrial State,* Boston: Houghton Mifflin, 1967. Herbert Marcuse, *One-Dimensional Man,* London: Routledge & Kegan Paul, 1964.]

18. [Adam Smith, *Wealth of Nations,* Glasgow edition, IV, viii, Indianapolis: Liberty Fund, 1982, p. 660.]

upon their estimates of what people are likely to want. In such circumstances they cannot create demand but can only elaborate or deflect it, and if they do think of something absolutely new, it has to conform to the standard of what is socially tolerable. In general, producers *respond* to demand.

In collectivist societies governments exert control over producers and in so doing influence consumption. It is not only a matter of satisfying demand or responding to it but also of seeing that it is of the right sort. An order of priorities is set up so that what is held to be a right and proper proportion exists between the things produced. Under such a system people have to consume in the proportions that are considered socially desirable or good for them rather than in terms of their own wishes. Their wishes may come to be influenced and altered by the government policies and in this way the influence of their upbringing on the nature of their demand will be lessened.

Individual and family spontaneity is likely to be greater under competitive capitalism than under collectivism. We might say that under competitive capitalism morality operates largely through consumption and demand, whereas in collectivist societies it operates to a much greater extent on production through a morally committed government. Under competitive capitalism it is consumers who set the moral tone, or rather, people set the moral tone in their capacity as consumers, whereas in collectivist societies the moral tone is set to a considerable degree by the policies of morally committed governments. In a democratic collectivist society the majority of the voters elect a government to implement a policy directed by a set of moral aims to which the minority do not fully subscribe. It is therefore the imposition of a moral outlook, an enforcement of morality (F. A. Hayek, *The Road to Serfdom*, London: Routledge, 1944).

The Morality of Self-Direction

Of course there are moral rules that are and must be enforced. These form the criminal codes of civilised societies. Murder, assault, theft and perjury are legally prohibited while at the same time it is hoped that many people will refrain from them because they regard them as wrong. A voluntary compliance with such rules is socially advantageous because if no one complied with the law voluntarily it might be impossible to enforce it. A considerable measure of self-direction, therefore, is essential for the very existence of society. But self-directed behaviour is also held to be better than behaviour under threat.

On what grounds can we say that it is better to be guided by rules that one accepts as reasonable than merely to submit to the threat of sanctions? There is the practical consideration that the individual who acts, as we say, from principle will conform to the law more consistently than the individual who acts under coercion, for he will conform even when the threat cannot be brought to bear on him. That self-direction is better than submission and coercion is a belief that permeates that liberal democratic creed which is such an important element in our political and constitutional arrangements. Perhaps one reason for the superiority of self-direction is that it is more mature. A child is disciplined for not showing regard for others, but as he grows up he is expected to be able to manage this part of his conduct for himself in terms of his own conscience. When he has reached this stage he can leave the home without bringing disaster on himself or others.

A society of individuals who can only be kept together by coercion is, therefore, inferior to one the members of which tend to do the right thing spontaneously. In the economic sphere their purchases will reflect a responsible form of life, and they will not need to be directed from above.

The system of competitive capitalism has been described as that in which the consumer is sovereign. The point of this description is that in the competitive system those things are produced which are demanded by consumers and in proportion to their demand. Certainly this does bring out the difference between the source of movement, as we may put it, in a free-enterprise economy where it is in the consumers, and in a collectivist economy where it is largely in the producers and the government. The consumer in a collectivist economy has to buy what some centralised body has decided should be produced, and so he is far from being sovereign.

Nevertheless, very large firms engaged in mass production do tend in one respect to diminish the influence of consumers, since they cannot respond very much to unusual demands but for reasons of cheapness produce large quantities of uniform goods. This is an unattractive feature of modern capitalism, but its importance should not be exaggerated. For mass production also enables large numbers of people to have goods which previously had only been available to small numbers of wealthy purchasers. What must be said is that the benefits of consumer sovereignty depend to a large extent upon the nature and nurture of the many sovereigns.

Competitive capitalism, then, gives scope for self-directed individuals to set and keep production going. What is produced depends upon what the consumers want. What they want depends upon how they have been brought up. If they have been well brought up, their patterns of demand will be morally acceptable. If they have been badly brought up, their patterns of demand will be morally unacceptable.

Moral principles are inculcated through their upbringing under the influence of parents, schools and churches. If, in a democratic society these agencies fail, there is nothing to be gained by transferring the function of education to government, since this will be elected by the same people who have failed to inculcate the right moral principles or have not been brought up to act on and respect them.

However, we now live in a society in which elected governments do interfere in all sorts of ways with the production and consumption of commodities, and capitalism must be reconsidered in the light of this. It must also be reconsidered in the light of the trade union movement which now provides a focus for the aims of so many industrial workers. A Samuel Smiles of our own day, were such an individual conceivable, would have to take these developments into consideration.

Unreal Labour Mythology

At the beginning of this lecture I referred to the mythology of the Labour Movement,[19] with its memories of Tom Mann, Keir Hardie and the Tolpuddle Martyrs. Employers are said to have persecuted and oppressed their workers, while the unions protected them and fought for industrial and legal justice. Nothing is said about union members who dynamited men considered to be blacklegs. In 1972, however, many of the unions are controlled or greatly influenced by leaders who say they are adherents of the Communist Party or other left wing bodies; furthermore, the Welfare State enables unions on strike to save on what used to be union

19. [Since Acton wrote, some of the issues that he discusses here concerning trade unions have been addressed through legislation.]

financed strike pay; and many strikes are not against particular firms or even industries, but are intended to force the
hand of the government in face of damage to the community
as a whole.

The present-day employer, therefore, has to walk through
valleys and face dangers there of which his nineteenth century predecessors knew nothing. His workpeople, too, are
very different. Most of them do not think of personal advancement, but surrender their future to a collective control
quite unlike anything that Samuel Smiles and his readers
could have thought possible. It is now just as dangerous for
a man to quarrel with his union as to quarrel with his employer, and his financial advancement can generally only
proceed *pari passu* with that of his workmates.

It would seem absurd, then, or even dishonest to preach
the virtues of self-help to men whose opportunities are so
limited. Even if it is so at present, I doubt whether it will be
so indefinitely. In the first place, what I have called the mythology of the Labour Movement is being increasingly dis-
sociated from the facts of the situation. People can tolerate a
lot of falsehood, but the stories of exploitation and cruelty
can hardly go on being applied to present-day industry in
these times of widespread car ownership and holidays in
Spain.

A very large proportion of union members already reject
these myths. Furthermore, in most unions only about ten
per cent of the membership take part in the election of offi-
cers and still fewer attend branch meetings. I do not think it
is any feeling of loyalty that leads union members to support
the 'militants', but rather the correct appreciation that they
bring in the increases and will go on doing so until the law
and present government policies are altered. The lack of
interest in branch meetings may be compared with the

small attendances of shareholders at company meetings. There is no loyalty in either case, just a concern for results.

My first point then is that the trade union mythology, although still in being, is beginning to lose its attachments. My second point is that it is through the firm rather than through the union that the workers are likely to obtain economic benefits, and if this were to be recognised the influence of unions would tend to diminish. Firms are much more coherent and creative organisations than trade unions. They not only produce the goods and create the jobs, but they also provide much of the social welfare, and will increasingly be seen to do so in the Common Market.

Large trade unions, at any rate, get their way now because they are feared rather than because there is belief in any cause they represent. Their success with wage demands results in dismissals and under-investment, and the general public's willingness to be harassed and chivvied, considerable as it is, can hardly be boundless. Surely the profitability and development of firms hold out more promise for those who work in them than wage demands that lead to losses. If managements had more confidence in their status and functions, they would make these things clear to the world. They would show how costly all this wage negotiating and striking is, and would employ handsome men and beautiful women to explain this to television viewers, instead of putting forward the battered and tongue-tied veterans who appear today.

Concern or Greed

Confidence in their status and functions, however, presupposes a belief in their moral standing, and it is this that collectivists have been trying to undermine for a hundred years and more. R. H. Tawney has been very influential in this regard, both through his arguments in favour of democratic socialism and through the account of the past which he gives in his writings on economic and social history. In the latter he makes a lot of the individual selfishness and lack of social concern which, he believed, the bourgeoisie exhibited as they broke free from the restraints of a Catholic society in which there was a genuine concern for the sick and the poor. Carlyle in *Past and Present* (1841), Pugin in *An Apology for the Revival of Christian Architecture* (1843) and Disraeli in *Sybil or the Two Nations* (1845) had all expressed a somewhat similar view for which, like Tawney, they produced some evidence.

In *The Acquisitive Society* Tawney held that 'the instruments through which Capitalism exercised discipline'— these are the power to require long hours of work, the freedom to pay what wages it likes, to bring pressure through dismissals and the threat of starvation—'are one by one being taken from it'. He urged that this 'discipline' should be replaced by 'professional feeling', 'enlisting in the conduct of industry the latent forces of professional pride'. Tawney's idea that this professional pride could be elicited in nationalised industries and that a Church with a renewed social concern would 'expect its adherents to face economic ruin for the sake of their principles'[20] has already found its way into the Museum of Lost Causes where hopeful and pleasing possibilities rest unrealised in showcases over which the blinds have been drawn. Diminution of the power in the hands of employers and the nationalisation of industries have not lessened greed but spread

20. [R. H. Tawney, *The Acquisitive Society*, London: Bell, 1921, pp. 175, 182–3, 184, 239; Fontana, 1961, pp. 139, 145, 146, 189.]

it wide and taught it to speak the bland language of fair shares.

Perhaps things would be done better if the aims were more modest. After all, business activity in its ordinary manifestations concerns individual wants and desires much more than any supposed total welfare. Work is something that has to come in between a desire and its fulfilment. People buy in order to get something they need or want, and they sell in order to get money to be spent on a variety of purposes. People whose wants are definite and urgent cannot wait on the good pleasure of some benevolent giver, but, in order to obtain what they need, must offer so much for such and such. In what ways is it possible for one individual to obtain what another individual possesses? He can take it, and this is spoliation or piracy. He can ask for it, appealing to the good nature of the other party, but then, as a beggar, he has no say in precisely what it is that he obtains. We may speculate that in a society of casual benevolent donations little progress is likely to be made in the arts of production.

The other possibility is for the individual who wants what someone else has, to offer something in exchange for it. This is the method of purchase, presupposing the institution of private property. Under this arrangement, each party, in order to help himself, has to help the other, or, to put it another way, in helping the other, helps himself as well. There is no call for devotion to the community as a whole, no self-sacrifice or self-immolation. These may be called for during dangers or emergencies but are not, as business is, the constant daily activity of society. It should not be forgotten, however, that in taking part in this activity an individual does not make himself a burden on others but pays for what he gets with the product of his own efforts. Self-help is not helping oneself to what others have but cooperating in a system of mutual aid. Neither beggar, nor thief, nor hero, the man of business may on occasion, like the mercenary at Thermopylae '[save] the sum of things for pay'.[21] But his prime function is to see that the things people need for life and civilisation are produced, modified, multiplied, protected, stored, moved and delivered.

Capitalism's Contribution

In conclusion may I suggest the following scheme of the capitalist's historical identity, to offset the scheme that Marxists have made popular. In the past, it would appear, the aristocracy have engaged in a mixture of piracy, conquest and public service involving a life of command and exploit. The peasantry have laboured in the fields, deferred to their masters, accepted their charity and manned their armies. The bourgeoisie, more scrupulous and more pacific than the aristocracy, and less deferential than the peasantry, so improved the arts of production that the system of warrior lords and dependent serfs was replaced by one in which large populations of free citizens enjoy a scope of living which goes beyond what the aristocracy formerly disposed of. Free speech, free movement, free trade, free thought, exploration of the earth and oceans, an ideal of peaceful domesticity, water colour drawing, conversation pieces, the novel and domestic drama—these are some of the things that the capitalist spirit has contributed to modern civilisation. Whether the multitudes who can increasingly share in all this will wish to do so, or whether they will prefer to bask in the exploits of a new aristocracy of entertainers

21. [A. E. Housman, 'Epitaph on an Army of Mercenaries', *The Collected Poems*, London: Jonathan Cape, 1939, p. 101.]

while themselves acting on the maxims 'one out, all out' and 'one up, all up' we do not know. Solidarity and monopoly are the dangers before which a system of freedom might have to capitulate.

THE MORALS
OF MARKETS:
AN ETHICAL
EXPLORATION

Preface [To The First Edition of *The Morals of Markets*]

I am very grateful for help (not always taken) and advice (from which I have greatly profited) from Arthur Seldon, Ralph Harris, George Schwartz, John B. Wood and Hamish Gray. I should also like to express my admiration for Mr Seldon's patience in allowing me to have second thoughts and rather long delayed ones.

March, 1970   H. B. Acton

CHAPTER 1
THE THEME OF THE ESSAY

The Unpopularity of Free Markets

The purpose of this essay is to examine, from the point of view of morality, the merits, for merits there assuredly are, and the defects, for there are defects in all human institutions, of the system under which goods are produced for sale at a profit in free markets. This system stands morally condemned by a large part of our population. In schools and universities the *laissez-faire*[1] philosophy is attacked by

1. The phrase *laissez-faire, laissez-passer* was used in the eighteenth century by a member of the group of French political economists known as Physiocrats. The Physiocrats criticised the so-called Mercantilist System under which the government controlled the manufacture and pricing of goods, the location of industries, and the movement of trade, with the aim of securing a favourable balance of trade for the country. The Physiocrats, as their name indicates—the Greek word *physis* means 'nature'—favoured a more spontaneous, natural and less artificial industrial and commercial system. Hence, *laissez-faire* meant 'let people produce' or 'let them get on with the job', and *laissez-passer* meant 'let people move around as they please'. Adam Smith was influenced by some of the arguments of the Physiocrats when, in *The Wealth of Nations* (1776), be argued that national prosperity is more likely to result from allowing goods to be freely produced and exchanged than from controlling production and exchange by governmental means. Carlyle used the expression *laissez-faire* in *Chartism* (1839), in a pejorative sense, implying that a government that does not intervene in economic affairs is failing in its duty. A striking feature of our own times is the revival of Mercantilism and a corresponding diminution of regard for economic freedom. In these circumstances *laissez-faire* tends to be an abusive term. It should be noticed that Adam Smith and his followers did not say that governments should never on any account intervene in industry and commerce.

many historians who describe and expose the harshnesses of its initial operation, and by almost all social scientists, who assume that it is outmoded and tell their students so. Competition is regarded as a form of strife, markets as 'jungles', and 'the profit motive' as disreputable. Collectivists, of course, by the very nature of their creed, wish to control and limit the workings of markets, but non-collectivists, too, have been influenced by their opponents and often believe that it would be unchristian to oppose the imposition of more control by governments over economic activities. Indeed, it is assumed that since for a long time now the tendency has been for governments to try to control the economy and to limit the extent of free markets, there is something quixotic, reactionary, or positively wicked in the idea of trying to move in the opposite direction.

Yet it is just when a social outlook has hardened into a dogma that it is most necessary to examine it in the light of possible alternatives. The time when 'we are all socialists' is the very time to reconsider the morality of the free market, which may be more often traduced than understood. If free markets are bad, the reasons why they are bad should be clearly stated. If they are not wholly bad, then the prevailing outlook needs to be modified. Past theories and policies and the lack of them have built up interests and influences whose presuppositions should not remain unquestioned.

Markets: A Preliminary Analysis

In the non-technical sense of the word, markets are *places* where goods are bought and sold. In small market towns farmers still bring produce to these places and wait for customers to come and buy. As the goods are on display, the buyers will look for the best goods at the cheapest prices. No one will knowingly pay sixpence a pound for potatoes when he can buy equally good ones somewhere else in the market for threepence a pound, and so the price of potatoes of similar quality tends to be the same, and a market price is established. In rather more sophisticated markets the goods have been bought from the producers by merchants who in their turn perhaps sell them to other merchants or to shopkeepers. In such markets both sellers and buyers are generally very well informed about what the producers have for sale and what demand there is from consumers. The goods are finely graded according to quality, and a market price for each grade is established as buyers ascertain what is on offer and how much of it there is.

When all or most of the products consumed in a society are distributed in this way, the society is said to have a market or exchange economy. In a market economy goods are produced with a view to their being sold through wholesalers and retailers. It is expected that the merchants who buy the products will give prices in accordance with the quality of the goods and in accordance with what they expect or hope to get from retailers or consumers. Merchants can choose between different producers, retailers can choose between the goods offered by different wholesalers, and consumers can go to the shop which seems to them to offer the goods they most want at prices they are willing to pay. When the system is competitive[2] merchants can buy from this producer or that, producers can sell to this merchant or that, and ultimately the consumer with money to spend can choose which shop to go to. Hence the producer tries to produce goods which merchants will want to buy,

2. Monopoly is discussed below, pp. 96–8.

merchants will try to buy goods which retailers feel sure they can sell, and consumers will go to the shop which they think offers them what they most want to have at prices which they think lowest for the quality they want.

A further feature of the market economy that must be mentioned at this stage is that the competing producers and competing merchants and shopkeepers are not, in general, individuals (although some of them are), but firms which employ individuals to work for them in exchange for wages or salaries. In a completely free market individuals could, subject to their contracts of employment, leave one firm and work for another which offered better terms, and employing firms could, again subject to their contracts with their employees, dismiss employees whose work they do not find satisfactory. The system is quite compatible with fairly long-term contracts between firms and employees, and with complex contracts between them on holidays, conditions of work and pensions.

Producing and merchanting firms are not only producers and merchants but also consumers of goods produced and distributed by other producers and merchants. For example, a producer of motor-cars is a consumer of steel which he buys (perhaps through a merchant) from a steel producer, and a merchant consumes in the course of his business at the very least notepaper and office furniture. Ultimate consumers, apart from children and retired and chronically sick people, are also producers, but of course each consumer consumes a much wider range of goods than as a wage earner he has helped to produce. It is important to notice that a very large proportion of the people who are active in the market economy are employed for wages or salaries by the firms which compete in producing and distributing the goods consumed in it. Within a market economy the most widely shared economic experiences are those involved in selling one's labour and in buying consumer goods. The more sophisticated economic experiences are confined to a relatively small class.

Some Presuppositions of This Analysis

The highly simplified sort of organisation so far described presupposes at least five sets of circumstances. Firstly it assumes a division of labour and normally the use of money. In it the producer of one sort of product sells it for money which he uses in buying products which he does not make himself.

Secondly it presupposes that those taking part in the transactions involved are all trying to do as well as they can for themselves and for their families. Producers and merchants want to get the best possible price for what they sell, and merchants and consumers do not want to pay more than they have to. In general, if someone pays too high a price or agrees to sell at too low a price, this will be through inadvertence, laziness, ignorance or a benevolent whim. If a man loses money for these reasons, he is not expected to blame anyone but himself, and if he does such things too often he will drop out of the system. Fraud and deliberate deception are, as we shall see, defined in the legal rules under which the system operates, and when detected they lead to punishments of various kinds. Dishonesty that cannot readily be dealt with in courts of law, such as denying or altering verbal agreements, is generally left to be countered by such methods as refusing to have further dealings with the perpetrator, as when consumers withdraw their custom. The various parties are expected to be honest, and it is hoped that if they are tempted to be dishonest they will be prevented by fear of losing business, if not by the strength of their moral principles.

Thirdly, although it is possible for goods to be exchanged without the existence of law and government,[3] continuous market operations require there to be laws against fraud and violence, and governments to enforce the laws. It can hardly be expected that no one will ever try to bully or to cheat in order to get what he wants. Even if all the parties were trying to be just, they could differ about the meaning of the agreements they have made and be obstinate in defence of their own point of view. The rules must be stated, interpreted and enforced, and for this framework of laws some sort of government is required. It need not be the state,[4] but where states exist the creation of this legal framework is a function they are universally expected to perform or to ensure that others perform. Just as some games require referees or umpires, so market economies require courts and police. Like football players, the participants are in general expected to institute and pursue their own strategies, but in both cases there are limits upon what they are allowed to do to one another.

Fourthly, it is generally agreed that private property is essential to the effective operation of the market economy. The idea has been that in buying and selling the seller receives money for what was originally his property and that the buyer, in passing over the money, gets in return the ownership of the goods. The market economy is thus generally regarded as an economy in which private enterprise predominates. Although markets may exist in socialist socie-

3. Indeed, it has been surmised that the earliest markets were held between the members of different hostile tribes who each needed what the other had and rather stealthily made the exchange in the wilderness.

4. The Stock Exchange and certain commodity markets draw up their own rules.

ties when quasi-independent producing bodies are allowed
to compete for orders from the government or when producing organisations compete in selling goods to the governmental retail stores,[5] our discussion is not concerned with
this socialist sort of market.[6]

A final presupposition of a market economy is that no
market or series of markets comprises the whole of a society. There have been societies without markets, and when
markets have eventually been set up in them some of the
earlier methods of distributing goods have continued, as
when clothes are made within the family, but the needles
and thread for making them are purchased from elsewhere.
When I said above that someone who persistently sells too
cheaply or buys too dear 'will drop out of the system', I did
not mean that he will vanish from society altogether. In all
societies with market economies some arrangements are
made to help casualties of the system. Again, it is not merely
the case that some sorts of thing that might be bought and
sold are not, but also that some sorts of thing ought not to be
for sale at all. There is not or ought not to be a market price
for everything. It would be quite easy to buy and sell parlia-
mentary votes, but it is illegal as well as morally wrong to
do so.[7] Again, a doctor or a shopkeeper may give his help in

5. See Margaret Miller and others, *Communist Economy under Change: Studies in the Theory and Practice of Markets and Competition in Russia, Poland and
Yugoslavia,* London: Institute of Economic Affairs, 1963.

6. Market *analysis* may also be appropriate to wholly planned economies
without competition to determine whether resources in the economy are being
effectively allocated. Professor Bela Csikos-Nagy, *Pricing in Hungary,* London:
Institute of Economic Affairs, 1968.

7. Of course, politicians endeavour to get votes, in exchange for policy
promises, but this is different from paying individuals for votes, which is wrong
for many reasons of which we may mention two. Buying individual votes
would favour richer candidates or parties. Further, it would turn voting into a
matter of individual gain, whereas the system of voting requires voters to consider the general interest.

exchange for money, but a parent does not expect payment for the help he gives to his young children, or grown-up children for the help they give their parents, or a friend for the help he gives his friend. Loyalty and love, as distinct from services or cupboard-love, are not in the market.

In market transactions all the parties are trying to make the best bargain they can. The whole mechanism presupposes that this is what they are doing. What they do with their rewards is for them to decide. Those who do well may, often do, give some to people in need, to charities or causes, social, religious or political, that they value. The market is not the place for generosity or self-sacrifice. Someone who accepts less than the market price or pays more is either under a misapprehension or else is giving something to people who do not expect to receive gifts, though no doubt they are very glad to have them. To be an unsuccessful business man is a stupid and inappropriate way of being generous. But although the market is not the place for directly exercising love and generosity, it is not the place for hatred or for treachery either.

In this section I have tried to give a brief preliminary account of competitive markets in order to prepare the way for discussion of the moral problems involved. Even at this early point of our argument, however, critics may object that the account I have given is unrealistic or irrelevant in the present era of large-scale firms and monopolies. Later in the essay I have suggested that large economic organisations which think themselves free from competition are nevertheless subject to its influence (pp. 69–73 and 96–8 below), and I have criticised the view that increasing monopoly and state control are inevitable (p. 135 below). The tendency towards size and monopoly should not be exaggerated. Although the numbers of people employed in manufacturing firms with more than 10,000 workers have increased very considerably over the last thirty years, and although the proportion of the total output for which these firms are responsible has increased even more, a large proportion of employees (36 per cent) and of the net output (32 per cent) is associated with firms employing fewer than 500 workers.[8] Furthermore, the proportion of large-scale to smaller-scale firms varies from industry to industry, and even in industries where a few large firms predominate, these generally compete with one another.[9] The tendency towards greater concentration of firms, furthermore, is in part a result of public policies which could be changed.

It may be objected that there is a steady trend towards larger and larger firms and towards nationalisation and state control. But if trends are to be accepted as pointers to an inevitable future, discussion about what policies we *ought* to adopt, or about what we should *try* to do, loses point, and nothing remains except to follow the fashion. Although it is true that human beings have sometimes behaved like lemmings, I take the view that they can, by altering their views about what is desirable, change trends and even reverse them. To deny this would be to deny that the criticisms of *laissez-faire* and the preference for collectivism that developed towards the end of the last century have had anything to do with the collectivist tendencies that have shown themselves since. Of course people are apt to fall in with fashion, especially in their early years, but they can also criticise and

---

8. Board of Trade, *Census of Production 1958*, Summary Table 12, London: Her Majesty's Stationary Office, and A. Armstrong and H. Silberston, 'Size of Plant, Size of Enterprise and Concentration in British Manufacturing Industry, 1935–58', *Journal of the Royal Statistical Society*, Series A, 128, Part 3, 1965, pp. 395–407.

9. R. Evely and I. M. D. Little, *Concentration in British Industry*, Cambridge: Cambridge University Press, 1960.

make it. Fashions in clothes change more easily than fashions in ideas. In a way, there is something absurd in the very notion of fashions in ideas, for if ideas are merely accepted as the shops supply them, they cease to be thoughts and turn into habits. The ideas of a society in which 'trendy' is a term of praise, need a lot of shaking up.

General Criticisms of the Market Economy

The shopkeepers and merchants who occupy such a central position in the market economy have been scorned, criticised and condemned from the earliest times. Plato, who explained how markets depend upon the division of labour and the invention of money, says in the *Republic* that in well-ordered communities shopkeepers are 'generally men not strong enough to be of use in any other occupation' and are even inferior to merchants who do at least brave the dangers of going into foreign countries.[10] Hence he placed traders of all kinds in the third and lowest class of his ideal republic, the class of those who were governed by their desires and were consequently unfit to take part in government. Aristotle, in his *Politics*, argued that it is somehow 'unnatural' and therefore bad to produce goods with the primary aim of selling them at a profit, since the purpose of production is to satisfy needs rather than to accumulate money. St Thomas Aquinas carried on the Aristotelian tradition in this as in other respects, and al-

10. [Plato, *The Republic*, translated with introduction and notes by F. M. Cornford, London: Oxford University Press, 1941, chapter 6 (Book II. 367 E-372 A). Acton discusses the views of Aristotle and Aquinas in more detail in 'Distributive Justice'.]

though he acknowledged that trading need not be 'sinful or contrary to virtue', he ruled that priests should not take part in trade since in so doing they would be diverted from spiritual things.

With the growth of economic science in the eighteenth century a rather more favourable view was taken of profits and of traders, and the classical economists, although sometimes very critical of them, argued that their activities were essential for a free and wealthy society. Thus Adam Smith in *The Wealth of Nations* wrote: 'The prejudices of some political writers against shopkeepers and tradesmen, are altogether without foundation. So far is it from being necessary, either to tax them, or to restrict their numbers, that they can never be multiplied so as to hurt the public, though they may so as to hurt one another.'[11] But this qualified approval turned out to be only a brief interlude in the continuing chorus of disapprobation. The collectivist movements of the nineteenth and twentieth centuries condemned the whole system of private competitive enterprise, claiming that it was bound to result in monopoly, injustice, widespread poverty, and eventual revolution. Influential writers of the Victorian period such as Carlyle and Ruskin criticised the system on moral grounds, and in more recent times J. A. Hobson and R. H. Tawney have revived and elaborated their arguments in order to recommend a form of socialism based on moral considerations.

Lord Robbins, in *The Theory of Economic Policy in English Classical Political Economy*, sets out to defend some of the classical economists from the charge of being 'very malignant creatures indeed', and in pursuing this object he

11. [Adam Smith, *The Wealth of Nations*, II.v, Glasgow edition, Indianapolis: Liberty Fund, 1982, p. 361.]

emphasises those particulars in which they departed from what complete *laissez-faire* would have required.[12] Anyone who today defends the competitive market economy is liable to be accused of favouring selfishness and inhumanity. The weary Victorian children sleeping at their machines, and the women dragging coal trucks underground are evoked to confuse and confound him.

Our present discussion is not concerned with the grandeurs and miseries of early nineteenth-century capitalism, for our questions are moral rather than historical. What we have first to consider are the grounds on which the free market economy is morally condemned. A preliminary view of them suggests the following main lines of criticism. In the first place there is the argument that the market economy, depending as it does on the 'profit motive', encourages selfishness and avarice and, indeed, exalts these vices to the rank of virtues. Then there is the argument that the competitive element in the market economy is a deplorable source of strife which should be replaced by cooperation and public service. Another criticism of the market economy is that competition inevitably leads to monopoly and so to tyranny—that what begins in freedom ends in bondage. Still another criticism is that in the workings of the market economy the purpose of production, which is the satisfaction of needs, is lost sight of, so that each individual, the capitalist or enterpriser as well as the worker, is in the grip of an impersonally operating system which takes no account of justice or morality because it is incapable of taking account of anything. Finally, the competitive market economy is contrasted with the socialistically planned economy to the detriment of the former: the

12. [Lionel Robbins, *The Theory of Economic Policy in English Classical Political Economy*, London: Macmillan, 1952, p. 5.]

competitive market economy is held to be chaotic and unjust by comparison with economies planned on socialist
lines.[13]

13. In *The Principles of Economic Planning*, London: Allen & Unwin, 1949,
third edition, 1969, Sir William Arthur Lewis objects to what he calls the
laissez-faire system, (1) that within it income is not fairly distributed, but is
distributed in accordance with the scarcity of the resources the individuals
possess, (2) that it gives no protection to employees, (3) that it is unstable, (4)
that it cannot keep control of foreign trade, and (5) that it cannot cope with
major change without being 'too slow and cruel', pp. 12–14; the quotation is
from p. 13. (3) and (4) are outside the scope of this essay.

CHAPTER 2
THE PROFIT MOTIVE

The Immoderacy of Profit

In this chapter we shall discuss the moral objection to the competitive market economy that, in depending upon the so-called 'profit motive', it encourages avarice and selfishness. This charge is complex, and we shall have to consider in turn various features of it.

One of the earliest criticisms of the market economy was put forward by Aristotle. He argued that when goods are produced for sale at a profit their use in satisfying needs is easily lost sight of and is replaced by the desire to accumulate as much money as possible. His idea was that whereas there is a limit or term to the satisfaction of needs, money can be accumulated *ad infinitum*. Hence the man who enters industry or trade in order to make money is led on by a desire that is by its very nature insatiable. The trader or money-maker introduces something inordinate and unnatural into society, and diverts attention from the satisfaction of satiable needs to the insatiable search for a limitless fortune.

It should be pointed out that any force this argument has applies not only to competitive markets but to any economy in which money is used. It is money values that can be conceived as being added to indefinitely, and these could be the gross national product of a socialist economy as well as the profits made in a competitive market economy. The contrast is really between the series of natural numbers on the one hand and satisfactions to which no numerical values in the sense of prices can be given on the other. The fact is that numbers can incite men to useless or harmful activity in any society that has a superstitious reverence for them. Profits themselves, of course, tend to be limited by competition between firms in a competitive market economy, so that any desire for the infinite is kept in check by the levelling processes of the market, so long as entry into it is free. In any case, perhaps Keynes was right when he said that 'It is better that a man should tyrannise over his bank balance than over his fellow-citizens'.[14]

The 'Mammon Gospel'

Thomas Carlyle's *Past and Present* (1843) contains much of the rhetoric that has since been used in moral criticisms of the competitive market economy. Certain phrases in it, such as 'cash nexus'[15] and 'captains of industry' have continued in use. Carlyle's device of contrasting the socially and ecclesiastically controlled medieval economic arrangements with the individualism of nineteenth-century capitalism has been copied since, notably by R. H. Tawney in *Religion and the Rise of Capitalism* (1926). Ruskin was influenced by it when he wrote his moral condemnation of the market economy in

14. J. M. Keynes, *The General Theory of Employment*, London: Macmillan, 1960, p. 374.

15. Carlyle wrote '*Cash payment* had not then grown to be the universal sole nexus of man to man' in his 'Chartism' in 1839. See, for example, his *Critical and Miscellaneous Essays*, volume 6, London: Chapman and Hall, 1872, pp. 148–9.

Unto this Last (1862). Friedrich Engels reviewed *Past and Present* when it first came out, and incorporated something of what he had learnt from it in an essay, *Outlines of a Critique of Political Economy* (1844),[16] from which much of the Marxist doctrine takes its origin. A paragraph from *Past and Present* (quoted by Engels in his review of it) may serve as our starting point:

> True, it must be owned, we for the present, with our Mammon-Gospel, have come to strange conclusions. We call it a Society; and go about professing openly the totalest separation, isolation. Our life is not a mutual helpfulness; but rather, cloaked under due laws-of-war, named 'fair competition' and so forth, it is a mutual hostility. We have profoundly forgotten everywhere that *Cash-payment* is not the sole relation of human beings; we think, nothing doubting, that *it* absolves and liquidates all engagements of man. 'My starving workers?' answers the rich Mill-owner: 'Did I not hire them fairly in the market? Did I not pay them, to the last sixpence, the sum covenanted for? What have I to do with them more?'—Verily Mammon-worship is a melancholy creed. When Cain, for his own behoof, had killed Abel, and was questioned, 'Where is thy brother?' he too made answer, 'Am I my brother's keeper?' Did I not pay my brother *his* wages, the thing he had merited from me? (First edition, pp. 198–9.)

In setting out, in chapter 1 of *Religion and the Rise of Capitalism*, the historical theme he proposes to investigate, Tawney contrasts 'the conception of society as a community of unequal classes with varying functions, organised for a common end', with 'that which regards it[self] as a mechanism adjusting itself through the play of economic motives to the supply of economic needs'; he also contrasts 'the idea that a

16. [See F. Engels, 'The Condition of England: *Past and Present* by Thomas Carlyle, London, 1943' in Karl Marx and Friedrich Engels, *Collected Works*, volume 3, London: Lawrence and Wishart, 1975, pp. 444–68; the passage from Carlyle is quoted on page 451. (The review originally appeared in *Deutsch-Französische Jahrbücher*, 1844.) The other reference is to Engels' 'Outlines of a Critique of Political Economy', ibid., pp. 418–43.]

man must not take advantage of his neighbour's necessity' with 'a doctrine that "man's self-love is God's providence" ', and 'the view of economic activity which regarded it as one among other kinds of moral conduct' with 'the view of it as dependent upon impersonal and almost automatic forces'.[17]

Both Carlyle and Tawney, it will be noticed, identify the market economy with society as a whole. They both consider that the market economy comprises or permeates the whole of society, and that in so doing it destroys relationships between people other than those contracted for economic purposes. Furthermore they assert that the society that has thus become identical with a market is one in which self-seeking, callousness and even downright maleficence are regarded as justified. But if, as I have indicated, the competitive market is only a part of any society in which it exists, then these criticisms are unacceptable. What would have to be shown is first, that where there is a market economy, it must permeate, and hence presumably corrupt, everything else in the society that harbours it. But second, even more fundamental than this is the claim that within the market itself men are necessarily dominated by avarice, lack of concern for others, and wish to harm them. Of course, if it is never right to look after one's own interests in competition with others, then the market economy must be fundamentally bad, since, as we have already indicated, all those participating in it are trying to do as well for themselves as they can.

This criticism must apply, not only to producing and merchanting firms, but to the ultimate consumers as well, for these aim to secure a consumer's surplus, that is, to make as

17. These quotations are from R. H. Tawney, *Religion and the Rise of Capitalism*, Harmondsworth: Penguin Books, 1964, pp. 26–7; on p. 73 Tawney writes that in medieval times 'the problem of moralising economic life was faced and not abandoned'.

large as possible the difference between what they pay in the market and what they would pay if they had to.[18] Thus we should not speak of profits as if they were, morally speaking, different from the advantages which all those who participate in the market economy hope to gain for themselves by selling, buying or working for a wage. The ultimate consumer is not generally as good at obtaining the advantages open to him as firms are good at making profits, for the purchasing of consumer goods is a less organised profession than it was in the days when most housewives specialised in it. But consumers' associations can bring expertise into the buying of consumer goods just as trade unions can advise and help men to make advantageous wage bargains. Profits, if they are honestly come by, indicate no more avarice than do wages and the purchases of shrewd and cautious buyers.

It might be objected that this only goes to show that in a competitive market economy all the participants, and not only those who set out to make profits, are engaged in self-interested activities which should be morally condemned. If the market were the whole of society this might be so, but the market is in practice an element in a society that extends far beyond it. Hence those who engage in market activities do so with aims that are related to the other aspects of the society in which they live. All men belong to a family, many of them have a religion, some of them have a care for social and philanthropic causes, an interest in art and science, a concern for their country. The interests they pursue in the

18. Alfred Marshall, *Principles of Economics*, London: Macmillan, ninth edition, 1961, Book III, chapter vi, pp. 124–37. For subsequent discussion of the idea see 'Realism and Relevance in Consumer's Surplus', in E. J. Mishan, *Welfare Economics: Ten Introductory Essays*, New York: Random House, 1969. The great subtlety of the metaphysics of the theory is unnecessary for the point that the purchaser aims to do as well as he can for himself and is thus in the same moral boat as the profit-seeker.

market, therefore, are not merely private and personal, but are imbued with ambitions and predilections to which monetary success is often subordinate. Most men's market dealings are linked with their desire to provide for their families, but they may also be concerned to promote concerns connected with churches, clubs, voluntary societies and other groups to which they give their loyalty. Firms themselves are influenced by the outlooks of their directors and managers, and purchases by individuals manifest 'profiles' which vary from one to another. It is true that some people are so taken with the market that they want money for its own sake, and there are others who chiefly want to outdo other people. But they are hardly typical. What should be emphasised is that whatever their non-market aims, motives and ideals, they will not promote them by buying too dear or selling too cheap in market terms.

Tawney, in the passage I referred to above, writes as if the principle that a man should not take advantage of his neighbour's necessity is opposed to the market system. To establish and exploit, say, a monopoly of food during a famine would undoubtedly be immoral, but such monopolies, I suggest, go against the market system, and cannot be taken as typical unless it is the case that competitive markets *must* tend to develop into monopolies. Sickness and poverty among those who cannot help themselves may have to be dealt with outside the market mechanism,[19] which may, as Lord Robbins emphasised, have to be suspended in times of scarcity imposed, for example, by the siege conditions of war.[20] But this is not to say that in the course of market activities people are taking unfair or otherwise reprehensi-

19. The advantage claimed for the reversed income tax is that it would redistribute income outside the market. See Milton Friedman, *Capitalism and Freedom*, Chicago: University of Chicago Press, 1962.

20. Lionel Robbins, *The Economic Problem in Peace and War*, London: Macmillan, 1947.

ble advantage of one another. The market, as a method of recording consumer preferences and allocating resources can respond to any distribution or redistribution of income. In one sense, indeed, people *are* taking advantage of one another, and it is a very good thing that they do so. For in competitive markets people who need goods and services receive them from people who see advantage to themselves in providing them. To take advantage of people's necessities in this way is not morally reprehensible unless it is always wrong to require payment for goods provided or for services rendered. The better one meets the needs of others, the more profitable market activity becomes. This brings us to a crucial aspect of the morality of markets.

Economic Harmonies and the 'Invisible Hand'

'Taking advantage of one's neighbour's necessity', we have seen, can mean two things. It can mean the exploitation by the strong of the weak or helpless by creating a monopoly and taking advantage of it; and it can mean the supplying for pay of goods and services that our neighbour wishes to buy. No one is going to defend exploitation by monopoly, but it should not be confused with responding to demand, and the question is whether the latter, which is the market method of helping one another, is to be morally condemned as well. Put in its very simplest terms, the question is: 'Is it always wrong to require payment for providing help?' The answer is undoubtedly 'No', and it is instructive to consider why.

Let us suppose a society in which there is division of labour and a belief among all its members that it is wrong to require payment for anything. In this society the man who grows potatoes wants to give them to those who need them, and the man who makes shoes wants to do the same. How do the potatoes and the shoes get to those who want them? Presumably these people go around and take some. But where do the potato-growers and shoemakers go for spades and leather? Has some kind man realised that these implements and materials will be needed and has he produced them for the potato-grower and shoemaker? He would have to find out what sort they required, but what would happen if they did not like them? After all, there is something indelicate about criticising gifts. Nor can gifts be demanded either, and yet the potato-grower may need the spade when his friend is making one for some other friend who is breaking the ground for a much needed house.

Such considerations make it clear that a society with division of labour and limited resources cannot rely upon gifts to get its products distributed. Benevolence is good, but it is business that is needed, and business means mutual agreements, times of delivery, specifications and quantities, contracts, exchange and sales. These agreements and deals take place in order that people's needs shall be satisfied. But the satisfactions are reciprocal. Each producer needs the products of some or all the other producers, and some or all of them need what he produces. In producing for sale what he is good at producing, each producer supplies the others with what they want. The buyer, unlike a recipient of gifts, can require the producer to make what is wanted. The producer or seller, unlike a bestower of gifts, is led to supply the types and quantities needed at times when they are of use.

This, I suggest, is what ought to be meant by the system of economic harmony. It is not that each individual seeks his own interest and that some 'invisible hand', to use Adam Smith's famous expression, sees to it that this results in benefits for all. For such a hand might lose its cunning or become paralysed. It is rather that the very structure or system of free exchange in a society with division of labour and limited resources is one in which what each party produces is for some others to have in return for what the producer would like to have from them. Benefiting oneself by providing what others need is the *raison d'être* of the whole affair. It is not that the good of others is a contingent byproduct of selfishness, but that each party can only benefit himself by benefiting others. He may from time to time benefit others without benefiting himself, by making gifts, or what comes to the same thing in a market, by selling below what he knows to be the market price. But persistently to do this would be to opt out of the system, the very functioning of which requires service to be by exchange rather than by gift. If there is to be business, it had better be business.

In *The Wealth of Nations*[21] Adam Smith seems to be recommending the method of exchange on the ground that it is better for an able-bodied man who wants what others have, to offer something in exchange for it rather than 'by every servile and fawning attention to obtain their good will'. He also suggests in the same passage that the methods of the beggar are not likely to be consistently successful, human selfishness being what it is, that they would lead to a great waste of time, and that they neither do nor can 'provide him with them ["the necessaries of life"] as he has occasion for them'. The last two seem to me to be the really compelling reasons, as they would still apply, as I have suggested above, even if human beings were primarily and fundamentally altruistic. For the system to work, even altruistic people have to look to their own benefit. Does this mean that they have to make themselves selfish?

21. Adam Smith, *Wealth of Nations*, I.ii, Glasgow edition. The quotations are from pages 26 and 27.

Not at all. What it means is that, whatever their outlook or their temperament, they must try to look after themselves while they play their part in the competitive market system. If they are honest and honourable men the part they play will be in keeping with their character. If they are not, they may still be kept in line by fear of the law or their knowledge that others will not do business with them if they are suspected of double-dealing. If they are misanthropic, they may try to forget that they cannot benefit themselves without providing other people with things they want to have. But if they provide what others do not want they will find themselves out of business.

The system was described very well in the eighteenth century by Le Mercier de la Rivière when he wrote:

> It is of the essence of [this] order that the particular interest of each individual can never be separated from the common interest of all; we find a very convincing proof of this in the complete freedom which ought to obtain in trade, if property is not to be damaged. The personal interest which this great freedom encourages, strongly and continually urges every individual to improve, to multiply the things that he wishes to sell; in this way to enlarge the mass of enjoyments which he can provide for other men, in order to enlarge by this means, the enjoyments that other men can provide for him in exchange. Thus *the world goes by itself* (va de lui-même); the desire for enjoyment and the freedom to enjoy, never ceasing to induce the multiplication of products and the growth of industry, impress on the whole of the society a motion which becomes a perpetual tendency towards its best possible condition.[22]

22. Le Mercier de la Rivière, *L'ordre naturel et essentiel des sociétés politiques*, 1767, volume 2, p. 447–8. Compare the edition by E. Depitre, Paris: P. Geuthner, 1910, p. 338. The passage occurs in a chapter describing the benefits of commerce. It is quoted by J. R. McCulloch in his 'Introductory Discourse' to his edition of *The Wealth of Nations*. Also see the edition of 1839, Edinburgh: Adam and Charles Black, and William Tait, p. xli.

We may no longer share the eighteenth-century writer's optimistic belief that all this will lead to 'the best possible condition', nor have we yet considered the relation of the analysis to freedom. But the central position, it seems to me, is correct, that is, the claim that in competitive markets individuals, whether firms or persons, provide for others in working for themselves. We might equally well say that in working for others they work for themselves. Hence, someone who was averse to helping other people would, once he understood the logic of the system, be rather disconcerted if he had to play a part in it. For business success depends on supplying people with what they want, and hence involves helping them.

It may still be objected that there is something paradoxical about the morality of urging people to act selfishly in order to promote the common good, for, it may be said, while someone is deliberately pursuing the common good he cannot be acting selfishly, and while he is acting selfishly he cannot be deliberately promoting the common good. Is there any real difference, it may be asked, between advising people to look after themselves on the one hand, and asking them to look after themselves in order to promote the common good on the other? Will not this be taken, and rightly so, as an invitation not to bother about other people? Historians of the subject say that Adam Smith was influenced by Mandeville's paradox that private vices are public virtues when he argued that an 'invisible hand' secured a result, viz. the interest of the society, that the individual had not intended. The word 'intend' was not very fortunately chosen by Smith, for we can hardly intend something as remote as the interest of the society, we can only aim at it or try to bring it about. What we intend are things much closer to us than the interest of the society. When we intend to do something it is something we think we know quite well how to do. Again, when Smith says 'It is not from the benevolence of the butcher, the brewer, or the baker that we expect our dinner, but from their regard to their own interest',[23] he is right but a little misleading, for in a competitive market economy these people do try to give their customers what they want. They must try to do this if they are to sell their goods. The word 'benevolence' suggests gratuitous or unremunerated help, and certainly butchers do not give their meat away. But remunerated help is help nevertheless, and the point of trading in a market is that the help that men can afford one another is extended over a wide area and rendered more efficient by the device of free exchange. Giving help and receiving it are united in one process. Not only is self-help rewarded, but misanthropy is rendered difficult by being made to result in self-injury.

The Market and Its Limits

From time to time ministers of religion assert that religion ought not to be confined to church and to private life and call for the application of Christian principles of conduct to economic affairs. More generally, critics of the market economy often say that moral principles should be applied throughout society and not only in the non-market sections of it. This is Tawney's view when, in the passage quoted above (p. 39), he contrasts the 'view of economic activity which regarded it as one among other kinds of moral conduct' with 'the view of it as dependent upon impersonal and almost automatic forces'. The suggestion is that there is an impersonal system going on like clockwork—and we here

23. Adam Smith, *The Wealth of Nations*, I.ii, Glasgow edition, pp. 26–7.

recall Le Mercier de la Rivière's world that 'goes on its own'—with no kind of moral conduct in it, and a world quite distinct from the economic world, in which moral conduct does occur.

But if Tawney's words mean what they say, then they certainly say one thing that is wrong, for it is obvious that moral conduct, in the sense of conduct that is morally right or wrong and is in general subject to moral standards, does take place in the market as it is and does not need to be imported into it. For in the market people can be just or unjust, honest or dishonest, reliable or unreliable, and these are moral characteristics. They can also be cautious or rash, and these may be regarded as moral characteristics too, although some might say that they belong to the sphere of prudence and its opposite rather than to morality. Whether or not we say that prudence belongs to the moral sphere, there is not necessarily anything *wrong* in it, and hence there is nothing necessarily wrong in the looking after one's interests that the market calls for. The suggestion, therefore, that people must be immoral or amoral in their market activities is quite unfounded, for, even if prudence is not to count among moral virtues, honesty undoubtedly must. If it is argued that it is not genuine honesty because it is enforced by legal or professional sanctions, the answer is that genuine honesty is no more removed from the world of business because there are penalties for cheating, than genuine love is removed from the non-business world because there are penalties for assault.

On examination, therefore, we find that there is absolutely nothing in the complaint that markets are by their very nature immoral or amoral,[24] although many of those who par-

---

24. Some are, of course, such as markets in men, love, scandal.

ticipate in them cheat or would cheat if they dared. All that remains to charge the market with on this score, therefore, is that in it the Christian virtues of humility, charity and self-sacrifice are not displayed, or are displayed markedly less than in the political management of the economy.

But how could humility, charity and self-sacrifice be shown in the market? If we ask how they could be exercised by business firms, the absurdity of the question becomes apparent. A firm can give away money that might otherwise have been distributed as profits, but it must be in a financial position to do this if it is not to fall into financial difficulties. The very idea of a firm showing humility or sacrificing itself is absurd, and the idea of these virtues being exercised by individual participants in the market is hardly less so. If a man constantly deferred to others and could not bring himself to accept an order if someone else would thereby fail to get it, he could not long survive in business. We shall have more to say about this when we discuss the morality of competition, but it should be pretty clear already that no one who does not try to make a profit, or, what is the same thing, to avoid a loss, can effectively take part in market activities. Nor can he long remain in a position to make gifts to good causes or be taxed for any means whatever.

But this does not mean that even the Christian virtues must be absent from the business world altogether. Between the members of a firm or between its employees there is plenty of scope for humility and charity, and perhaps even for self-sacrifice as well. For example, a man might allow a friend to be promoted to a position which he would have liked to occupy himself. But this, although it happened in the business world, would not in itself be a market activity. There just would be no sense in a firm's allowing another firm to take its business from it. I hardly think, either, that we should regard it as humility or self-sacrifice if an employee took no steps to prevent his employer from underpaying him, unless his employer were a friend or a charity which the employee hoped to help thereby. Furthermore, those expending funds for good causes have a duty to make their expenditures as economically effective as possible.

In *Unto this Last* (1862), Ruskin says that it is the duty of a soldier to die rather than to leave his post in battle, of a physician to die rather than to leave his post in a plague, of a pastor to die rather than to teach falsehood, of a lawyer to die rather than to countenance injustice. Then Ruskin asks: 'The merchant—what is *his* due occasion of death?' His answer is that the merchant's function is to provide for society and that he must therefore face death or damage 'rather than fail in any engagement, or consent to any deterioration, adulteration, or unjust and exorbitant price of that which he provides'. Furthermore, the merchant must so conduct his business as to promote the welfare of his employees: 'And it becomes his duty, not only to be always considering how to produce what he sells, in the purest and cheapest forms, but how to make the various employments involved in the production, or the transference of it, most beneficial to the men employed.'[25]

The comparison of the merchant and the industrialist with the soldier was repeated by Tawney in *The Acquisitive Society*:

> The idea that there is some mysterious difference between making munitions of war and firing them, between building schools and teaching in them when built, between providing food and providing health, which makes it at once inevitable

25. [See John Ruskin, 'The Roots of Honour' in *Unto This Last*, 1862. Also see Ruskin, *Unto This Last and Other Writings*, ed C. Wilmer, Harmondsworth: Penguin Books, 1985, pp. 177–8.]

and laudable that the former should be carried on with a single eye to pecuniary gain, while the latter are conducted by professional men, who expect to be paid for their services, but who neither watch for windfalls nor raise their fees merely because there are more sick to be cured, more children to be taught, or more enemies to be resisted, is an illusion only less astonishing than that the leaders of industry should welcome the insult as an honour and wear their humiliation as a kind of halo. The work of making boots or building a house is in itself no more degrading than that of curing the sick or teaching the ignorant. It is as necessary and therefore as honourable. It should be at least equally bound by rules which have as their object to maintain the standards of professional service. It should be at least equally free from the vulgar subordination of moral standards to financial interests.[26]

This passage occurs in the course of a section headed: 'Industry as a profession'. Like Ruskin, Tawney contrasts businessmen, whose aim is to make profits, with professional men who do not 'watch for windfalls'. Industry, he says, is organised for the protection of rights, 'mainly rights to pecuniary gain', a profession 'for the performance of *duties*', the measure of their success being 'the service which they perform, not the gains which they amass'.[27] Thus, the suggestion is that if professional men acted on commercial principles, doctors would raise their fees during epidemics, teachers would demand more pay when the numbers of their pupils increased, and soldiers would do the same in time of war. The argument based on this suggestion is that since doctors, teachers and soldiers would regard it as wrong to do these things, businessmen should behave more like professional men and look to other things besides pecuniary gain. Curing the sick, it is said, counts most for the

26. R. H. Tawney, *The Acquisitive Society*, London: Bell, 1921, pp. 110–11. See the Fontana edition of the above, London: Collins, 1961, pp. 91–2.

27. Ibid., Bell, p. 108; Fontana, p. 89.

doctor, getting children to think and to exercise skills counts most for the teacher, defending the country counts most for the soldier. By analogy, therefore, supplying the needs of his customers should count most for the businessman who should not, therefore, have 'a single eye to pecuniary gain'. We must now proceed to examine the analogy and the argument.

Business and the Professions

There are so many different factors involved in these comparisons that it is very difficult to disentangle the essential from the irrelevant. Professions, for example, are very much concerned with their members' rights, and trades and industries and firms have to recognise all sorts of duties to suppliers, customers and employees. This was so in 1921, when Tawney was writing, as well as today, and hardly seems to present a fruitful topic for examination. As the businessman is compared with a number of different professions, perhaps it will be best if we first consider his side of the comparison.

Does the businessman have 'a single eye for pecuniary gain'? From what we have said about the competitive enterprise system this is true, in so far as the businessman is in business to avoid losses or to make a profit. If he gives anything away, this, unless it is a part of his marketing activity, is outside his business dealings, the very point of which is that he gets what he can by supplying goods and services that are in demand. What he can get is determined by what the buyers can and will pay and by the quality of his goods by comparison with that of the goods offered by other suppliers. He is required to be honest, to keep his promises about dates of delivery, to refrain from misdescribing his goods. He is not called upon to die for his customers, although keeping his promises to them may require him to work very hard on their behalf as well as on his own—and in a competitive system, in doing the latter he will be doing the former as well.[28] A lazy distributor of insulin or of 'heart machines' is not only unbusinesslike but also insensitive or callous.

Now let us suppose that there is a shortage, not of his contriving, of the goods that a merchant supplies. This will bring the price up, but it may not bring more profit to the merchant, for the volume of his sales may diminish. If there were a very serious shortage and the price went high, the poorer customers might have to buy less or nothing at all. If, however, the suppliers did not put up the price, the goods would be bought up by the earliest buyers, probably those who first realised that there was a shortage. If in such conditions there was only one supplier, he might be able to make very high profits, especially if there were no substitutes for the product he sells. The profits of each would be limited if there were competition between the sellers. If the shortage were a general shortage of food it would be considered wrong to allow the demand to push the prices up to such an extent that the poorer people were brought to starvation or near to it, and in such circumstances a publicly controlled system of rationing would be introduced. A new law, penalties for

28. In an overstretched economy suffering from wage inflation, he will not be able to *keep* his promises about deliveries, and if he does not *make* the promises he will not get the orders. This is one way in which inflation corrodes basic morality. To compare the selfishness of business men with the public spirit of professional men in such circumstances is fatuous, but it is only fair to mention that Tawney had in mind quite a different set of economic conditions in a non-inflationary economy.

breach of it, the registration of individuals, the issue of ration books would then become necessary.

We may now examine the contrasting cases cited by Tawney. The doctors he had in mind are supposed to be working privately for fees. What happens when there is an epidemic? Tawney assumes that they would not think it right to put up their fees. But they would then have to see more patients and would in consequence receive *more* in fees, even though the fees had not been raised. But perhaps the epidemic is so great that not all patients can be treated by the existing body of doctors. Then each doctor would be expected to treat those who needed treatment most, as far as he could find this out. It is important to notice that he can judge the varying needs of his patients much more easily than a shopkeeper could judge the varying needs of his customers, for the doctor examines the patient, even goes into his home, whereas the shopkeeper, unless he serves a village, does not know much about the personal circumstances of his customers. Hence a doctor can act as his own rationing authority and, indeed, might be *better* at it than any Ministry of Health. Treating patients is a very different sort of service from selling goods, and the differences between what is reasonable from shopkeepers and merchants in times of famine and what is reasonable from doctors in times of epidemics depend on this distinction. Perhaps a reason why traders are criticised in times of famine more than doctors are in times of epidemic is that the former can often get food for themselves whereas doctors run the same risks of disease as everyone else, if not more.

We need not consider the case of doctors employed by a national health service, as the comparisons we need may be examined by relation to teachers and soldiers, the other cases mentioned by Ruskin and Tawney. According to Tawney, then, teachers would not consider it right to demand salary increases in return for teaching more children. But if this meant that they would have to work much harder, it would not be wrong of them to make such a demand and the increased salary may be essential to attract more people into teaching and away from other employments. The difference between teachers and traders is largely due to differences in what they do. Teachers have continuous personal relationships with considerable numbers of children, and are bound to them by likes (and dislikes) and by their understanding of their characters and personalities. They are expected to give encouragement and to have sympathy and loyalty. These are not qualities much required in the processes of marketing, and businessmen exercise them, if at all, in their relation to colleagues within the firm. What is necessarily central in the activity of teaching is peripheral in the activity of trading. Hence it is inappropriate that the professional attitudes of teachers should find their way into industry and commerce, even though in business certain teaching functions are necessary here and there. It is worth noticing, too, that whereas a teacher's pupils are, so to say, his final products, the businessman's subordinates are links in a chain of production and distribution.

The comparison with soldiers raises some points of interest. It would be disgraceful for soldiers to demand more pay in time of war with the threat of not fighting at all unless the increase was granted. Yet the trader will not forgo a rise of price in times of scarcity. But for the trader's action in not raising prices to have any point he would have to ration his supplies, and his customers might not like that at all—he needs the authority of the state to do such things. The soldier is part of the state's authority, and if he refuses to fight he mutinies, and if he does so successfully, he seizes authority from its former holders. Why should not the merchant risk his life for something or other as the soldier risks his life for his country? Under a system of division of labour the merchant's circumstances do not generally require this. His function is to take another sort of risk, that of financing a transaction before its total costs are known and before the demand from customers is known either. The soldier is housed and fed and clothed by the state, while the entrepreneur takes the responsibility for these things himself and faces economic uncertainties. Here, again, therefore, the idea of transferring the responsibilities of a soldier to the man of business is seen to rest on similarities too slight to produce any conviction, once the negative analogies are brought to light.

It is absurd, then, to criticise the man of business for not exhibiting the devotion of a hard-working doctor, the sympathy of a schoolteacher, or the self-sacrifice of a soldier. His circumstances do not normally call for these virtues, but for foresight, honesty, reliability in keeping promises, and a readiness to accept the consequences of the risks he has to take.

Is Private Trading Wicked?

It may be argued that we have still failed to identify the central moral defect of profit-making, which is to be found in the very process of bargaining itself. There is, it may be said, something essentially ignoble in the higgling of the market. Traders are engaged in wicked work. We are not surprised to find such an attitude in the writings of Plato and of other upholders of an aristocratic form of society, for trading has always been looked down upon by the nobility, who use traders and sometimes have pillaged them. But why should this aristocratic attitude survive into presentday society? Can any convincing reasons be put forward in support of it?

The best attempt to do this that I know of was that of J. A. Hobson. One of Hobson's earliest books was his *John Ruskin* (1898), in which he expounded and upheld Ruskin's economic theories. In his later writings Hobson applied Ruskin's ideas about non-economic goods to the social problems of the nineteen-twenties and nineteen-thirties, and endeavoured to show that dealings in markets are essentially bad. In *Wealth and Life* (London: Macmillan, 1929) Hobson wrote:

> Save in the rare case when both parties are equally strong in finance, knowledge, and organization, business bargains distribute the gain unequally and proportionately to an economic force which, in its final issue, means the power 'to starve the other out' (pp. 211–12).

In the same passage he also wrote:

> By their very nature the bargaining processes inhibit the consideration of the good of others, and concentrate the mind and will of each party upon the bargaining for his own immediate and material gains . . . this constant drive of selfish interest involves a hardening of the moral arteries (p. 213).

And in a lecture entitled *The Moral Challenge to the Economic System*, given to the Ethical Union in 1933, he said:

> Sometimes the market is favourable to the sellers, sometimes to the buyers. What does that mean? It means that a superior bargaining power belongs to one side or the other, and that the price will be determined by this superiority of power, distributing the gain in accordance not with equity but force.[29]

29. [*The Moral Challenge to the Economic System*, London: The Ethical Union, 1933, p. 15.]

Let us first consider the claim that in market dealings it is 'force' or 'power' that prevails over 'equity'. Does force or power prevail in practice? Certainly not in the sense in which it would prevail if, instead of there being an exchange or sale, the stronger party had taken from the weaker party what he wanted from him. Markets can only operate when force of this sort (what Bastiat called 'spoliation') has been eliminated. Competitive markets require law and peace and order if they are to work at all. Thus, 'power' and 'force' must mean something else, 'the power to starve the other out' mentioned by Hobson in *Wealth and Life*. But no such power is exercised when the prices of cabbages, meat, bread and other foods are settled in ordinary markets. Of course, the producers and owners of these things need not sell them and could, if they could concert to stop all rival suppliers, hold them back until their customers got really hungry. But the producers and merchants are in business to sell, and if one firm tried to make its customers feel the pinch of hunger, other firms would sell to them. In a competitive market a price, so to say, *emerges*, by reference to the demand and to the available supply. If someone cannot pay the market price, then he has to go without, and hence the very poor cannot satisfy their needs as well as the rich can satisfy theirs and may have to be given additional money. Force is present in that if the very poor tried to *take* what they could not *buy*, they would face arrest and punishment. But if very many were in this position, the price would have to come down, otherwise the goods would not be sold. It should not be forgotten that not only do consumers wish (or need) to have, but that producers and merchants want to sell. Furthermore, employers may have fixed capital investment at stake, whereas their employees can walk out and leave them with the consequences.

Force or power are much more apparent, I suggest, when there is *no* market, as when governments in time of war barter large quantities of goods or contract bulk sales and purchases with governments of other countries. In such circumstances there cannot be a market and, as experience showed in the last war, the parties finally settle because they have to.[30] Even so, it is not necessarily the *stronger* that gets his way. For the weaker party can bargain from its very weakness, arguing, sometimes successfully, that the stronger power has more to lose in the event of the weaker power's collapsing. So called 'oriental' bargaining, again, is either a form of amusement, or else possible only because one or both of the parties is ignorant of the state of the market. In developed competitive markets there is very little bargaining because there is no need for it among those who understand the supply situation.

I suggest, therefore, that Hobson's account of bargaining in a market is more like bargaining in the absence of markets. It is indeed, more like politics than trade, and one must conclude that, in spite of his discoveries about the effects of over-saving, he did not really know what goes on in markets.[31]

Another element in Hobson's indictment of the market is that the price is not determined by equity. By this he means that the market price is not a just price. The passage we have quoted from his Ethical Union lecture suggests that Hobson thought that a price would be just, or at any rate less

30. At that time the Russians searched through Western trade journals to find the highest prices quoted in them for the commodities they wished to sell.

31. His interesting *Confessions of an Economic Heretic*, London: Allen & Unwin, 1938, bears this out. Hobson lived in the world of books and journalism and was sheltered by a private income. He complains that no university department of economics in the country ever *asked* him to take a job with them (see p. 83), but he does not say that he ever *applied* for one.

unjust, when there is no large discrepancy in bargaining power between buyers and sellers. It is certainly an appealing picture of economic justice that Hobson sets before us, in which no one is under pressure from anyone else and everyone exerts the same economic influence as all the others. In order that such a situation could exist, it would be necessary for no one to be so poor that he paid prices that he regretted having to pay. In such a situation, sellers too would not be forced to receive less than their goods had cost them. There would be no shortages, no commercial miscalculations, no governmental muddles, no obstinate or arbitrary men making use of an advantageous position. That is, in order that just prices could be established supplies would have to be ample and yet not constitute a glut, and a population of reasonable, moderate men, free from inordinate desires, would have to be in possession of incomes that made them invulnerable to economic pressures. This may be an ideal situation; it is neither a real nor a likely one. The prices established in a competitive market have the function of getting goods and services from suppliers to consumers in the conditions that prevail. With increasing prosperity these prices might get established with less urgent pressures on the parties involved and so approach nearer to Hobson's conception of justice. But to complain that they are not just in this sense is to refer to an unavoidable consequence of the world's scarcities and man's imperfection.

In a part of his Ethical Union lecture which I have not quoted, Hobson shows that a major injustice in the settling of market prices which he has in mind, is the price paid for labour. The 'vital resources' of employers, he argues, are larger than those of their employees, so that employees are forced by their employers to accept lower wages than they would do if they had no fear of losing their jobs. Hence, it is wage bargaining in a competitive market which he considers to lead to particularly unjust results.

Hobson was writing at a time when there was much unemployment and when, therefore, employees were at a disadvantage because the employer could generally find someone else to do the job if the employee were disposed to press his demands. But the position now is very different. When there is less unemployment and when most employees are ready (or are persuaded) to strike when their unions require them to do so, the bargaining advantage is on the side of the wage-earners. According to Hobson's view of justice, therefore, at a time of full or overfull employment it would be employers who are unjustly treated, and justice can only be made possible when employment is less than full, and in consequence employers have a prospect of resisting some of the claims the unions make upon them. His notion of a just wage, therefore, comes very close to that of a wage established in a competitive market between parties who have alternative bargains open to them; in this case, between employees who can offer their services elsewhere and employers who can hold their employees to their agreements without thereby risking a strike. It is interesting to note that Professor Michael Fogarty, in his defence of the scholastic theory of the just wage, assumes a fairly freely working labour market in which monopolistic and monopsonistic positions are not exploited.[32]

Another difference between Hobson's day and ours is that unemployment benefits are now less inadequate, and receiving them is not regarded as a stigma. To this extent, the employee is under less pressure in making his wage bargain and is therefore less forced than in the past. His choice is not

32. M. Fogarty, *The Just Wage*, London: G. Chapman, 1961; see especially pp. 12 and 264–5.

now between accepting the employer's terms or starving and becoming an object of contempt. It is rather between working for a higher remuneration or striking and receiving strike pay himself and state assistance for his family. He might even find another job while the strike is on. Leaving moral considerations out of account, a man might opt for leisure and lower remuneration rather than for work with higher remuneration. In so far as fear of unemployment is fear of idleness or of loss of dignity, it presupposes the value and dignity of work and of providing for oneself and one's family. If voluntary unemployment and idleness ceased altogether to be regarded as disgraceful, and if it were legally possible and sufficiently well provided for, wage bargaining would be of interest only to the more energetic, ambitious and conscientious members of the community. Trade unions, therefore, have a material interest in the dignity of labour, and stand to lose their functions if it is belittled or denied.

Profits and Wages

It is implied in the Carlyle-Ruskin-Tawney-Hobson line of thought that profits are morally inferior types of remuneration by comparison with professional fees or wages and salaries. In a free and competitive system profits are obtained by laying out monies in buying or producing goods and selling them when they are produced or demanded. The entrepreneur has to buy materials, engage workmen, pay for transport, cover the costs of all this and recoup them by the sales he makes. He runs the risk of not recouping his outgoings, for he may have paid too readily or too highly, or the goods he has bought or has been responsible for manufacturing may no longer be in demand, or may be less in demand than when he set the transaction in motion. He contracts to sell his goods or products, but he contracts with no one to give him a profit and he may in the event make a loss. Whether or not he makes a profit, and its amount if he does make one, depend on his skill in forecasting and in organising, and on luck as well.[33] The entrepreneur has to be willing to back his judgment and chance his luck. Like someone who backs horses, he hopes to strike lucky but, again like him, he may fail.

Wages and salaries are very different. The employee has to find an entrepreneur, or a public firm or corporation, who will employ him. He then contracts for a wage or salary for a certain period. He is remunerated for doing particular sorts of things in an already existing organisation which he does not control. His remuneration is something prescribed for a definite period. By contracting for it, he is on to a near-certainty for the period of the contract,[34] but he has no hope of striking lucky as the entrepreneur might do. In a letter dated 25 September 1857, Marx asserts that wages were, in their first beginnings, payments known as *peculium castrense*, service money, paid to soldiers in the Roman army.[35] I doubt whether he is right in this, but it does bring out an important feature of wages and salaries, namely that they are payments made by an employer to those who serve or work for him. There is someone definite who pays out the wages contracted for. Profits, on the contrary, are what are left over when this man or firm has completed the transaction of making, moving, selling the goods.

33. Inflation lessens his risks and makes it easier for him to make profits.

34. The employee takes a risk when he acquires a skill, which at some later date, may not be needed.

35. [For Marx's letter of September 25, 1857, see Karl Marx and Friedrich Engels, *Collected Works*, volume 40, New York: International Publishers, 1983, pp. 186–7.]

These differences are of central importance. If all remuneration were by means of wages and salaries, everyone would have to be employed by some individual or by some firm or corporation. In these circumstances there would be no individual entrepreneurs at all. Could there then be individual firms? Hardly, for what would a firm be in the absence of possible profit or loss? Suppose there were several 'organisations', as we might call them, providing the same type of goods, say shoes, and suppose they were not trying to make a profit. What output would they decide on? Who would their customers be? How would they fix their prices? In the absence of the test of profitability, the firms would have to make these decisions by agreement between one another, or, if they could not agree, someone would have to tell them what to do.[36] If firms cannot make profits and losses, they must become administrative or productive units within an organisation where everyone is paid for his services to it. Profits, therefore, belong and are essential to independently operating economic units, wages and salaries to those who serve them or who serve other bodies such as armies or nationalised concerns. Profits are bound up with one main system of economic organisation. Wages are payable under all except slave systems. Profits are not contracted for, wages are. Profits have no definite limits, up or down. Wages have as their lower limit what is necessary to keep the wage-earner alive and fit and willing to work, and as their upper limit what an employer would be prepared to pay rather than do without the wage-earner's services.

Because of these fundamental differences, one would expect wages and profits to carry different moral implications.

36. In centrally directed societies they are told by the state, although in recent years such societies are finding it necessary to use the profit and price system.

Wages are contracted for, and therefore impose specific duties on those who pay them and those who receive them. The former must endeavour to pay the same wages for the same work, the latter to do the work they get the wages for doing. Since profits are not contracted for, there can be no very definite idea of a just or fair profit. Profits are essentially residual, variable, problematic. To use the word 'remuneration' both for wages and for profits is to suggest that they are more alike than they really are. The profit-seeker has expectations and hopes but can make no claim to any particular rate of profit. The wage- and salary-earner can claim what was agreed on and what is appropriate for the amount of work he does. To apply to profits the moral principles that are applied to wages is to abolish, or to wish to abolish, profits altogether, and that would be to abolish or wish to abolish the system of competing firms and entrepreneurs in favour of a universal employer or combination of employers.

At a period of continuing inflation, a large proportion of entrepreneurs and firms make profits, and very few fail to do so. As a result, the risk-taking aspect of profits appears to be diminished and they appear more like fees or wages. Furthermore, when governments intervene in the fixing of wages and prices their accountants, in arriving at the levels they propose, are bound to think of a level of profits which firms may be reasonably expected to make. In consequence, profits are made to appear more like fees or discounts than they are under conditions of competition. Again, when politicians dispute on the hustings about the distribution of wealth and the level of incomes, they tend to lump profits and wages together, as competing forms of remuneration. When the 'pay-freeze' of 20 July 1966 was instituted the government said it must apply to dividends as well as to wages, even though they were aware that the deflationary steps they were taking would reduce or eliminate many profits in any case. When government intervention leads to the conception of 'reasonable' profits, then governments and the firms that feel bound to cooperate with them imply that a profit is something to which a firm has a *right*, or to which it is *entitled*, something that can be *fixed by agreement*. But a profit then becomes more like a fee or a discount, and the whole structure of industry is being looked at in a different light.[37] For the 'profit' is now regarded as a cost of the enterprise, as something that must be allowed for, even if not paid out, like interest or bank loans, or like wages.

We shall consider this further when we examine the ethics of systems alternative to the competitive market economy. In the meantime it is sufficient to notice that, since profits are not rights or entitlements, they are, morally as well as legally, very different from wages, and different, though not as different as wages are, from fees and discounts.

37. As in H. F. R. Catherwood, *Britain with the Brakes Off*, London: Hodder and Stoughton, 1966. It is significant that the Director-General of the NEDC,* who wishes to draw businessmen into a state-controlled system, tends to write of 'return on capital' when others would say 'profit', and to emphasize the weaknesses of competition.

*[NEDC—the National Economic Development Council—was set up in 1962 as an exercise in corporatism in which representatives of trade unions, employers and the government were to study problems of economic policy and make recommendations.]

CHAPTER 3
THE ETHICS OF COMPETITION

Competition, Strife and Rivalry

Critics of competitive markets often contrast the competition that is essential to such markets with non-competitive cooperation. They believe that competition goes along with such characteristics as aggression, emulation, rivalry, conflict and strife, and that cooperation belongs with mutual aid, benevolence, modesty and harmony. In their view it follows, therefore, that economic competition is morally inferior to cooperative, non-competitive modes of commercial and industrial organisation. Right-minded people, it is assumed, are against strife and in favour of harmony and mutual aid. Modestly conducted cooperation, therefore, is superior to aggressive competition, and hence collectivist organisation is to be preferred to what these critics call 'the law of the jungle'. Collectivists are on the side of the angels while supporters of competitive markets are the Devil's disciples, helping him to bring misfortunes on the hindmost. Some, even, of those who support capitalism do so in a shamefaced way,[38]

38. See again Catherwood, *Britain with the Brakes Off.* In *The Christian in Industrial Society*, London: Tyndale, 1964, Mr Catherwood had proposed the setting up of what were later called 'Little Neddies'* (p. 37).

*[Little Neddies were bodies set up for particular industries, on the model of the national NEDC. The suggestions of Catherwood's to which Acton refers are not to be found in the third (1980) edition of his book.]

as they are convinced that in itself collectivism, being a form of cooperation and harmony, is morally superior to capitalism, even though, alas, human egoism makes capitalism inevitable.

We must now ask whether competition in free markets does have the morally obnoxious features we have just mentioned. Is it a species of strife, rivalry, emulation? Is it opposed to altruism, cooperation and harmony? Is the only moral justification for competitive markets and capitalism that socialism is an ideal beyond human capacity to realise?

According to Dr Samuel Johnson, competition is 'the action of endeavouring to gain what another endeavours to gain at the same time'.[39] Johnson expresses this definition in morally neutral terms and brings out the central idea that in competition two or more people want and try to get what only one can have. He does not say anything about *how* they try to get it, since this depends upon what it is that they want and how it *can* be got. There certainly are what we might call competitive jungle situations in which animals seize food and run away with it or fight among themselves for it. Human beings sometimes do similar things, as when the members of a Bingo Club jostled each other as they pillaged presents intended for children at a Christmas party. Those who gain them do so as a result of strength or agility, but although some animals fight to the death, human beings generally confine their scramble within rules. With animals there may be no rules at all, and no conception of what is fair or unfair.[40] When 'all's fair in love or war' human beings approach the jungle situation.

39. [See the citation of Johnson in the entry for 'Competition' in *The Oxford English Dictionary*, volume 2, p. 720.]

40. Animals do generally confine their fights within rules, and so may be said to have some conception of what is permissible.

But let us now consider the sort of situation in which human beings compete for a prize or a job. In such situations the competitors may not meet one another and may not even know one another. When a prize is offered, say, for the best essay on Balzac or for the first correct solution of a mathematical problem, the winner of the competition is the competitor who does the required thing best or first. There has to be an awarding authority which makes the award according to certain rules. The essay has to be of such and such a length and has to be sent in by such and such a date. Applicants for a job have to submit accounts of their qualifications, specimens of their work, and so on. If there is only one prize or only one job, then at least one competitor has to be unsuccessful.

We may now compare prize competition situations with competitive jungle situations. In the latter, let us suppose, there are no rules and no awarding authorities. In the absence of rules, jungle competition may take place when there is enough for all, even though it is intensified when there is a scarcity. In prize competition situations, there is never enough for all, and there must be losers. Jungle competition often takes place by means of fighting, but this is not necessary to it, since by eating its food or occupying its space, a group of animals may destroy another group it does not come into contact with. For competition of either sort to involve rivalry, the competitors have to know one another, for when 'rivalry' does not mean the same thing as 'competition', it means the attempt of individuals or groups to outdo other individuals or groups, and this requires the rivals to have some knowledge of one another. It is possible to compete without knowing that one is competing, for someone might endeavour to obtain a prize or job without knowing that others are after it too. The essence of competition is that each competitor strives after what he wants. The essence of rivalry is that each competitor strives to outdo the others. In competition, the failure of the losers is a consequence of the success of the winners, not something that the winners aim to secure. Rivals, on the other hand, set out to *defeat each other* as well as to win the prize. To aim at defeating someone else comes somewhat closer to malevolence than mere competition does. Someone who endeavours to write the best essay in order to win the prize, may have no desire to defeat anyone else, but rivals do endeavour to defeat one another. Friendly rivalry is possible, as in games, but even this can easily spill over into hostility.

In jungle competition, then, the competing parties may fight, and may act as rivals to one another. But even in this primitive kind of competition, fighting *need* not occur, and does not when a species of animal unwittingly destroys the food of another species. In prize or job competition, there is an awarding authority proceeding according to rules, as there is not in jungle competition. As in some sorts of jungle competition, the competitors for prizes or jobs may not know one another or have any personal contact with one another. If they know one another they can behave as rivals. Rivals can be friends, as in games, but rivalry has kinship with hostility and malevolence, because rivals endeavour to outdo one another as well as to do what will win them the prize. The existence of rules for competitions for prizes and jobs limits the things that can be done to win. Competitors at local flower shows have been known to destroy their rivals' blooms. But this sort of behaviour is against the rules.

How, then, is economic competition related to the forms of competition we have now considered? It shares one important presupposition with them, that there is not an abundance of everything for everybody. If everyone could always get everything that he wanted, there would be no economic activity and no competition. Competition of all sorts presupposes scarcity, or at any rate a *belief* that what is wanted is scarce. (There might be enough food for all the animals who fight for it, but they fight because they do not know this.) Now competitive markets are not places where people fight, nor places where they pursue their rivalries. We have already seen that the attempts to outwit one another in what is called 'oriental' bargaining are not features of developed markets, but can only make sense for parties who are ignorant of conditions of supply and demand. Rivalry comes in when political considerations are important, as with pre-emptive purchases in time of war. But in general, economic behaviour in competitive markets is a peaceful sort of thing. Piracy and confiscation are uncommercial activities and trade flourishes when goods can be inspected and moved about without danger from marauding bands. Exchange, as we have seen, is morally preferable to spoliation or entreaty.

These, however, are very general considerations, and we must now consider some forms of economic activity in more detail, in order to see what morally relevant forms competition may take. Let us consider, then, competition between firms for a contract, competition in the labour market, and competition to sell to ultimate consumers.

(a) Competition for Contracts

When firms compete for a contract they are in a situation analogous to that between competitors for a prize or a job. Each firm tries to get the order for itself by considering its own technical resources and probable costs in relation to what it considers the ordering firm is willing to pay. Its knowledge that other firms are tendering discourages it from asking too much, and its desire to make as good a profit as possible makes it unwilling to ask too little. Knowledge, intelligence and luck all affect the success of the enterprise. Rivalry need not enter into the situation at all, although, of course, it often does. A spirit of rivalry could cloud the judgment of a firm or individual and lead to unprofitable courses. In trying to obtain an order, of course, the tendering firm does more than quote its price, it will laud its product. Its representative may entertain the potential buyer and flatter him. But a buyer who signs a contract because of the charm of the salesman rather than because of the economic merits of the deal may come to regret it and certainly will do so if he makes a practice of acting in that way. Both parties will judge the success of the contract in terms of eventual profit or loss and, in a competitive situation, are led by the hope of profit to cut their costs as much as they can.

It should be noted that there is impersonal competition between firms, just as there is impersonal competition between animals in the jungle. We have said that a group or species of animal, even without fighting, may deprive another group or species of its food or space, and in so doing may lead to its extinction. In the process of natural selection those animals which do not succeed in adapting themselves to their circumstances eventually die out. They may be devoured by others, or they may just be deprived of what they need by others which do not ever meet or recognise them. Something analogous happens between firms. A firm which makes and uses a new invention may cause other firms to go out of business or even bring about the extinction of a whole industry. The defeated firms or industries are not assaulted or threatened; they just cease to get orders. But the extinction of a firm or an industry is not the same sort of thing as the extinction of an animal or a species. When the last are rendered extinct, particular animal organisms die and have no descendants. Physical death occurs. But the extinction of firms and industries does not necessarily involve the physical death of human organisms, even though a stockbroker may jump from the roof or handloom weavers die of hunger.[41] Bankruptcy may be described as economic death, but it is quite different from physical death. Firms themselves, indeed, may survive by changing the scope of their activities, and even if they are extinguished, the men who direct the work for them go elsewhere and work for other firms. Herbert Spencer's phrase 'the survival of the fittest'[42] applies, therefore, to firms as well as to animals and animal species, but in its economic application it does not imply the physical death of those that fail to survive, but only the cessation of some groupings and activities and the assumption and organisation of new ones.

(b) Competition Between Suppliers of Labour

We may now consider some moral implications of competition in the market for labour. When workmen compete with one another for jobs and firms compete with one another for workmen, wages vary in terms of its supply and of the demand for labour. It is well known that for several generations from the end of the eighteenth century employers in industrial countries had the upper hand over those who worked for them. The population was increasing, new industrial methods were making traditional skills useless to

41. The bankrupt stockbroker is generally 'hammered' and the employees of dying industries are nowadays retrained, redeployed or pensioned.

42. [Herbert Spencer, *The Principles of Biology*, volume 1, New York: D. Appleton & Company, 1884, p. 444.]

those who had them, and combinations among workmen were legally regarded as criminal conspiracies. Furthermore, the society within which the industrial revolution was taking place was already divided into classes and accustomed to the exercise of authority from above. In these circumstances workmen tended to be the losers in wage bargaining, and their situation was improved when legal obstacles to the formation of trade unions were removed, and improved still more when trade unions were given legal immunity from claims for damages.

Nowadays groups of employers negotiate with trade unions and in many industries no workman can get a job if he does not belong to a union, and may lose it if he does not strike when his union gives the order. Furthermore, it is a function of unions to prohibit unusually productive or efficient workmanship on the part of its members, and in this way competition between more efficient and less efficient workmen is prevented. Because of their need for votes, democratic political parties dare not seem to falter in advocating full employment. When there are more jobs than there are workmen to fill them, employers bid among one another for skilled men and in this way the total wages paid are often much higher than those negotiated between unions and employers' associations. At the same time there has been a growth of egalitarian sentiment, so that workmen are less inclined to fall in with their employers' wishes than they were in the nineteenth-century aftermath of aristocratic society.

(c) Competition Between Employers of Labour

When there is full employment and unions bargain on behalf of men who have little fear of losing their jobs, there is competition between firms for the skilled labour they find it difficult to obtain, but little competition between workmen applying for jobs. If competition promotes efficiency, then the absence of competition among workers is likely to lessen their working efficiency. Trade unions, furthermore, tend to discourage speed and efficiency of work, and in so doing they tend to diminish pride in achievement and workmanship. In such conditions unions are not the protectors of the workers against grasping employers—the employers may *want* to grasp, but they just cannot do so—but aggressive fomenters of increased claims. If they did not act in this way they would not retain their members, since the terms of trade favour the workers in any case. The trade unions are thus tempted to require all workers to become union men and to regard themselves as united claimants from what the employers wilfully withhold from them. It is no longer a question of individuals competing for jobs as if they were prizes, but of the whole group extorting a collective prize for everyone. Bargaining comes into its own again, and the employers do well if they manage to settle for something less than the original demand. Instead of individuals competing with one another for scarce jobs, there are large organisations, manœuvring, compromising, bluffing and striking to secure collective transfers of wealth. Instead of competing with one another, the workers support organisations which threaten and fight for them.

Under conditions of full employment, then, employers compete for labour, even when they do not compete with one another in other ways. Employees, however, do not compete among themselves, but pay spokesmen to bargain for collective benefits on their behalf. It is not a situation of emulation and rivalry between individuals, but one of conflicting collectivities. But even in these conditions the *impersonal* competition I mentioned above still continues. As invention proceeds, for example, some industries decline by comparison with others. Thus oil and gas gain by comparison with coal, and road transport by comparison with the railways. Declining private industries may get state subsidies, declining nationalised industries may get both subsidies and other privileges. But unless they can be kept in being as museum pieces, like the Swiss Guards at the Vatican, they are reduced or eliminated just like the unsuccessful firms in competitive market conditions. This competition is inseparable from the attempt to improve. Whenever someone tries to do something in a better way than it has been done before, others are faced with the choice of doing likewise or of being squeezed out. There may be no rivalry, no emulation, no struggle, no fighting, but just an exercise of originality or ingenuity by someone who has no intention of competing with or outdoing anyone.

(d) Competition to Sell to Consumers

We now come to competition to sell to ultimate consumers and the ethics of the relationships involved. There is a sense in which the ultimate consumers compete among themselves, in that a buyer who is unwilling to buy at the price that is asked may realise that there are others who will pay that price. The sellers, of course, compete with one another in providing what the consumers want at prices they will pay. The sellers also compete with one another in offering the consumers commodities they had not thought of before.

Competition between sellers is not unlike competition between firms for contracts and raises no new issues except those connected with advertising. Competition between buyers is hardly felt as such in competitive markets. This is because most consumers arrange their purchases according to their means, and go to those shops where the things they can afford are on sale. In societies divided into classes, few individuals think much about expenditures outside or beyond their ability to pay. But the situation is rather different when everyone thinks it possible or thinks it right that he should buy everything that is on offer. Then he may come to regard the rich man who pays high prices as competing against him, with superior buying power, for goods that he would like to have but is prevented from affording. When there is a single, classless market, the feeling of being, so to say, 'out-bought' by others is engendered. This encourages both demands for higher pay and demands for reductions in the spending-power of the richer consumers. I suggest that competition between consumers is not emulative when they think of their budgets in terms of their resources. It tends to become emulative when they take seriously the idea of expenditure beyond the limits of their present income. In the nineteenth century and earlier twentieth, those who had such ambitions aimed first to acquire the money necessary to satisfy them. They tried to get better paid jobs and they saved. But many consumers now hope for these results by collective measures exerted through trade unions and political parties. This is the reason why hopes and demands outrun resources and intensify the struggle for them. Whereas in the earlier forms of free competition individuals were encouraged to rely on their own efforts and abilities, in the system of cooperative conflict that has now emerged individuals hope to satisfy their desires by collective protection and pressure groups. The activities of individuals are merged into those of groups and masses.

Opponents of competitive markets often criticise the part played by advertisements in stimulating desire and demand.

They assert that when competing firms advertise in order to encourage expenditure on their goods they stimulate a materialistic outlook and mould men's lives in doing so. It is true that advertisement can lead to increased sales,[43] but commercial advertisement is only part of the apparatus of persuasion that operates so massively in contemporary society. Ever since the eighteenth century political leaders have been saying that each individual has the right to pursue his happiness, and the results of this belief are being experienced in our day. The 'scramble' for consumption goods is due to the misleading belief that there is increased wealth to be had effortlessly for all rather than to economic competition. Individuals would be less willing to buy what advertisers tell them if they were more inclined to accept limitations on their desires. When, furthermore, governments encourage inflation, thrift becomes pointless except for those with very large incomes or very small outgoings or both. The inflation characteristic of our day results from the happiness-seeking moral outlook of our time as well as from clumsy attempts to apply Keynesian economic theories in democratic societies. Indeed, Keynes's economic theory was in part an expression of his opposition to the strenuous moralism of the Victorian era when it was generally considered right first to save and then to spend. This comes out in a passage of *The General Theory of Employment, Interest and Money* (Macmillan, 1936) where he writes, with reference to Mandeville's criticisms of the evils of saving:

> No wonder that such wicked sentiments called down the opprobrium of two centuries of moralists and economists who felt much more virtuous in possession of their austere doctrine that no sound remedy was discoverable except in the utmost of thrift

43. Ralph Harris and Arthur Seldon, *Advertising in Action*, London: Hutchinson for the Institute of Economic Affairs, 1962.

and economy both by the individual and by the state. Petty's 'entertainments, magnificent shows, triumphal arches, etc.' gave place to the penny-wisdom of Gladstonian finance and to a state system which 'could not afford' hospitals, open spaces, noble buildings, even the preservation of its ancient monuments, far less the splendours of music and the drama, all of which were consigned to the private charity or magnanimity of improvident individuals.[44]

In *The Fable of the Bees*,[45] Mandeville called prodigality 'that noble sin', and elaborated this by saying: 'I mean the unmixed prodigality of heedless and voluptuous men, that being educated in plenty, abhor the vile thoughts of lucre.' Keynes, like his friend (and rival) Lytton Strachey, disliked the puritanism inculcated in Victorian times, and Mandeville's easygoing hedonism was congenial to him. It has now become congenial to large sections of the population and in doing so has served to increase both the effective demand for consumer goods and the belief that they ought to be available for the asking. It is in this moral climate that advertisers of consumer goods operate, and there will be a 'scramble' for them as long as this fundamental weather does not change. There is no consistency, and little honesty, in criticising competitive advertising and at the same time proclaiming the right of everyone to as much as they can enjoy.

44. J. M. Keynes, *The General Theory of Employment, Interest and Money*, London: Macmillan, 1936, p. 362. Compare the passage from the *Treatise of Money* (1930) quoted in Sir Roy Harrod's *The Life of John Maynard Keynes*, London: Macmillan 1951, pp. 406–7; Harmondsworth: Penguin Books, 1972, pp. 478–9; where the relation of thrift to enterprise and profit is most carefully stated. The anti-Victorian ambit of Keynes's outlook is made clear by Harrod in chapter 5 and elsewhere. [See too Keynes, *A Treatise on Money, volume 2, The Applied Theory of Money*, in his *Collected Works*, volume 6, London: Macmillan and Royal Economic Society, 1971, p. 132.]

45. [See Bernard Mandeville, *The Fable of the Bees*, ed. F. B. Kaye, Indianapolis: Liberty Fund, 1989, pp. 25 and 103.]

Market Commodities and Non-market Goods

In Chapter 1 (p. 27) I indicated that casualties of the competitive market system, those who are unable to maintain themselves by their own exertions, may need to be supported by non-market means. Children as such are hardly casualties, but, apart from family allowances and school tuition and meals, and medical care, they are supported by their parents, and, to a decreasing extent, incapacitated parents are supported by their children. Insurance is a means of dealing with casualties within the market mechanism itself, and in this way both firms and individuals may guard themselves against the effects of death, accident, illness and other human risks. If there are people who cannot afford to pay the premiums, and if there are misfortunes that the market cannot insure against, then casualties may have to be helped by other than market means to enter the market, except that the incapacitated may need personal care in kind.

It was because the market was thought incapable of helping people in need of help that poor relief, unemployment benefit and medical care was provided, by private charity, voluntary insurance or publicly financed agencies. Thus people get incomes they do not work for, to pay for food and clothing they could not otherwise buy. They also get subsidised lodging and 'free' medical treatment, although they might have money (or vouchers) to pay for them.[46] Sometimes, but rarely, the gratuitous benefits are forced from private individuals in what amounts to confiscation, as happens when the rents of private houses are controlled at

46. Ralph Harris and Arthur Seldon, *Choice in Welfare*, London: Institute of Economic Affairs, 1963 and 1965; A. T. Peacock and J. Wiseman, *Education for Democrats*, London: Institute of Economic Affairs, 1964; and E. G. West, *Education and the State*, London: Institute of Economic Affairs, 1963.

uneconomic rates and the landlords in consequence have to house their tenants at their own expense. But for the most part, the casualties of the system receive help paid for by money collected in rates and taxes. As incomes rise the casualties become fewer because they can insure against sickness, accident, death and other uncertainties. When we say that the market cannot deal with the casualties of the system we are faced with the possibilities of voluntary private provision (charity), involuntary private provision (enforced gifts, as with some controlled rents), voluntary public provision (as with public appeals for victims of natural disasters), and involuntary public provision (as with taxation). It is the last that people generally have in mind when they speak of providing for needs outside the market.

We need not spend time considering the ethics of involuntary private provision. There is no morally defensible reason at all for forcing some individuals, irrespective of their incomes or circumstances, to give pecuniary help to beneficiaries whose incomes and circumstances have not been inquired into. In this way benefits are provided for people who may not need them by people who may not be in a position to afford them. The public at large say that certain classes of people should be helped, and then take no steps to see that the help goes to those who need it or that it is provided by those who, in equity, should provide it. The existence of this system is a sign of moral abdication, and those who oppose its abolition can have no concern for justice.

For the charitable methods of helping the casualties of the market to be feasible there must be wealthy people and wealthy organisations, or there must be widespread ability and willingness on the part of friends and neighbours to help their unfortunate fellows. In contemporary society families are so scattered and friendships are so dispersed, that less help comes from personal and family loyalties. Fewer people think they ought to help one another in these ways, although they are increasingly able to do so, and people in distress no longer expect to obtain much help this way. No doubt this unconcern has been encouraged by the establishment of public relief organisations, but whatever the reasons for it, the fact remains. When help is dispensed by charities and other organised bodies, enquiries may have to be made into the extent and nature of the need. But these bodies may not have the power to obtain the necessary information, and in any case their representatives may think that too close enquiry will destroy the charitable atmosphere. They may prefer to be deceived by some artful dodger rather than to probe too far into his affairs, and as a result honest need may pass unnoticed and unhelped. Furthermore, when the subservience of immediately post-aristocratic society diminishes, many of those in need have an aversion to receiving gifts of this sort. They know they have no *right* to gifts, and they think they do have a right to some other sort of assistance. Givers, even those giving to relieve distress, can give to whom they please. People in distress who are *not* relieved naturally come to think they are unjustly overlooked. Thus there arises the belief that those in distress have a right to receive assistance.

It is at this stage that it comes to be accepted that such assistance should be provided by monies raised through taxation. For if the indigent have a right to assistance, and if there is no one in particular against whom this right can be claimed, then it is the public at large who have to fulfil it. Agencies of the government can demand the information necessary to distribute assistance to those who need it in proportion to their need. In this way, the help is less subject to private whim and accident than private charity would be. Indeed, in large populations it might not be possible for charity to provide the necessary help on the requisite scale. In a democratic community the citizens are presumed to approve of the expenditure they pay their taxes to meet, and in general the presumption is well-founded.[47] The plight of the needy is brought to their attention and they do not wish to see them starved or rendered desperate.

But in housing, medicine and education the matter has been taken further than this. Let us take first the example of housing. At one time private bodies such as the Peabody Trust built blocks of flats to be let at cheap rents to those who could not afford unsubsidised accommodation. Local authorities then joined in and financed such accommodation by subsidies from the rates. Then the central government added to these subsidies and a position was reached in which a considerable proportion of the population live in publicly subsidised dwellings. In some areas, indeed, a majority of the population are so provided for. It then comes to be said that housing is and ought to be a 'social service' and should not be left to be brought and sold in markets. This might be put forward as part of an argument for a socialist system of society, but we are not now discussing it in that light. The arguments we are concerned with are (1) that when housing is scarce it should be distributed in accordance with need, just as food should be rationed in times of famine; and (2) that housing is something very special, in that without places to live in people cannot go about their other affairs. The assumption here is that some things are too fundamental and important for

47. Recent research suggests, however, that the public does not generally approve of indiscriminate 'universal' social benefits; see Arthur Seldon, *Welfare and Taxation*, London: Institute of Economic Affairs, 1968.

individual survival for them to be left to be settled by market decisions.

On the first of these two arguments, we need to know about the nature and causes of the scarcity before we decide that rationing of subsidised housing by officials is the only way out. Scarcity is a function of effective demand, and if large numbers of people who cannot afford them nevertheless demand *new* houses, there are likely to be difficulties in supplying them. In general, the idea that everyone has a right to accommodation of the sort that he considers desirable is bound to lead to the idea and even to the creation of a shortage. Again, the legislation controlling rents has made it very unlikely that private companies will build houses to rent. Thus the legislation controlling rents has forced the provision of such houses on to the public sector. Once the local governments and central government agencies are organised for this purpose, interests are built up in our society which regard it as natural that they should expand and extend. These do not consist only of the officials and administrators, but also of the 'experts', that is to say, specialists who know about the organisation and statistics of the matter. Once local authorities have large housing departments, they regard extension of them as the most natural and effective way of dealing with housing shortages, and do not ask whether other measures could be taken which would lessen or remove the responsibilities of their departments. The combination of large organisations, interested 'experts' and lazy-minded good nature forms a public opinion that is unlikely to be critical.

It is the second argument, however, that takes us to the heart of the problem. If the most fundamental and important things must not be left to be supplied and bought in markets, then it is not housing alone that will be claimed as essentially a social service. Similar, indeed, more extensive claims, are made in respect of medical care and of education. There are at present no influential voices calling for the abolition of private house ownership, but there are many who say that no one should be allowed to buy or sell medical attention or education. Medical attention is a matter of life or death and education or the lack of it can make or mar a whole career. (Food or the lack of it is also a matter of life or death, but the nationalisation of food provision is not advocated on that ground.) Such important matters, it is said, should not be left to be settled by the purse, for if they are, the better-off will live longer, healthier lives and have better careers than the poorer members of the community.

Before we consider the moral issues involved in this attitude, it will be as well to notice a similarity between housing, medical care and education. In all three cases a large organisation has been first set up, 'experts' have collected around it, and what was first regarded as a rescue operation for some is now regarded as a right or perhaps even a necessity for all. Now that the National Health Service has been working for twenty years it is suggested that it is *morally wrong* for individuals to pay for medical care. The main argument used is that in so doing they divert to their own use medical skill which, if used in the National Health Service, would be used for people most in need rather than for those who can pay for it. What began as an organisation for ensuring that no one would go without medical care for lack of means may possibly turn into the only permitted source of such care. People would then be prevented from paying for better medical care. When, several years ago, doctors withdrew from the National Health Service in order to provide medical care for a group of paying patients, they were criticised on the ground that they were diminishing the amount of care available in the National Health Service and providing their paying patients with more than their due.

Similarly, the organised network of local authority schools is gradually ousting fee-paying schools, even though public education was first provided in order to ensure that parents should not escape their obligation to see that their children are educated. It is now being claimed that it is wrong for people to pay for education outside the public system. For in doing so, it is alleged, they are unfairly buying advantages and privileges for their children at the expense of those whose parents are less well-off. It appears that when the public bodies concerned with education and health grow very large, arguments are produced for swallowing up the remaining private concerns. Perhaps it is only because millions of people now own their houses and many children still hope to inherit from them that it is not likewise being argued that in buying a house for himself a man is 'jumping the queue' and obtaining unfair advantages for himself and his family.

An interesting example of the way in which this institutional imperialism works may be seen from the arguments devised in order to equate the relief of taxation allowed for interest payments on house mortgages with subsidies for council houses. The tax reliefs were granted at a time when house-ownership was being encouraged and when well-off people tended to buy houses for cash. Owing to inflation and high taxation it pays many more people than it used to to buy their houses by means of mortgages, and a good sum of money would be saved by the Treasury if this concession were withdrawn. Because of this, it is said that the wealthy are being subsidised in buying their houses just as the poor are subsidised by having houses at less than their economic rents. But the wealthy came to use this system of finance because inflation and high taxation made it financially advantageous for them to do so. Furthermore, if house-ownership were still regarded as a worthy object of public policy then it could be encouraged among the less well-off. As it is, the major effort is put into subsidised rented housing, and critics of this policy are then told that well-to-do house-buyers are also being subsidised. Yet it is public policy by way of inflation, high taxation and publicly provided housing that has made it appear that tax relief on house mortgages is a form of subsidy.

We must now consider the argument that some needs are so fundamental that their satisfaction should not be left to the market, but should be provided publicly. This amounts to saying that in what concerns their basic needs people should not be left to fend for themselves. Social reformers in the past have said that no one should be allowed to go without shelter, medical care and education of some kind. But now the view is that no one should be allowed to *buy* these things for himself, but should be allotted his fair share of them under a publicly organised scheme. Taxes would be paid in accordance with ability, and benefits allotted in accordance with need. In this way the communist rule 'from each according to his ability, to each according to his need', would be applied, not to economic activity, but to the sphere of welfare. Not to organise things this way would be to support injustice, privilege, discrimination.

My first comment is that this dual system of economic inequality and welfare equality contains within itself, to use Saint-Simon's expression, 'the seeds of its own destruction'. For few people, in the long run, are likely to work and contrive their utmost if they are to be in no better position, as regards the fundamentals of living, than the helpless, the

lazy or the unlucky. The more egalitarian the welfare distribution, the less enthusiasm there is likely to be for the competitive economic activities that produce the wealth. Within
the system of competitive capitalism the individual is supposed to do the best he can 'for himself', which generally
means also for his family and any causes he has set his heart
on. But if he is prevented from using his income or his profits for things that *he* wants, if he is forced to send his children to schools he does not like and to go to a doctor he
does not trust, then he may well wonder whether his business activities are worth while. He would be discouraged
still further if housing became entirely a matter of welfare,
to be allocated only in accordance with need. Thus, the extension of welfare and so-called 'fair shares' from one field
to another is not compatible with the system of competitive
capitalism. Believers in capitalism who set no limits to the
extension of the 'fair shares' principle are helping to stake
out the ground in which their graves will be dug.

It will be said, however, that it is wrong to wish to buy
privileges with superior wealth. We may now see the issue
in this way: it is said by some that education and medical
care are so important and fundamental that they ought not
to be bought and sold, and by others that, just because they
are so important and fundamental, they should be the responsibility of each individual. The conflict would appear to
be between these two policies: (*a*) providing basic welfare at
public expense and in accordance with need, and (*b*) each
individual regarding himself as responsible for providing his
own and his family's basic welfare according to his resources and his wishes.

Now it should be remarked in the first place that (*a*) is a
much more cumbrous way of proceeding than (*b*). For under (*a*), the money has to be collected in taxes and used to

pay for the doctors and hospitals to which the individual taxpayers then present themselves, whereas under (*b*) they pay the doctors and the hospitals direct. What reasons are put forward for preferring the roundabout way?

One reason is that it is a means of making the well-off pay towards the welfare of the poor. But this would only justify taxation to cover the welfare expenses of those who could not afford to pay for themselves. Yet what is being advocated is taxation to provide a service which is to be the *sole* service for everyone. Why, then, should those who can afford to, not pay for the welfare services they require for themselves and their families? Having contributed towards others, shouldn't they be free to look after themselves with what remains to them? Two reasons are given for answering these questions in the negative. The first is that if the better-off members of the community paid for private welfare services for themselves and their families, they would be enticing skill and other resources away from the state system and in this way lowering the level of the services it can provide. The second reason is that it is unjust that some people should have different and better welfare services than others, since welfare should be in accordance with need, not in accordance with ability to pay.

The first of these reasons is the less radical. It depends on the fact that a state system already exists, and is then put forward as the claim that nothing should be available outside it. It can be answered in the following way. Either only a few want services outside the state system, or many do. If only a few, then the effect on the whole system is small and there is no need to trouble about it. If many want services outside the system, this shows that many people can and do wish to be responsible for their own arrangements, even after they have been taxed to provide for others. Furthermore, the more people there are who wish for private provision, the fewer there are who need public provision. Again because they are paying for it themselves, those who opt out of the system are likely to employ existing resources more economically than do those who remain in the system.

Of course, it is the second, more radical reason that moves most of those who object to the buying and selling of medical care and education. They think it is unjust for people to spend money on schooling or medical care for themselves or their children, for in doing so they are buying privileges, and privileges should not be bought. If a privilege is merely an advantage, then the more intelligent and shrewder people are constantly buying privileges, since they constantly buy to better advantage than other people. If, however, a privilege is an *unjust* advantage, then to talk of buying privileges in these connections, is merely to assert that it is wrong to buy medical care or education.

Which things, then, is it right to buy and sell, and which things should be excluded from markets altogether? Professor R. M. Titmuss[48] thinks that human blood should not be bought and sold, but rather given and taken, and then only within the British National Health Service. Not many people object to the selling of human hair, although Kant thought the practice 'not entirely free from blame'.[49] All civilised

48. In *Choice and 'The Welfare State'*, Fabian Tract No. 370, February 1967, pp. 13–16. According to Professor Titmuss *sellers* of blood try to sell too much and so weaken themselves. Furthermore they tend to be 'Skid Row' characters and their blood is not always up to standard.

49. *The Metaphysics of Morals* (1796) in *Werke* (Prussian Academy Edition), volume 6, p. 423. Kant thought that to 'give away or sell a tooth' or 'to submit oneself to castration in order to gain an easier livelihood as a singer' were somewhat akin to self-murder. Hair, as a *part* but not an *organ* of the body, was rather different, but even so in selling it, an individual was treating a part of himself (and hence himself?) as a means rather than as an end in himself. Blood seems to be neither an organ nor a part of the body. In *The Price of Blood*, London: Institute of Economic Affairs, Hobart Paper 41, London, 1968, Michael

peoples think it wrong to buy and sell human beings, yet these same societies regard the selling of one's labour, which is an activity of one's self even if not a part or organ, as morally acceptable. One can list some objects and activities which are universally regarded as morally unsuitable for purposes of buying and selling, e.g. votes, knowledge that would be useful to a foreign power, knowledge about a friend which would be of interest to a newspaper and its readers, sexual complaisance or sexual activity, a man's services as thief or killer. There are some things and activities which by their very nature *could* not be bought or sold. Love and tenderness, for example, presuppose a spontaneous concern on the part of the person who, as we say, *gives* them, and just could not be made available in return for a payment offered. On the other hand, care and attention can be bought, even though they can only be sold by someone who is conscientious and skillful.

However, we are not here concerned with any argument to the effect that medical care and education *cannot* be bought or sold, but with the argument that, like votes, knowledge acquired in friendship, and one's country's military secrets, they *should not* be. The last two are forms of betrayal and the first is bribery, and the relevant actions are wrong because betrayal and bribery are. Selling one's services as a thief or murderer are wrong because theft and murder are wrong, and prostitution is wrong because it denies human dignity on the part of both supplier and customer. Betrayal of a friend in the way mentioned above is not a *criminal* offence, but fidelity is not regarded as open to financial offers.

H. Cooper and Anthony J. Culyer argue that 'payment, provided that it is separated from donation, would induce further supplies' and that 'payment for blood can be both sensible and humane' (p. 45).

On the face of it, education and medical care are not, like treachery, bribery or theft, morally wrong or criminal and hence not rightly bought or sold for that reason. For many generations private doctoring and private schooling were not only tolerated, but were highly respected activities. Has anything happened, then, to change their moral quality? I suggest that it is the growth of the large state organisations connected with them that has led many people to change their moral attitudes towards them. When in the past a doctor set up in practice or a scholar opened a school, all he had to consider were his patients, pupils or colleagues. But nowadays the state educational and medical systems, and the 'experts' associated with them, join to accuse him of antisocial behaviour. It is not enough for him to help a number of particular individuals who pay him to do so, for, it is said, there are other individuals who need the help more, and in any case the people's representatives and the state apparatus they control know better than he does where doctoring and schooling can best be deployed. It is not the business of the law to interfere with a man's choice of a car, a diet,[50] or a form of sexual behaviour, but education and medical care are held to be quite different; inequality is permissible in the former, but not in the latter, because in the latter they are too important to be left to individual choice. Buying education is, indirectly, buying chances in life, and buying medical care is, in effect, buying life itself. The implication is that life chances ought all to be equal, that health and life should be equally considered through public authority, and that these equalities can in practice be achieved in these ways.

50. Of course the state has a duty to require standards of food production and manufacture, since buyers are frequently unable to ascertain whether the food is poisonous, adulterated, etc. Similarly, the state justifiably requires school teachers, doctors, etc., to have certain qualifications.

Now the critic of this outlook may deny that equality can be achieved in these ways. He may suggest that powerful people, politicians and their hangers-on prominent among them, would get advantages for themselves and their families which in the free system had been obtained by rich people. He may also suggest that sometimes those who pay for what they consider better things may be very much mistaken. But the main line of criticism, I suggest, ought to go to the implications of imposing an equality as regards education and health and of leaving individuals to pursue freely chosen lives in other ways. I have already suggested (pp. 87–8 above) that equalised welfare and a competitive economy are not likely to be able to exist together for very long. I now suggest that when they do live together their union is morally questionable. Broadly speaking, what is advocated is forcible communal and equalised provision of what is considered most fundamental to the individual, and freedom as regards the less fundamental, particularly the inessentials and luxuries. The government consider this to be 'getting our priorities right', since they see themselves organising the people so that they *receive* the fundamentals before they can concern themselves with anything else. The priorities are those of the government and presuppose that the government controls what people can do. But from the point of view of the individual the moral situation looks very different. Under the compulsory welfare system we are considering, schooling and medical care are organised in ways over which the individual has little control. They are not among the things that *he* has to work and save for—or so it seems to him, for the money for them is taken from him before he receives his pay. In the very process, therefore, of being made *social* or *governmental* priorities, education and medical care cease to be *individual* priorities in the economy of the individual. As he is not allowed as an individual to spend money on these things, whatever sense of priorities he may have must be expressed in other directions. His responsibility in the spending of his money starts only after these fundamental services have been provided for him.

The consequences of publicly providing people gratis with services which would be of fundamental personal and moral importance if they had to provide them for themselves, are likely to be very far-reaching indeed. When the government imposes *its* priorities it alters the balance of the choices which the individual can make for himself. In the past it has been regarded as an individual's responsibility to direct his expenditure in the best possible way. This involved him in ensuring that he had dealt with essentials before he embarked on inessentials and luxuries. Some people made a better job of this than others, and there were, as we have emphasised, some whose mistakes or misfortunes made them casualties. But under the system we are now considering, no one is to be allowed to have personal control of his expenditure on some of the basic matters. But the more his needs are satisfied in this way, the more important will his expenditures on other things seem to him. Some of these other expenditures, such as those on food[51] and clothing, will be important enough, but luxuries and superfluities will play a large part among them. His sense of responsibility for what he is not allowed to decide for himself is likely to diminish, and it is possible that he will be less concerned for

51. Diet is of great importance for individual health ('Der Mensch ist was er isst', said Feuerbach). See *Die Geheimniss des Opfers oder der Mensch ist was er isst;* cp. L. Feuerbach, *Saemtliche Werke,* ed. F. Jodl, Stuttgart: Frommann Verlag, 1862, p. 22. But no one proposes that diets should be publicly devised and imposed, even though bad diet must increase the calls upon the National Health Service. Subsidised school meals, however, have been defended on the ground that parents may fail to provide nourishing meals for their children.

his health and his children's education than for his amusements. The very quality of his amusements, it may be suggested, varies in accordance with whether they are engaged
in after he has himself provided for the fundamentals of his
life, or whether they are the major part of the mere residue
of personal choice allowed to him by a paternalistic society.

Let us consider the situation of a man who is not allowed
to spend from his own income on his health or his children's education. Let us suppose, too, that his housing is
subsidised and is of the standardised type usual for such
accommodation. His control over the medical attention he
and his family get, and over his children's schooling and his
house is small. He can vote at national and local elections,
and he can sometimes change his doctor or make protests
about how the schools are organised. A man in this situation
would give expression to his personal aims in spending the
income he takes home from work after taxes have been de-
ducted. Because his taxes are paid on his behalf by his employer, and because they finance what is publicly provided
for him, his take-home pay appears to him to be his total
pay. From this he has to buy food, clothing and furniture,
but apart from such items it is amusements and luxuries that
his 'wages' appear to buy for him. A likely consequence of
this would be that the connection between work and the
provision of the state-provided fundamentals is obscured.
The individual would be encouraged to believe that provision for such fundamentals as health and education is not
his concern. When he presses for increased wages what he
is likely to have in mind is the income he can spend as an
individual, and he will probably think that the pre-empted
taxation gets in the way of this. Unless he has strong religious convictions, or a concern for public work or for the
exercise of some skill or artistic ability, he is likely to think

that work is for food and amusement. Adam Smith said that 'it is perfectly self-evident' that 'consumption is the sole end and purpose of all production',[52] but to the inhabitant of a secularised Welfare State, it is amusement and luxury that are likely to appear as the main ends of production. For in such a society the system of taxation and of welfare expenditure conceals the connection between work and production on the one hand, and the consumption of welfare services on the other. We may call this the mystification of the Welfare State. If, on the other hand, people pay directly for their doctor and for their children's education, they are likely to approach the rest of their expenditure in a different and perhaps a more responsible manner.

Monopoly and Cooperation

We have already discussed in the first section of this chapter, the idea that economic competition is a form of strife or rivalry and should therefore be morally condemned. We may now briefly consider the idea that competition is bad because it is opposed to cooperation which, as a form of harmony in human affairs, ought to be promoted as much as possible.

Deliberately organised cooperation is not, in itself, necessarily good. A cabal or gang may cooperate most amicably in carrying out an evil design, and hence the purpose for which the cooperators deliberately harmonise their actions and policies is relevant to the goodness or badness of what they are doing. Furthermore, people may cooperate without deliberately setting out to do so. This indeed is what generally happens when commodities are produced under com-

52. Adam Smith, *The Wealth of Nations*, IV.viii, Glasgow Edition, p. 660.

petitive market conditions. In his *Harmonies Économiques,* Bastiat wrote of the mining, smelting, manufacturing, transporting, financing and storing involved in producing a cheap lamp for sale to a French workman. Firms and individuals all over the world had worked together in producing it, but no one man or body of men had organised all these processes so as to fit them together into a whole. There was detailed cooperation in hiring men, miners or metal-workers or dockers, buying materials, moving finished or semifinished products, and so on. But there was no single plan for lamp-manufacturing, organised from a single centre and requiring the acquiescence, obedience or enthusiasm of all the participants. The mineowner, the miner, the metalworker, the carrier, each pursued his own ends, and, without even considering the lamps that resulted, cooperated in producing them and getting them to the shops and to the purchasers. Competitive cooperation, therefore, is not a contradiction in terms, if we mean by it the working together that takes place without conscious participation in some comprehensive plan. There must, of course, be deliberate cooperation within firms, and between firms that contract with one another, but in a competitive economy the firms are not cooperating to execute a plan agreed between them all or imposed upon them.

Competition, then, is not opposed to cooperation, but rather to deliberate and comprehensively organised forms of it, as described, for example, by Engels in his *Fundamental Principles of Communism* (1847) in the words: 'When industry is conducted in common and in accordance with plans determined by the whole of society . . . '[53] Competition

53. *Marx-Engels: Werke,* Berlin, Dietz Verlag, volume 4, 1964, p. 376; compare Karl Marx and Friedrich Engels, *Collected Works,* London: Lawrence and Wishart, volume 6, 1976, p. 353.

then, is not opposed to cooperation but is opposed to monopoly. There may be occasions when a monopoly is justified, as, for example, when the cost of producing a commodity is very much less when the total output is produced by one firm and there are substitutes to which consumers may turn if the price goes too high. But competition is not compatible with agreements between firms for limiting or eliminating it. On the practical effects of legislation to prevent monopoly, I am not competent to judge. But it should be emphasised that when there are substitutes for the monopolised commodity, and when it is open to new firms to come into the market, undesirable monopolies are not likely to persist. A competitive economy can put up with some monopolies and even publicly organise some to its own advantage. It is when competition has already been seriously undermined that calls for anti-monopoly legislation are heard, and then it may be too late for them to be of much effect. Such may be the situation in Great Britain today.

CHAPTER 4
THE EGALITARIAN
COLLECTIVIST
ALTERNATIVE

Egalitarian Collectivism and Distributive Justice

The form of collectivism we are now concerned with advocates help by the state for the casualties of the competitive system and the provision of basic welfare such as medical care, housing and education in accordance with need rather than in accordance with ability to pay. Two principles are relevant here. First there is the principle of a basic minimum, and second there is the principle that certain basic requirements and services should be distributed in accordance with need rather than in accordance with the financial resources of the recipient.

The liberal accepts the principle of a basic minimum without accepting the principle that medical care, education and the like should not be marketable goods. He argues that in a humane and wealthy society the poorest should not be left to suffer from illness and exposure and forced to remain without education in the basic skills. To help those in distress, he holds, and to respond to the call of humanity, is a moral demand that no one can reason-

ably question, but this response is concerned with reliev-
ing suffering, not with achieving justice. It is one thing, he
argues, to bring help in order to relieve suffering, and
quite another to bring help in order to achieve justice. The
first does not necessarily lead in an egalitarian direction
whereas the second tends to do so. If the poor or the casualties of life are helped because it is *unjust* that they should
remain as they are, then the way is opened for saying that
it is unjust that some people should be less well-off than
others. But if the help given to them is given on *humanitarian* grounds, then there is no presumption in favour of continuing the process of redistribution beyond the point at
which distress is relieved. Of course, what constitutes distress will vary to some extent with the level of wealth of
the community. But this is a very different thing from saying that everyone should be equally well-off.

The collectivist we are now considering, then, is concerned at the injustice of inequality as well as by the distress
of the needy. Wealth, he argues, gives its possessors advantages which it is unjust that they should have. Basic needs,
be believes, should be satisfied in accordance with their
urgency, not in accordance with the financial resources of
those who have them. Thus while everyone believes that
suffering calls for relief, the egalitarian collectivist claims
that inequality calls for remedial redistribution.

Distributive Justice and Commutative Justice

The philosophical discussion of justice started with Aristotle's account of the matter in Book V of his *Nicomachean
Ethics*. Here Aristotle distinguished between distributive justice on the one hand and corrective or remedial justice on
the other. He also appeared to have in mind a form of justice

which has since been called catallactic or commutative justice, and there has been discussion whether this is a species of corrective or remedial justice or a distinct kind. In his *Aristotle*[54] Sir David Ross writes of three forms of justice, the third of which he calls 'commercial'.

By distributive justice Aristotle meant justice in the distribution of such things as property, honour or bodily safety. In his view, a distribution was just when the goods (or evils) distributed were distributed equally or fairly, and they were distributed equally or fairly when they were distributed according to merit. By 'merit' Aristotle did not mean a person's individual moral worth, but rather his just claims on the basis of status or contributions to the society. Aristotle appears to have been thinking of the distribution of profits in accordance with shares in a business and of the distribution of some public gain by an authority with the right to allocate it. By 'distributive justice' he therefore meant distribution in accordance with the rightful claims of the parties to and between whom the distribution was to be made. We may illustrate one aspect of his view of distributive justice by considering how prize money used to be distributed in the British Navy, when each individual received his share of the prize in accordance with his rank, the admiral receiving a large sum, the captains a smaller share, and so on.

By corrective justice on the other hand, Aristotle meant the form in which a party has a right to redress against another party, either because one of the parties has failed to fulfil a contract, or because one of the parties has injured the other. In such cases justice is secured when the situation has been adjusted or put right, by obtaining fulfilment of the contract or payment in lieu of that, or by payment of damages in the case of assault.

54. W. D. Ross, *Aristotle*, London: Methuen, 1923, 1949, p. 212. [For further discussion of Aristotle and Aquinas, see Acton's 'Distributive Justice' below.]

Aristotle's view of catallactic justice, or justice in exchange, appears to be that justice is secured when the producers of the goods exchanged receive payment in proportion to the real value of what is produced or the merit of the producers. Aristotle's meaning is not clear, but he appears to assume that, although demand is what gives rise to exchange value, and although money is a means of facilitating exchange, there is some natural or just relationship of value between the various types of manufactured goods, such that, to use his examples, a bed or a house is really worth so many pairs of shoes.

St Thomas Aquinas took over Aristotle's general account of justice, interpreting it in his own orderly manner. He retained Aristotle's adjective 'distributive' for the one form of justice but introduced the word 'commutative' for the other, arguing that justice in exchange is a form of commutative justice in which goods are bought and sold at prices which reflect their real values. In his *Commentary on Aristotle's Ethics* St Thomas says that an exchange is just when there is a just reciprocity (*contra passum juste*).[55] Before we pass on to consider later views, we must call attention to some important features of the Aristotelian–Thomist analysis of justice.

First, it must be emphasised that both Aristotle and St Thomas thought of distributive justice in terms of the distribution of some public gain or windfall among citizens or members of a partnership. They both recognised that this has to be done by some authority in the light of the merits or claims of the parties between whom the distribution is being made. They both took it for granted that this was happening in a society in which there was an established order and system of property. Neither of them had

55. [*Exposito in decem libros ethicorum Aristoteles ad Nicomacum*, ed. Raymundi M. Spiazzi, Turin: Maretti, 1949, p. 270.]

in mind the reform of society by means of a redistribution of goods and services in terms of some ideal system of social justice.

Second, Aristotle and St Thomas thought that there was a just price at which goods should be sold and that this was a price that reflected the 'real' value of the goods. They thought that as food is to shoes, or as farmers are to leather workers, so the relative prices of food and shoes should be. It followed that they regarded prices as matters of justice and hence of morality. If what I said in Chapter 2 above is correct, then they were wrong in believing this. Injustice occurs in a trade transaction when a party does not fulfil his contract, and the injustice is corrected when he is made to do so or to pay compensation. But in competitive markets prices are settled by supply and demand, and no price is just or unjust as long as buyers and sellers are honest with one another. If 'just price' means anything, it means only the price that the buyer and seller have agreed. The analysis of justice began to be wrongly stated when Aristotle included justice in exchange as a form of justice, and it went still further awry when St Thomas used the word 'commutative' to mean both what Aristotle called remedial justice and the supposed just price in the exchange of goods.

Third, it should be noticed that authorities play a different part in distributive justice from the part they play in exchange transactions. The distribution is *made* by an authority. If there were no authority to make it, there could be no distribution, just or unjust. On the other hand, individuals exchange goods between one another; it is they who determine who gets what, not some authority over them. Government is needed, of course, to prevent violence and fraud, but the government is not a party to the exchanges. It sees that the agreements are not broken with impunity, but it does not make them. It is natural, therefore, to use the term commutative justice to mean just dealing between individuals, and just dealing between individuals is dealing in which agreements are freely made and honestly kept. Distributive justice is exercised by an authority, commutative justice by and between individuals.

We may now consider distributive justice in more general terms. It is the distribution of goods or services or burdens (as with taxation or military service) in accordance with some rule. According to Aristotle, this means distribution in accordance with merit, but by 'merit' he appears to mean something like 'just claims', and this does not take us very far. Professor Chaim Perelman in *The Idea of Justice and the Problem of Argument*[56] mentions the following types of rule that have been considered distributively just: the same to everyone, i.e. equal distribution; to each according to his merits (moral merit?); to each according to his works; to each according to his needs; to each according to his rank; to each according to his legal entitlement. Professor Nicholas Rescher in *Distributive Justice*[57] does not list the rule of rank, but amplifies the rule of merit with the phrase 'ability or merit or achievements', and adds further rules, one of which is 'according to their efforts and sacrifices' and the other 'according to a valuation of their socially useful services in terms of their scarcity in the essentially economic terms of supply and demand' (p. 73).

This last is not a rule of distributive justice at all. For distributive justice involves an authority who makes the distribution in accordance with a rule, but in competitive markets individuals exchange goods with one another and their

56. Chaim Perelman, *The Idea of Justice and the Problem of Argument*, London: Routledge & Kegan Paul, 1963, p. 7.

57. N. Rescher, *Distributive Justice*, Indianapolis: Bobbs-Merrill, 1966. This book contains a comprehensive bibliography.

gains or losses are not *allocated* to them by anyone, but accrue according to their luck or perspicacity. There is no need for any authority to distribute in accordance with scarcity and supply and demand, for that happens anyway in a competitive market. To say that such a distribution is distributively just is to suppose an authority where there is none. To say that such a distribution is commutatively just is merely to say that no one has used force or fraud.

Through competitive markets, opportunities, incomes and wealth come to people according as they are lucky, clever, industrious, or have some rare ability that is in demand. Doctors (once established in a practice) earn more than filing clerks, school teachers less than air pilots. Businessmen may hope to make fortunes, poets can reasonably hope only to have their works read and admired. No one has *decreed* these things, for they are the unplanned consequences of history, convention, chance, relative scarcity and many other things besides. There is no one who distributes things in this way, no one who says that doctors should get so much and teachers so much less, no one who makes poets seek for jobs in a bank rather than hope to earn a living from their poetry. These incomes come about as a result of all sorts of particular bargains, acquiescences, resistances, windfalls and expectations.

Is what emerges in this way just or unjust? I suggest that the question, as generally put, is a confused one. If the doctor's client cheats him, if the teacher fails to keep up to date in his knowledge, if the businessman fails to deliver what he has promised, then breaches of commutative justice have taken place. But what is just or unjust about the whole situation in which they find themselves? If no one is responsible for bringing it about, no one can reasonably be commended for arranging it justly or blamed for arranging it unjustly.

The rain that falls upon the just and upon the unjust cannot be condemned for its lack of concern for moral distinctions. Neither can a social order be condemned as unjust if no one has planned and controlled it. If a whole system of social and economic relationships is held to be unjust, this must really mean that *if* someone had made the distribution deliberately, *then* it would have been unjust. But something that merely *happens* can be neither just nor unjust. It is not unjust for a good man to die in an accident and for a bad man to live long and happily.

When, therefore, the socialist says that it is unjust for opportunity and wealth to depend largely on luck and birth he is implying that they *should be* deliberately distributed in accordance with some rule or standard.[58] This *follows* from his wish to establish justice in society as a whole. Distributive justice implies a distributor, such as a judge, teacher or parent, who acts in accordance with some rule of distribution. He intervenes to bring something about that would not otherwise have happened. In a world in which wealth and opportunity are not the same for everyone all sorts of inequalities arise and tend to be accentuated. To introduce distributive justice into it, some man or body of men must alter it in terms of a system of rules. The differences between the incomes of doctors and air pilots and filing clerks and poets must be settled in accordance with principles of justice. Known and accepted rules must be followed by those who re-model the social order. There must be some govern-

58. It is significant that when Henry Sidgwick discusses the socialist distribution of wealth he compares it with Divine Justice, secured by the will of the Deity. 'If the Socialistic Ideal . . . could be realised without counter-balancing evils, it would certainly seem to give a nearer approximation to what we conceive as Divine Justice than the present state of society affords.' See *The Methods of Ethics*, London: Macmillan, seventh edition, 1907, 1930, p. 289. God is not only the Creator of the world, but also its supreme lawgiver and regulator.

mental organisation which, like Mr Aubrey Jones and his Prices and Incomes Board, combines the functions of judge, teacher and parent, and the population must accept their authority. In seeking for distributive justice in the community as a whole in addition to distributive justice in families and firms, egalitarian collectivists require there to be some public father or non-commercial board of directors to arrange the distribution.

Before passing on to the next section, I should like to consider Professor John Rawls's views on justice in general and on distributive justice in particular, since his treatment of these topics cannot be ignored in any contemporary discussion of justice in society. According to Rawls, the notion of fairness is fundamental to that of justice.[59] He asks his readers to imagine a number of free and rational individuals considering, before its formation, what rules and institutions they should give to the society they are about to form. We imagine them, that is, in process of entering into a social contract. In order that they shall not be tempted by considerations of their own personal interest, they must be supposed ignorant both of their own past position, and of their own powers and abilities. Nevertheless, they must be supposed to have actual or potential family ties and a regard for such things as religious truth. These individuals would, if rational, choose a set of institutions of such a nature that they would not mind if their enemy decided the place they were to occupy in it. For with families and other interests at stake, and in ignorance of their own prospects of success or failure, they would opt for institutions that would not be atrociously hard on anybody. They would, in consequence,

---

59. John Rawls, 'Justice as Fairness', in P. Laslett and W. G. Runciman (eds), *Philosophy, Politics and Society*, second series, New York: Barnes and Noble, 1962, pp. 132–57.

come to accept two principles of justice. According to the first, each person involved in the institution of the society would have to have an equal right to as much freedom as is compatible with a like freedom for the others. According to the second, the institutions set up should be such as to be to everyone's advantage, and the offices in them should be open to all. A basic idea here is that of reciprocity. The contracting parties would try to set up a system in which no one is assigned a purely sacrificial role. This, in brief, is Rawls's account of justice in general.

Distributive justice, he holds, is concerned with the inequalities in income and wealth, and in social prestige and status, required in order to fulfil the two principles mentioned above. It is the second principle of justice that is most important here. A system of inequalities in wealth and income can only be justifiable if it is in the interest of a representative member of the general body of people. This would mean that the amount of inequality that is permissible would be the amount necessary to provide incentives for entrepreneurs so to conduct trade and industry that increases in wealth would accrue even to the least advantaged. Those who are favoured by nature would be enabled to gain only on terms that would also improve the wellbeing of the least endowed.

> Thus, we suppose that, in addition to maintaining the usual social overhead capital, government provides for equal educational opportunities for all either by subsidising private schools or by operating a public school system. It also enforces and underwrites equality of opportunity in commercial ventures and in the free choice of occupation. This result is achieved by policing business behaviour and by preventing the establishment of barriers and restriction[s] to the desirable positions and markets. Lastly, there is a guarantee of a social minimum which the government meets by family allowances and special

payments in times of unemployment, or by a negative income tax.[60]

This idea of a minimum is very important. Clearly, the contracting individuals described by Rawls will have possible misfortune in view, and will wish to ensure that if misfortune is to be their lot, it will be as bearable as possible. This leads Rawls to consider how the proportion of the society's resources that ought to be allocated for savings could be fairly decided. An extra factor here is the fairness of imposing savings on one generation for the benefit of future generations. On Rawls's view, this means that the contracting parties choose as if they did not know to which generation they belong.

> The saving of those worse off is undertaken by accepting, as a matter of political judgment, those policies designed to improve the standard of life, thereby abstaining from the immediate advantages which are available to them. By supporting these arrangements and policies the appropriate savings can be made, and no representative man regardless of generation can complain of another for not doing his part.[61]

Saving for what Rawls calls 'various grand projects' would not necessarily coincide with saving justly. He concludes his main discussion as follows:

> This account of distributive shares is simply an elaboration of the familiar idea that economic rewards will be just once a perfectly competitive price system is organised as a fair game. But in order to do this we have to begin with the choice of a social system as a whole, for the basic structure of the entire arrangement must be just. The economy must be surrounded with the appropriate framework of institutions, since even a perfectly ef-

60. John Rawls, 'Distributive Justice', in P. Laslett and W. G. Runciman (eds), *Philosophy, Politics and Society*, third series, New York: Barnes and Noble, 1967, pp. 58–82; see p. 69.
61. Ibid., pp. 75–6.

ficient price system has no tendency to determine just distributive shares when left to itself.[62]

In an article entitled 'Justice and Fairness',[63] Professor John W. Chapman criticises Rawls's first account of his view, that is, his account of justice as fairness prior to his later account of distributive justice. Chapman argues that Rawls's account of justice, by placing fairness and reciprocity at the centre of it, fails to take account of rights and of needs. As to the former, Chapman points out that on Rawls's view the contracting parties might agree to the institution of slavery. Rawls accepts this consequence, but in doing so has in mind a society in which military victors have the right to kill the conquered. As to the latter, Chapman considers that justice as fairness cannot deal with the idea that it is just that certain basic needs should be satisfied even if the person in need makes no contribution to the society. I should say here that help given in such circumstances is given not on grounds of justice but of humanity. Rawls's discussion of justice in saving seems as if it may have been written with Chapman's paper in mind, for the level at which unfortunates can be maintained depends upon the productivity of the society and upon the general willingness of its members to forgo immediate consumption for themselves.

With Rawls's central theme that fairness and reciprocity are central to justice I agree, although I have taken my terminology from the Aristotelian–Thomist tradition and have drawn conclusions with which Rawls might not agree. A point I notice in his 'Distributive Justice' is that at the beginning he lists as items to be distributed, incomes and wealth, and social prestige and status, and yet in the body of his

62. Ibid., pp. 78–9.
63. J. Chapman, 'Justice and Fairness', in Carl J. Freidrich and John W. Chapman (eds) *Justice (Nomos 6)*, New York: Prentice Hall, 1963, pp. 147–69.

article he discusses only the first two. Perhaps he was right not to deal with the second two ideas, for they not only differ between themselves—prestige is more general and more informally awarded than status is—but they both also differ from wealth and income. Wealth and income can be increased in total amount and spread more or less equally. Wealthy people might become more wealthy at the same time as poor people become less poor. But it is not so clear that everyone's status could be increased in this way, for an improvement in status for those who, if the expression be allowed, have less of it, is likely to be obtained at the expense of those with more. Status is concerned with how people regard one another, the respect or deference they accord to one another, and this seems to belong to the region of recognition, of pride and respect, rather than to that of justice.

We have seen that Rawls emphasises the importance of equality of opportunity for securing justice. Education, on his view, is to play a part in this by subsidies for private schools or by operating a state system. It will be noticed that he does not regard publicly provided education as the only method of working towards equality of opportunity. It seems important, however, to look more closely at what equality of opportunity implies. We may speak of *making* opportunities, of *taking* opportunities, and of *being given* opportunities or of *being presented with* them. Is equality of opportunity the equal chance of making opportunities for oneself? This would appear to assume an energy and intelligence that few people have, so that it would be straining the expression to use it only for the freedom to make opportunities for oneself. On the other hand, it would be straining the expression the other way if it were taken to mean that everyone is to have opportunities lying, so to say, ready to hand, requiring little or no trouble to be utilised. Indeed, this is hardly possible, since any individual can fail to utilise or to take an opportunity offered to him. I suggest, therefore, that *taking* opportunities is central to the very concept of equality of opportunity, which in consequence presupposes a certain spontaneity and activity on the part of the taker. If this is so, we may expect that those who wish to equalise opportunities for everyone in the sense of placing opportunities before them within government-organised educational systems, will find that only a proportion of those to whom this is offered will accept the offer. The equalisers are then tempted to put more and more emphasis upon *giving* and *presenting* and this is likely to involve placing hindrances in the way of the makers and the takers. This means that a policy that began as an attempt to increase freedom turns back upon itself and imposes monopolistic prohibitions. This is how state education in some Western countries, not least Britain, has developed.

Distributive Justice in the Satisfaction of Needs

The establishment of distributive justice, then, as between all the members of a democratic state, would require a government that decided what each type of citizen and worker ought to receive, and a population that was in general agreement with the government on what the principles of distribution should be. The difficulties in the way of establishing acceptable principles of distribution are well known. Should distribution of income be in terms of merit, effort, output, or, if in terms of some or all of these, what system of weighting should be used? These questions are so difficult that most collectivists nowadays have given up the attempt to answer

THE EGALITARIAN COLLECTIVIST ALTERNATIVE **113**

them and concern themselves chiefly with the distribution of basic needs such as health, housing and education. In this realm they consider the principle of distribution to be the fairly simple one of requiring that each individual should receive in terms of his *needs*. For a distribution to be made there has to be a distributor, and this, in the case we are considering, is to be the democratically elected government. It is assumed, for example, that it is easier to ascertain that a doctor needs such and such an education and that a filing clerk needs such and such a different education, than to decide what the doctor's salary should be in comparison with that of the filing clerk.

But the question that then has to be decided is: who is to be trained to be a doctor and who is to be trained to be a filing clerk? Those, it would seem, who have the necessary desire and aptitudes for the jobs in question. How, then, are the aptitudes to be ascertained? In the collectivist scheme of things aptitudes would be ascertained in the light of progress through the comprehensive schools which egalitarians favour. In Britain, the great majority of posts available for medical men are in the National Health Service, and the training given to fill them is financed by the state. If, as is the case, more people want to become doctors than there are opportunities for training, those who get into the medical schools do so as a result of *competition*, which is no different from the so-called 'rat-race'[64] that takes place in the schools. If, again, medical

64. What is this 'rat-race'? In the course of their school careers children exhibit aptitudes, talents and ambitions of various sorts in varying degrees. By some means or other those who can and want to undertake the most exacting types of work that require long training must be distinguished from the rest. An attempt to give this training to children who do not want or cannot complete it must lead to misery and waste of effort. If all were capable of undertaking it, only some could be selected to do so. Selection of some sort is unavoidable and the expres-

care is distributed by the state, then the number of those who can receive medical training depends on the number that the National Health Service employs. Does this number depend on *need*? There is no doubt that in this country many more doctors would be employed if *the wishes* of the population for medical attention could settle the matter. But this number would be much larger than could be met by the financial and physical resources likely to be allocated for it by the state out of taxation. As patients, people want more medical care than they wish to pay for as taxpayers. The egalitarian view is that this scarce care should be distributed in accordance with need.

It is clear, however, that 'need' is and will be interpreted in more than one way. The individual *to whom* the distribution is made does not always have the same conception of need as the individual *by whom* the distribution is made. The recipient tends to interpret it in terms of what he wants. If he wants a medical examination, for example, that is what he 'needs'. The distributor, on the other hand, is more likely to distinguish between what the recipient thinks he needs and what in the distributor's opinion he really needs, and to wish to make his distribution in terms of the latter. If everything that anybody wanted could be supplied to him, then distributive justice would be unnecessary. It is because not all wants can be supplied that some rule of distribution, some 'rationing' has to be established. Needs, then, are generally held to be wants that are in some sense basic, wants the non-fulfilment of which destroys or severely hurts the individual who has them. Distribution of medical care, then, in accordance with need, would be distribution of it to those who would die or suffer serious harm if they received

sion 'rat-race' serves only to vituperate the inevitable.

no care, and distribution among the members of this category in accordance with the degree of their possible loss or injury.

The type of health service, however, which egalitarians support, is one to which everyone belongs and from which everyone can claim medical attention, without fee, for slight as well as for serious illnesses. Everyone, then, is to receive in accordance with his wish, want or basic want, in accordance with his whim or in accordance with his dire need. Since the resources for supplying medical services are limited, it can be said that in general there is competition for these services between all those entitled to them, so that the mildly ill compete with the desperately ill. This is to some extent concealed because not *everyone* competes for the services of the brain surgeon or the 'heart-machine'. But the services of nurses and non-specialist doctors are, so to say, *diluted* between those who are seriously ill and those who are hardly ill at all. The patient with a cold takes up time and expense that might have been employed in giving a more thorough diagnosis to someone else. Furthermore, in a comprehensive scheme of this sort, the selfish, the demanding and the well-connected can gain attention at the expense of others.

In an egalitarian scheme, therefore, in which everyone can gain some attention on demand and without fee, the services given are likely to be diluted, the givers of the services are likely to be overworked, and the most selfish are likely to get attention at the expense of the more conscientious or amiable members of the community. When some quarrelsome individual enters a group he causes disputes and perhaps violence even though the other members of the group are pacific. The desire of the others for peace cannot preserve peace if there are a few who do not want it. It is somewhat similar, I suggest, with unreasonable or unnecessary demands on a public service. If a few individuals start to push their claims too high, others are induced to make similar claims to ensure their 'stake' in the available resources. There is something rather like Gresham's Law, and irresponsible behaviour tends to drive out responsible behaviour. The egalitarian collectivist, therefore, in removing the competiton that arises from cash demand, substitutes for it competition by means of entreaty or bullying. It is nowadays regarded as rather indecent to refer to the abuses to which collectivist schemes are liable. The suggestion is that the critics of such abuses are self-righteous and show a contempt for the poor. But in a collectivist system such as the National Health Service to which practically everyone belongs irrespective of his income, some of the well-to-do are likely to be much more effective in obtaining special benefits than the less articulate among the poor.

The conclusion I draw from this is that basic welfare should not be removed from the market and provided for everyone out of taxation. Poverty and misfortune are evils but are not injustices, and the moral demand they make is for help on the ground of humanity. In matters as basic in their lives as health, housing and the education of their children it is best for people to allocate their own resources as far as they can, with public provision (when possible as purchasing power) in reserve for what they cannot individually pay for. If they are not allowed so to provide for themselves out of their disposable income they will come to regard their basic requirements as somebody else's business and to regard amusement as the chief aim of their free choices.

This is a convenient point at which to consider briefly the position of those well-off people who favour the enforced universality of publicly provided health and educational services, but meanwhile pay for private treatment in hospital for themselves and private schooling for their children. They can defend this *Interimsethik* by saying they are justified in so behaving while they support the coming of a system in which money can no longer buy such advantages. Their assumption is that individuals are morally justified in taking full advantage of privileges they believe they ought not to have as long as they support their eventual abolition. Whether they would consider a vote at an election as sufficient to constitute support I do not know, but, leaving this aside, it appears that they must believe that it is right for them to do what they consider wrong as long as other people who do not think it wrong are not legally prohibited from doing it. They will not act on their principles unless other people are prohibited from acting on theirs.

They may argue, of course, that if they were to refuse to take advantage of what they consider to be unfair privileges others, with different views, would go on benefiting from them, and their own principled actions would have no tendency to alter the system. This may seem rather like the individual in the State of Nature depicted by Hobbes who will not refrain from aggression on others until there is a power capable of coercing *everyone* to keep the peace. There is an important difference, however, between the position of the wealthy egalitarian 'queue jumper' and the apprehensive natural man who longs for peace, but is reluctant to give away his advantages meanwhile. For everyone may be supposed to wish for self-preservation and the peace that fosters it, whereas large numbers of people see no harm in paying for extra services for themselves and their children, especially if they have earned the money to do so. To refuse to act on a moral principle unless and until everyone is forced to observe it, irrespective of their moral beliefs, is a strange way of showing one's adherence to it. It seems to me that someone who takes this view would feel justified in taking personal advantage of whatever new system was set up. Once fee-paying schools were abolished, for example, the wealthy could congregate in districts where there are particularly good schools and hospitals, arguing that they are justified in doing this as long as the good teachers and doctors have not been forcibly spread equally all over the country, or as long as a 'busing' system for children and patients has not been instituted. The stress all the time is on the system, and the individual considers himself free to try to beat it whenever he can, and more particularly whenever it is not perfect, which, of course it will never be. Yet no system can work well unless individuals are prepared to govern their *own* actions by principle irrespectively of what others do.

Two Collectivist Objections Considered

There are two main objections to the view summarised on the previous page. The first is that if left to themselves people will not provide these things for themselves even if they have the wherewithal to do so. It is hard to know what to say in reply to this argument, which seems to assume that problem families are typical of the community as a whole. A forcibly imposed system of universal welfare might *make* people become like this, but it is premature to suggest that the transformation has already taken place. Dr E. G. West has shown[65] that before the Education Act of 1870 most parents were proud to make personal payments towards the

65. E. G. West, *Education and the State,* London: Institute of Economic Affairs, 1965, pp. 140–4 and 171.

education of their children. But that was over a hundred years ago and perhaps presentday parents, it may be objected, are no longer like that. Ralph Harris and Arthur Seldon[66] have ascertained that many people nowadays would *like* to make their own choices about welfare and pay more for them rather than rely wholly upon what the state provides. The remarkable thing is that such eminently responsible individuals are criticised by egalitarians as 'queue jumpers' if they so express themselves. One cannot help suspecting that egalitarians think there is something morally evil in the desire to foster the development of one's own children, to look after one's own health and to own one's own house, even in a society where minimum standards are at a level undreamed of by the pioneers of the welfare state.

This brings us to the second objection to the idea that in an economically advanced community individuals should be free to make and pay for their own choice of welfare. Dr Brian Barry[67] has argued with force and subtlety against some of the socialist arguments in favour of confining medical care and education to the publicly provided system. Nevertheless he appears to favour this course on other grounds—'because one places value on integration as such'. We may note, he says, that from the point of view of integration 'every departure from a complete ban on private provision must be regarded as a concession.'[68] He also suggests that integration is bound up with democracy in the following way:

As far as each parent determining the education of his child is

66. Ralph Harris and Arthur Seldon, *Choice in Welfare 1965: Second Report on Knowledge and Preference in Education, Health Services and Pensions,* London: Institute of Economic Affairs, 1965.

67. Brian Barry, *Political Argument,* London: Routledge & Kegan Paul, 1965, chapter 7.

68. Ibid., p. 132.

concerned private schools offer as much scope as public in principle since private schools may be run by the parents of the
children attending them. But if what one values is that the members of the community should determine as one group how the
next generation is to be educated, there is no substitute for public schools.[69]

The emphasis here is upon the *oneness* of the group that
determines how the next generation shall be educated. Dr
Barry does not notice, however, that the one group will also
be *treating the next generation as one,* so that parents and
non-parents of one generation will be imposing a uniform
mode of education on the next. He does not, nevertheless,
regard integration as a very strong value, even though he
does consider it essential to some collectivist arguments, and
he puts forward three other arguments for eliminating private choice in welfare. He argues that a society with a variety
of methods for providing welfare 'is liable to serious splits to
heal which there will be no shared experiences and standards'.[70] Furthermore, in such a society there will be ineffi-
ciency, because wealth rather than ability will secure entry to
positions of power. And finally he asserts that in an integrated
system of welfare, the powerful would have a strong motive
for improving the forms of welfare that are publicly provided,
since they themselves would have to use them and would
therefore want them to be as good as possible.

This last argument has been implicitly met by Professor
Hayek in *The Constitution of Liberty*.[71] He points out that
in a society where the free market has scope, the better-
off tend to pioneer various types of consumption which are

69. By 'public schools' Dr Barry means, of course, schools provided without
fee out of taxation. See pp. 133–4.

70. Ibid., p. 134.

71. F. A. Hayek, *The Constitution of Liberty*, London: Routledge & Kegan Paul,
1960, pp. 42–6.

then made available for larger sections of the population. The same principle, I suggest applies to welfare, especially to education where private schools have set standards and carried out experiments which the publicly provided schools have then made beneficial use of. As to Dr Barry's second argument, it seems to me that a free market economy is less prone to hierarchy than is the bureaucratic sort of society that socialism requires. This topic will be discussed later. As to the alleged 'divisive' effects of a society which permits free choice in welfare, one is back with 'integration' once more. Societies such as those in France, the United States and Great Britain contain all sorts of institutions, traditions of thought and action, regional idiosyncrasies and cultural oppositions. The distinctions between Catholics and free thinkers, between North and South, between England and Scotland have sometimes led to violence and are continual sources of strain. But if they were all eliminated the nations within which they exist would lose much of their energy and creative power. The suggestion that the people of these countries would be made better by forcing them all to go to the same schools and the same doctors in organisations administered by bureaucrats under the sort of control that democratic government permits is incredible in itself and dangerous because of the disappointments its realisation would give rise to.[72] I have already argued that under such a system individual effort would be guided by trivial aims because individuals would be prevented from directing their energies on the things that concern them most.

In a beautifully argued letter to the *Spectator*[73] Antony

72. It is possible that such disappointment is one reason for the bad temper and violence that are so widespread in Great Britain in the later nineteen-sixties and early seventies.

73. Antony Jay, 'Handsome is as Newsom Does', letter, *The Spectator*, 2nd August 1968, p. 177.

Jay indicates that if, as the Royal Commission on the Public Schools assumed, it is 'divisive' for parents to pay for their children to go to public schools, it is equally 'divisive' if some people are allowed to operate private cars when a public transport system exists. Owners of private cars, for example, 'can use their wealth to buy access to parts of the country which are denied to their fellow citizens who through no fault of their own have to rely on the state transport system'. If everyone, including Cabinet Ministers, had to make use of the public transport system, there would be more pressure on it to improve, and furthermore, by being forced to use public transport people would get 'enriching experience' and be saved from 'the arrogant isolation and social privilege of the private car'. The majority on the Commission on Public Schools wanted half the places at them to be used for children 'in need' of such education. Mr Jay suggests that places in those private cars that remained in a society where public transport predominated could be allocated to 'those suffering from infectious and contagious diseases, halitosis, agoraphobia and diseases of the central nervous system'.

Collectivist Organisation

As soon as the shape of modern society began to become apparent a distinction was drawn by students of it between forms of organisation in which uniformity was obtained by means of force and societies in which harmonious development is obtained by means of freely made agreements. In 1817 in *L'Industrie*[74] Saint-Simon distinguished between

74. *Oeuvres de Saint-Simon et d'Enfintin*, Paris, 1865–76, volume 18. See Frank E. Manuel, *The New World of Henri Saint-Simon*, Cambridge, MA: Har-

military and industrial forms of society. The military form, he held, was obsolete and its decline was made inevitable by the French Revolution. The old military and landed aristocracy was being replaced by a form of society in which employers, workmen and traders cooperated in ways which rendered armed force and nationality irrelevant. Later in the century Herbert Spencer distinguished between what he called 'militant' and 'industrial' social types. In his *Principles of Sociology* (1876–96) he said that in militant forms of society the whole people is nationally organised like an army with ranks, a chain of command and an imposed *esprit de corps*. For the latter to be possible the leadership has to combine political with religious and ceremonial functions. In such societies the industrial and commercial activities are subordinated to the requirements of the government, for which they constitute a 'permanent commissariat'.[75] In industrial types of society, on the other hand, cooperation is secured by voluntary means. 'Multitudinous objects', Spencer wrote, 'are achieved by spontaneously-evolved combinations of citizens governed representatively.'[76] In industrial types of society free exchange is the central economic feature, and freedom and the keeping of agreements are basic moral requirements. Thus the unity, hierarchy and use of force in the militant type of society are contrasted with the differentiation and freedom of the industrial type.

Saint-Simon's view of 'industrial' society was largely based on J. B. Say's account of the economic system, which in its turn was derived from Adam Smith's critique of mercantil-

---

vard University Press, 1956, chapter 20.

75. Herbert Spencer, *The Principles of Sociology*, third edition, volume 1, 1885, New York: D. Appleton and Company, page 549.

76. Ibid., p. 556.

ism.[77] Spencer, for his part, was a liberal of the old school who watched with alarm as governments that called themselves liberal interfered more and more with economic affairs. The distinction between military and industrial[78] types of society was drawn, therefore, from an antisocialist, or at any rate an antimercantilist point of view. Furthermore, neither type exists without some admixture of the other, and existing societies are more or less military, more or less industrial. Indeed, from what we have said already in chapter 1 it is clear that if the 'industrial' type of society is to keep going there must be a government that enforces contracts and punishes fraud and violence, and hence some features of the military society are inevitable if anarchy is to be prevented. Since Spencer's day the movement towards collectivism which he saw and deplored has accelerated to such an extent that the sort of spontaneously regulated society he favoured seems very remote to us now.[79]

But these are not adequate reasons for neglecting the important truths that are expressed in the distinction between 'military' and 'industrial' or 'contractual' types of society. Advocates of state-provided welfare have generally considered themselves to be pacific and internationalist in their aims. But in spite of this the twentieth century has been a particularly warlike period. Collectivism, egalitarianism and neomercantilism, indeed, have been prominent features of a civilisation in which whole peoples have been slaughtered. The growth of science and technology has undoubtedly

77. Manuel suggests that Saint-Simon was not sincere in writing this, as he says that 'in 1817 Saint-Simon posed as the popularizer of extreme *laissez-faire* liberalism . . . '; see *The New World of Henri Saint-Simon,* p. 241.

78. 'Industrial', in this usage, does not mean 'technological'. Perhaps 'commercial' or even 'contractual' would have been a more suitable designation.

79. There are signs in some communist countries of a movement towards 'industrial', i.e., 'contractual' forms of organisation.

made this slaughter more efficient, but the coincidence of war and welfare state collectivism should make us think it possible that egalitarian collectivism and militarism are not as opposed to one another as is generally supposed.

Should Distributive Justice Overrule Commutative Justice?

Near the beginning of the present chapter it was argued that distributive justice requires a distributor. This is not a purely verbal point—indeed, the phrase 'distribution of wealth' does not itself imply that someone has distributed it. The point is this. A complex society that has developed through many vicissitudes of history is neither justly nor unjustly organised. When, however, people want it to be justly or-ganised they imply that, since God has not done so, man must take it in hand and do what God has failed to do. As soon as people want society as a whole to be justly or-ganised they imply that it should be brought under some unitary human control so that the government secures the just distribution that does not come about on its own. In a democratic society the voters are expected to elect a govern-ment to do this.

Now the question that needs to be considered is whether a state organised to move toward distributive justice can at the same time be organised to maintain commutative justice. Are these consistent aims or must they clash with one an-other? I suggest that there is a fundamental opposition. Com-mutative justice is found when freely made agreements are kept, and it is maintained when there are laws for punish-ing fraud and for enforcing the fulfilment of contracts. The state's prime functions are the prevention and repression of crimes and the maintenance of honest dealing. Humanity requires it to provide such help for the unfortunate as other agencies cannot ensure. But it is most unlikely that the ownership of wealth and incomes which results from this will coincide with what the political parties in a democratic electorate will consider just. In particular, collectivist parties consider that the just distribution of wealth and income would be a more equal distribution, and hence they use taxation as a means of equalising wealth and incomes as well as a means of paying for the enforcement of law and for helping the unfortunate.

Since taxation is not a voluntary payment, in democratic societies the better-off are forced to give up wealth in order to conform to the electorate's desire for distributive justice, and even if the distinctions of wealth are not very large, taxation is used to enforce the majority's view of what sort of distribution is proper. If someone is unwilling to contribute towards the cost of crime prevention, we feel he ought to be made to do so. If someone is unwilling to contribute towards the cost of helping those who are in dire want, we do not think it is wrong for taxation to be put upon him. But to be forced to make payments in order to secure a just distribution of wealth is a different matter, since there is no universal view on what such a distribution should be, and the individual is being forced to pay for something he may consider wrong. Furthermore, the larger the proportion of his income that is taken for purposes of public expenditure, the stronger the likelihood of inflation, and in consequence financial agreements of all kinds are interfered with because of the erosion in the value of money. Again, in the pursuit of distributive justice agreements between landowners and houseowners and between landlords and tenants are altered or abrogated. Trade unions, for one reason or another, are freed from the necessity to keep to their agreements, and bequests are diverted from the purposes intended by the donors. Thus the scope of coercion is widened and the possibilities for free agreements are diminished.

Trade unions were given their present privileged legal status at a time when their bargaining position was weak, and retain it at a time when it is very strong. It is now agreed by 'experts' whose convictions are formed under the influence of the trade union bureaucracy that it is impossible in this country to make changes in trade union law towards the sort of legal system that exists in other countries. The report of the *Royal Commission on Trade Unions and Employers' Associations 1965–1968* shows how difficult it is, to quote Andrew Shonfield's phrase (p. 288), to get consideration for 'the degree of regulation which should properly be applied to organisations wielding great authority in communities where the average citizen becomes progressively more vulnerable to what they do', in the face of an organisation defended by experts who can easily exploit the practical complications involved in the making of any change whatever.[80]

It may be argued that it is quite right for commutative justice to give way before distributive justice, since the former is often based on a bargain imposed under unfair conditions in which the wealthy have all the advantages. We discussed the idea that buying and selling is unfair in capitalist societies when in chapter 2 we considered J. A. Hobson's account of the matter. We there concluded that Hobson unwittingly assumed that a fair bargain would be

80. ['Note of Reservations by Mr. Andrew Shonfield', *Royal Commission on Trade Unions and Employers' Associations 1965–1968*, London: HMSO, June 1968, pp. 288ff. (Cmnd 3623; British Sessional Papers, 1967–1968, volume 32, pp. 731ff.)]

one carried out in the conditions of a competitive market. But the point that now needs to be made is that when distributive justice is placed above commutative justice, force is being advocated at the expense of voluntary agreement. Force, of course, is inseparable from government, and has to be used in order to prevent or punish murder, assault, fraud and theft. Everyone is against these crimes and everyone favours the force of government that is used to prevent them. But there is no such unanimity about what constitutes a failure in distributive justice in the community as a whole. I have suggested that the very conception of it assumes that there should be a distributor. Quite apart from that, the claims of desert, merit, achievement, effort and need complicate the issue to such an extent that egalitarians themselves have in recent years given up the attempt to assess their relative weightings. There are disagreements about what constitutes justice in a voluntary bargain, but they are capable of settlement and have been worked out over centuries in the law of commerce.

In practice, in democratic societies the answer to the question what constitutes a 'just' distribution of wealth varies as different groups and interests gain the ear of politicians. The prevailing interests try to get economists, sociologists and journalists to justify their policies, and are generally able to find some who are willing to do so. What a democratic collectivist government would most like to have would be a widespread belief that the principles behind its policies are morally necessary. In democratic societies this moral consensus is obtained, if at all, after much discussion and argument. But when a democratic government is deeply involved in economic affairs, there is a tendency for the discussion to take place within the terms of the immediate problems the government is facing. Criticism that calls the prevailing trends into question is apt to be regarded as irresponsible. Businessmen, academics and journalists are tempted to look at events within the context of governmental policy.

Since trade unions, professional organisations and industrial associations are constantly being asked to help in government, their leadership tends to get into the hands of men who are thought to be 'responsible' and 'constructive'. Businessmen are put in a difficult position, for if they refuse to cooperate in governmental plans they are accused of injuring the public interest, and if they do cooperate they are inevitably associated with the collectivism they may not agree with. In particular, as lines of production are costed by accountants employed by the government, the notion of a 'fair' or 'reasonable' profit gets accepted. But this, as I argued in chapter 2, is, in effect, to abandon the conception of profit altogether and to assimilate it to a fee or to a salary—at any rate to something that can be contracted for. I do not think that this particular aspect of governmental planning has been sufficiently noticed. Once a certain rate of profit is regarded as 'reasonable' or 'fair', profit is no longer playing the part it used to play in economic affairs, and the retention of the word only serves to disguise the essential change that the economic system is undergoing. Sometimes 'fair' profits are profits which monopolists in collusion with governments hope to obtain as a result of their collusion.

However that may be, it is clear that democratic collectivist governments, concerned as they are with distributive justice, concerned, that is, with distribution by the government in terms of a moral rule, are bound to want this rule to be accepted by everyone. Now there is a moral principle which all civilised peoples accept, the so-called Golden Rule, according to which people should treat others as they would wish others to treat them. What this principle enunciates is the idea that no one should expect others to treat him as a unique and special case, as entitled to more consideration than others just because he is the individual he in fact is. As regards commutative justice this means that no one is entitled to argue that, whereas others must keep their engagements to him, he is under no obligation to keep his engagements to them. Certainly if someone were to argue in this way, or were to act as though he had taken up this point of view, he would be going against a central feature of civilised morality.

But does the Golden Rule apply to distributive justice as well? Egalitarian collectivists appear to suppose that it does, in that they argue that it is a violation of distributive justice for an individual to be discriminated against, that is, for him not to get the same treatment as others when there is no difference in his situation that requires this. Someone, for example, goes into a nursing home for private medical treatment, whereas someone else who cannot or will not afford it (i.e. prefers to spend his money on motoring or something else) waits much longer and goes into a hospital where he cannot get the privacy he would like. Egalitarians would regard this as a violation of distributive justice if both people were in need of private treatment for, it is supposed, in these circumstances there is discrimination in favour of the man who pays, and two individuals whose needs are similar receive unequal treatment just because one is willing to pay and the other will not or cannot.

But we must ask who does the discriminating here. There would be unjust discrimination[81] if those responsible for al-

---

81. It is significant of the trend towards an unthinking egalitarianism that the word 'discrimination', which in aesthetic contexts is regarded as essential and desirable, is, in moral contexts, taken in a pejorative sense, so that 'unjust dis-

locating beds under some national health scheme gave more favourable conditions to one than to another who equally needed them when it was possible to give similar conditions to both. But when there is freedom to pay for the conditions that some people want, no one discriminates when one person has less favourable conditions than another whose plight is the same as his. To talk as though there is unjust discrimination in such circumstances is *to assume* that all medical care *ought to be* under a single public control, and such an assumption will only be made when a large part of it already is. To attack 'discrimination', therefore, rather than callousness or poverty, is really to call for a single state system. Now while it is true that the Golden Rule prohibits selfishness, fraud and lack of consideration for others, it can hardly be taken to imply that there should be no private medicine, housing or education.

Someone whose duty it is to administer a rule must do so justly, that is, he must follow the rule in such a way as not to favour some by comparison with others. He is required to treat equal cases equally, and if one party is treated differently from another there must be some relevant ground for this. But it does not follow from this rule of distributive justice that *no one* should treat one person differently from another without reason for doing so. If it did, then friendship would be impossible, since friends do not generally have reasons for being friends. People have reasons for being allies or business partners or political associates, but it is possible to have friends who are none of these, and hence to have friends for no reasons whatsoever. The existence of friendship, therefore, is a proof that the Golden Rule does

crimination' tends to become pleonastic. Similarly 'segregation' is taken to mean 'undesirable segregation' and 'selection' to mean 'undesirable selection'.

not imply that distributive justice should prevail in all human relationships.[82] If what I have said is right, then distributive justice is applicable only where there is an authority applying a rule of distribution. To press for universal distributive justice, therefore, is to press for a universal authority.[83] It is generally admitted that totalitarian socialism requires such an authority, but it is now clear that democratic socialism requires one too. Forced fraternity or compulsory integration is an essential characteristic of egalitarian collectivist society.

We have now seen what truth there is in Spencer's idea that socialist societies are types of 'militant' society. In socialist societies the governments hope for a much wider range of moral agreement than obtains in non-socialist societies, and endeavour to obtain it, not only by argument and persuasion, but also by prohibiting behaviour which many members of the community regard as right or permissible. Thus in socialist societies the political leaders endeavour to secure a moral authority for their aims, and although moral authority is different from ecclesiastical authority it is the nearest approach to it that a secular society can offer. For it involves at least the suggestion and frequently the assertion that opponents of the government are wicked men. When

82. Compare Dr Aurel Kolnai's paper, 'The Moral Theme in Political Division', *Philosophy*, 1960, pp. 234–54, especially page 254: 'The basic moral intuitions of mankind—which Right and Left alike cannot but take for granted as a premise for their respective moral appeal—provide no solution, except in a prohibitive and limiting sense, for the permanent or topical problems of political organization and choice.'

83. Compare R. P. Dognin's 'Échange et "Justice" Commutative selon K. Marx', *Archives de philosophie du droit*, 12, 1967: 'Marx et le droit moderne', p. 13–32. Professor Dognin quotes from Proudhon (*De la justice dans la révolution et dans l'église*): 'The family is the sphere of authority and subordination; and if communism is to be logical, it will recognize that in taking the family as the model for society, it ends in despotism' (p. 32). Perhaps there is less despotism in families now because it is being transferred to the state.

governments claim to speak with moral authority on topics that permit of genuine moral disagreement they act as a sort of secular church fulminating against heretics. In the end, however, the heretics against democratic socialism are not likely to be burned, but smothered rather by the weight of officially generated opinion.

The resulting form of society need not be hierarchical but it must be bureaucratic.[84] Professor Hayek has pointed out[85] that a centrally organised economic plan can no more be drawn up or executed by democratic discussion of details than an army can carry out a campaign by democratic procedures. Bureaucrats are needed, not merely because they are experts—frequently they are not—but because men are needed to take decisions as events unfold, and neither legislators nor elected ministers are often in a position to intervene. Nationalised industries, government departments and state welfare organisations all have to be organised in bureaucratic forms with controlling directors and committees and chains of command and responsibility. Recruitment into them may be by merit and hence they may offer a career to talent. But when there are more of such bodies and they increase in numbers, as necessarily happens with the move towards collectivism, fundamental changes take place in the society as a whole. Democratic control and independent criticism must be made more difficult. When a large part of the information about economic statistics or administrative arrangements is collected and issued by the government, investigators and critics are forced to approach the very officials they may criticise for the information that might give substance to their criticisms. The officials will generally de-

---

84. In the 'redeployment' of labour executed by the government in 1966–67, by far the largest number went into government agencies.
85. F. A. Hayek, *The Road to Serfdom*, London: Routledge, 1944, chapter 5.

fend themselves, their superiors and the system in which they hold positions of responsibility. 'Cooperative' and 'public-spirited' enquirers will be favoured. Writers who hope for these favours will insensibly find themselves supporting a 'public interest' that the government itself has defined. Even in the merely partial collectivism under which we now live, consultative committees, parents' associations and other such bodies are treated with a somewhat contemptuous toleration. But as collectivism is further extended, these bodies become agencies for explaining and justifying the government's decisions, as the trade unions have become in the 'people's democracies'. There are the beginnings of such developments in the society we live in, but if they are recognised they can be dealt with. If on the other hand, they are not recognised, a social order will grow up from which independent thought and action have been unwittingly excluded.

CHAPTER 5
SOME REFLECTIONS ON PLANNING AND PREDICTING

Is a Centrally Planned Economy Inevitable?

So far I have endeavoured to do two things. First, I have criticised the arguments and assumptions of those who oppose systems of free market enterprise on moral grounds. Second, I have argued that the egalitarian collectivist alternative to a system of competitive markets is bound to lead to the authoritarian imposition of a state-controlled morality. In my discussion so far I have assumed that a system in which consumers, individual entrepreneurs and firms compete in their various ways is possible, and that potentially maleficent monopolies can be somehow got rid of. But in his Reith Lectures delivered in 1966[86] and in *The New Industrial State* (London: Hamish Hamilton, 1967) Professor J. K. Galbraith has argued that the growth of large-scale technology has made competitive markets obsolete.[87]

86. [J. K. Galbraith's Reith Lectures, 'The New Industrial State', appeared in *The Listener*, 17 November 1966, pp. 711–14; 24 November, pp. 755–58; 1 December, pp. 793–95 and 812; 8 December, pp. 841–43 and 853; 15 December, pp. 881–84; 22 December, pp. 915–18.]

87. He says that in the United States, 'faith in free enterprise is one of the minor branches of theology', *The Listener*, 17 November 1966, p. 711. Galbraith, of course, expects his readers to conclude that it is therefore quite ridiculous.

Galbraith asserts that in consequence of the types of technology now in use, even very large firms cannot take risks
in employing the large amounts of capital needed for the
development of their products. They therefore ensure that
their product is bought by preparing the way for it with
advertisement, and they see to it that there is no competition
in settling the price. In effect, according to Galbraith, they
make the consumers want what the producers wish to sell,
and they determine the price so as to cover their outlays
and to provide capital for future developments. But they
can only do this if the consumers they 'manage' (Galbraith's
word) have the money to pay the prices; and to see to it that
they have, the government is encouraged to step in to maintain total demand by monetary management, to limit wage
demands, to provide the training needed in the technological industries (hence the growth of higher education in recent years), and to undertake the very great risks involved in
such new industries as those concerned with atomic power
and space travel.[88] 'We may assume', he says, 'that there
has been an interaction between state and firm which has
brought the two to a unity of view.'[89]

According to Galbraith modern industrial planning is autonomous in the sense that it is a primary agency that makes
other practices and institutions follow in its wake. Hence the
modern style of industrial production puts the old style of
industrial entrepreneur out of business, yet at the same time
it makes it impossible for democratic politicians to control
it. For the decisions of large-scale industry are, 'if it is to be
efficient, somewhat authoritarian'.[90] He concludes that the

88. *The Listener*, 8 December 1966, pp. 841–2.
89. Ibid., p. 853.
90. 'The technical complexity and planning and associated scale of operations, that took power from the capitalist entrepreneur and lodged it in the
body of the firm, removed it from the reach of social control,' *The Listener*, 15
December 1966, p. 882.

differences between what is falsely called 'free enterprise' in the United States and the socialist societies of Eastern Europe have been much exaggerated, and that there is little that individuals can do to alter the technological autonomy which leads to their convergence. What individuals can try to do is to set up aesthetic objectives which are not engendered within the industrial organisation itself. But if individuals oppose the state they will only be helping the industrial organisation to extend its control for, according to Galbraith, industrial organisation is so powerful that it is only through the state that it can in any way be limited. 'It is through the state', he writes, 'that the society must assert the superior claims of aesthetic over economic goals, and particularly of environment over cost.'[91] If Galbraith is right, then, the inevitable future is a society under the 'somewhat authoritarian' control of industrial managers who may be persuaded by the state to pay some attention to the beauties of the human and natural environment as they manage consumers, fix prices and expand their operations.

This view of Galbraith's is an elaborately modulated outcry of helpless disillusion rather than an analysis of our present social situation, but even so it calls for a number of comments. Galbraith argues as if what a determined advertising campaign may achieve for an individual detergent manufacturer can be achieved for the whole of industry, but the near-collapse, to take one example, of the shipbuilding industry in this country is evidence to the contrary. The successes of advertising take place when a demand exists that can be evoked, extended or transferred from one product to another, but to create demand or even to manage it is a very different proposition. I endeavoured to show in chapter 2 that markets are not independent of the society in which they function, but presuppose all sorts of other activi-

91. *The Listener*, 22 December 1966, p. 918.

ties. In societies where many different activities flourish, this variety will be reflected in the many different things that people want. Wants can be managed by industrialists and by governments only in societies where there are few centres of independent activity. In effect, Galbraith is arguing that in our own day technological and industrial management is the sole source of independent ('autonomous') activity. He is implying that men's wants are so limited and so feeble that a fairly small group of scientists, technologists and business administrators can control them. In his view of our society the only possible counterbalance to large-scale industry is the desire to enjoy beauty, while religion, intellectual self-development, the concern for justice and for freedom, and the striving for moral integrity are assumed to be ineffective.

Galbraith is so far correct in that the very intellectual development which encouraged the growth of modern science and its technological applications has discouraged religious beliefs and has weakened religious institutions. Furthermore the cult of youth and of contemporaneity tends to attribute merit to what is new and to lessen concern for monuments of the past, whether in landscape, buildings or literature. (Conservationists are apt to be of a conservative frame of mind.) Traditional morality, too, tends to be regarded as outmoded. It is possible however, to recognise that this is widely believed without going to the extreme of holding that the wish for aesthetic enjoyment is the only curb on complete technological control over society. If this were so, then the case would indeed be bad, since aesthetic taste is variable and very easily modified. But I suggest that there are many people with a concern for freedom and spontaneity whose wants are not manufactured by the large industrial concerns. To ask them, as Galbraith does, to put their trust in state intervention on their behalf is to acquiesce in the existing or emerging *status quo.* It has been said[92] that Galbraith's views may have released powerful and radical forces, but surely what they suggest is that there is practically nothing that can be done to alter the present trends, and that therefore the ruling authorities have to be submitted to in the hope that they will not destroy too much beauty. Whether Galbraith thinks that nothing else is worth preserving or that everything else has already gone without possibility of return he does not say.

It is interesting to notice that in *The New Industrial State* Professor Galbraith considers that universities have a part to play in influencing governments to allow scope for cultural (which for Galbraith seems to mean aesthetic) activities.[93] This might be useful, although not all university planning experts put beauty before industrial growth, and professors of Fine Art may not be listened to. Indeed, universities might be torn apart if one expert is paid to testify on one side and another on the opposite, even if by this means sweetness and light are brought to the tribunal proceedings. But universities are now being invaded by the idea that markets are essentially wicked and that demand is created and corrupted by irresponsible business corporations. Professor

92. *The Times Business News,* 4 September 1967, p. 21, in an editorial, referring to *The New Industrial State:* 'If the ideas of this book do gain wide acceptance, the professor may turn out to have loosed far more powerful and radical forces than his own gently chaffing tone suggests. For his critique is at least as ambitious in scope, as appealing in its simplicity and as alarming in its implications as Marx's ever was.'

93. Compare Raymond Ruyer, *Élogue de la société de consommation,* Paris: Calmann-Levy, 1969, pp. 119–20: 'The remedy proposed by Galbraith: development of countervailing powers: universities, scientific research, astronautics, consists in adding to the military plans, cultural plans financed by the taxpayers. These will be less monstrous but in the end perhaps just as mortal, as is shown today by the enormous expenditure on universities and the instruction at great expense of an intellectual proletariat. Galbraith wants to cure the plague by inoculating the patient with cholera.'

Herbert Marcuse, the rich man's Galbraith, puts forward Galbraithian ideas in sub-Galbraithian prose, writing of 'free competition at administered prices, a free press which censors itself, free choice between brands and gadgets'.[94] Marcuse's admirers in the universities seek to destroy the organisations that Galbraith thinks we must submit to and might influence, and they think that universities themselves are creatures of the corrupting bodies. What can a follower of Galbraith say in the face of all this?

Professor Galbraith's views on the organisation and economic power of large industrial concerns have been criticised in some detail by Professor G. C. Allen[95] who points out that giant concerns meet with troubles, fluctuations and even disasters, and gives evidence to show that it is false to suppose that there is 'a steady progression from highly competitive markets to monopoly'.[96] He points out that large firms compete with one another, and although they do sometimes create demand (small firms do this too), they do not manage and control it to the extent that Galbraith's argument requires. Those who have studied British industry have not found it dominated by monopoly, and the monopoly of the nationalised Coal Board has not been able to prevent the demand for competing fuels. 'In 1950', Allen writes 'the National Coal Board enjoyed a virtual monopoly of fuel supplies in this country. Today it is one of several powerful competitors for the fuel and power market.'[97]

Galbraith has no regrets for the competitive markets

94. Herbert Marcuse, *One-Dimensional Man*, London: Routledge & Kegan Paul, 1964; paperback edition, p. 23, London: Sphere Books, 1968.

95. G. C. Allen, *Economic Fact and Fantasy. A Rejoinder to Galbraith's Reith Lectures*, London: Institute of Economic Affairs, Occasional Paper 14, 1967.

96. Ibid., p. 21.

97. Ibid., p. 29.

which he says have now ceased to have importance, and yet he seems to view with distaste the inevitable subjection to large firms in league with government which he says have replaced it. Perhaps he would have preferred democratic socialism, but since he thinks this is now impracticable, his only hope is that the democratic remnant will influence the state to provide oases of beauty in a world of machines, bureaucracies and standardised mass amusements. By adopting a collectivist attitude towards industrial authoritarianism, Galbraith and his followers make it clear that they intend merely to sit back and take what comes. But if Galbraith is wrong in his diagnosis, there are good prospects for opposition to monopolies of all kinds and opposition to attempts by governments to plan economic circumstances from the centre. If industrial monopoly under the aegis of the state is not inevitable, then there is much to be gained by criticising the collectivism that fosters its formation. Galbraith is not likely to release powerful and radical forces, but is rather a prophet of the bandwagon disguised as Solomon Eagle.[98]

Centralised Planning and Technological Advance

We have seen that according to Galbraith modern industrial and technological planning is 'autonomous'. There is no

98. According to Daniel Defoe in *A Journal of the Plague Year*, Solomon Eagle was an 'enthusiast' who during the plague of London 'went about denouncing of judgement upon the city in a frightful manner'. 'What he said, or pretended, indeed I could not learn,' said Defoe, and Galbraith's intentions are similarly obscure. Compare Daniel Defoe, *A Journal of the Plague Year*, ed. Anthony Burgess and Christopher Bristow, Harmondsworth: Penguin Books, 1966, p. 119.

need to accept the whole of his view to recognise that the development of natural science and technology is an extremely powerful element in contemporary society. The researches of Lord Rutherford, for example, led to the atomic bomb and to atomic fuel, to destruction, constant menace, new military strategies, new methods of curing diseases and new forms of motive power. Rutherford's discoveries were developed by technologists under the stress of war, and present soldiers, politicians and ordinary citizens with new dangers and new hopes. New materials, new machines, new methods of prolonging life constantly affect human relationships.

Some of the social effects of new discoveries can be foreseen, but it is unlikely that they all can be. Will the widespread use of contraceptive pills in advanced countries, for example, stabilise the population there or will it lead to a reduction? No one knows. No one knows, furthermore, what new discoveries and inventions will be made. Industrial firms, of course, have research workers trying to solve particular problems, and governments develop particular types of weapon in response to what they believe other governments are doing, and hence reasonable forecasts can be made about the probable results of these researches. But discoveries are sometimes made by accident, or as byproducts of a line of enquiry with quite other objectives. Sometimes discoveries involve quite a new way of looking at things, as when the concept of inertia was conceived, or as when light was conceived in terms of waves instead of in terms of corpuscles. The trouble with accidents, byproducts and new conceptions is not that they are *difficult* to predict, but that it is and must be *impossible* to predict them. For in predicting accidents, byproducts and new conceptions the predictor would already have made the discovery or formed the new conception and would not be predicting.[99]

We have seen that scientific and technological discoveries have considerable effects on the development of society. It follows that societies in which scientific and technological discovery is particularly frequent must be societies in which predictions of their future condition is particularly hazardous. Our society is certainly such a society, and hence all predictions of its future must be tentative.

Certain qualifications now need to be made. A scientific discovery may not have social repercussions for some considerable time after it has been made, and may not, indeed, have any such effects at all. Again, once a scientific discovery has been made, some of its technological and social effects may be foreseen and provided for. Furthermore, a technologically educated government (or firm) may foresee certain effects of a new invention and take steps to prevent it from being developed. Like 'Breakages Limited' in Shaw's play,[100] it may even suppress a new invention or postpone its use. Nevertheless, the general effect of rapid scientific and technological advance is rapid social change and a failure to foresee what form it will take. The more rapid and widespread the technological advances are the more

99. I made this point in 'Comte's Positivism and the Science of Society', *Philosophy*, 26, 1951, pp. 291–310, where references are given. Sir Karl Popper in the Preface to *The Poverty of Historicism*, London: Routledge & Kegan Paul, 1957, gives another argument (first formulated by him in 1950), to show that 'we cannot predict by rational or scientific methods, the future growth of scientific knowledge' (pp. ix–x). F. H. Bradley had argued to a similar conclusion in his *Presuppositions of Critical History*, Oxford: Oxford University Press, 1875. Carlyle, in an early essay, stated the point without argument.

100. [G. B. Shaw, *The Applecart*, in *The Collected Works of George Bernard Shaw*, volume 19, New York: William H. Wyse & Company, 1930, pp. 169–277. See page 237: ' . . . because every new invention is bought up and suppressed by Breakages Limited'.]

likely it is that social changes will occur that no one has anticipated.

But 'planners' of all parties urge *both* that rapid technological advance is desirable, *and* that the economy should be brought under centralised control. But any technological advance, whether by private firms or governments is bound to make control of the economy more difficult, and to defeat, from time to time, the schemes of the planners. The planners could try to keep the time-gap between scientific discovery and technological application as wide as possible. They could try to keep new inventions in cold storage until their implementation was opportune. They could withdraw funds from research or switch them from one area of investigation to another. But the range of scientific discovery and technological invention is enormous, and as specialisation increases, it becomes more difficult for any man or even committee to know what is afoot everywhere. Even if planning of the whole economy were a valid concept (in fact it is a confused one), and even if it were a feasible economic exercise (and this may well be doubted), the planners would still be faced with the paradox that the more successfully science and technology are pursued the more uncontrollable they become and the more social surprises they will give rise to. Scientists and technologists necessarily make the central planner's task impossible.

In an article in *The Economist*[101] entitled 'A Superior Snakes and Ladders' reference is made to a conference[102] at Strathclyde University attended by market researchers, economists, systems analysts, mathematicians, logicians, sociologists, pure and applied scientists and businessmen.

101. 'A Superior Snakes and Ladders', *The Economist*, 6 July 1968, pp. 53–4.
102. The papers from this conference were published in *Technological Forecasting*, ed. R. V. Arnold, Edinburgh: Edinburgh University Press, 1969.

The object of the conference was to consider how scientific advances and technological inventions and the resulting social repercussions and changes in demand could be predicted. The author confirms my doubts expressed above, that discoveries that involve looking at established facts in a new way are particularly hard—I would say impossible—to predict, but he seems to think that, because scientific research is now so well organised, even such discoveries might be predicted with some fairly high degree of probability. He recognises, however, that the problem of predicting *when* a new technological discovery will be made is extremely difficult, and that forecasts of demand based on the so-called 'Delphi' technique of collecting the opinions of large numbers of experts are bound to be risky. After going on to note the difficulties that arise in integrating the evidence of mathematicians, technologists, economists, etc., he concludes: 'The magnitude of the problems can be gauged from our continuing inability to produce a workable and up-to-date input–output table of the economy, despite all the statistics. Without one, any closely engineered national plan will break down—just as the first one did.' This seems to call for the following comments.

(*a*) Accidents and new ways of regarding the facts *cannot, logically* cannot, be predicted. To attempt to do so is merely to attempt to hasten up scientific and technological advance by shock methods.

(*b*) It is true that those in the know can sometimes foresee various *types* of scientific or technological discovery that are, so to say, already in the pipeline. Even then, as the writer in *The Economist* points out, timing is very important, since the course of events may be very different if the order of two discoveries or inventions is different. In any case, these limited predictions can be made only if it is assumed that no very fundamental discovery will make them irrelevant.

(c) Once it is admitted that predictions of further discoveries and inventions only allow of probability, it has also to be admitted that their practical utility must be limited, and it always remains possible that plans based on them will turn out disastrously.

(d) If we could be quite sure that no other unforeseen occurrences would interfere with our social plans, we could make them with confidence. Those who want to plan human society on a very large scale are therefore tempted to try to keep large parts of society as stable as they can. As their plan progresses they will get more and more irritated at anyone who plays the joker. They can only stop him by preventing him from playing at all. There can be no important place in such a society for spontaneous behaviour. Social prediction on a large scale is easiest in repetitive or traditional and hardest in progressive forms of society. Those who want to predict and make sure cannot allow private initiatives. They are driven towards totalitarianism.

The events in France during May and June 1968 are very instructive in this context. The French 'planners' had devised what *dirigistes* elsewhere have commended as a well-organised and successful set of financial, economic and industrial measures which secured a strong franc and an apparent unity. The completely unexpected students' revolution and the confused reactions to it brought about a situation which no one had foreseen. Within a few days the whole economic outlook was transformed in ways which the planners had not wanted.

(e) A further difficulty in the way of long-term planning for the future is that it seems likely that future generations will want different things from what we want, or, to put it pompously, will have different systems of values from ours. If this is so, to plan for the sort of thing that the present generation wants would be to produce a gigantic white elephant that future generations would not know what to do with. 'Futurologists', therefore, as those who study how to plan and foresee the future call themselves, find it necessary to consider how people are likely to evaluate the choices open to them in the year 1985[103] or the year 2000.[104] A large number of learned articles have been written on this subject, and in 1967 a journal called *The Futurist* was founded in the USA by the World Future Society. A contributor to this journal suggests that in the future such literary themes as adversity, death and sexual frustration will mean little 'in a world of affluence, near-immortality and instant sex'.[105]

Attempts are made at a serious assessment of this problem in *Values and the Future*.[106] One of the contributors, after commenting on the rapid social and hence 'value change' in our own generation, looks forward to the institution of a new profession of 'value impact forecasters'. Professor Rescher gives some analysis of what can be meant by 'value change', suggesting that it can mean a growth or diminution of the adherents of a specific value, a greater or less commitment to it by its adherents, extension or diminution of the

103. The Horizon 1985 Commission in France.

104. H. Kahn and A. J. Wiener (eds), *The Year 2000*, New York: Macmillan, 1967.

105. [The quotation from *The Futurist* is from a citation in I. Taviss, 'Futurology and the problem of values', *International Social Science Journal*, 21, no. 4, 1969, pp. 574–84 (see p. 581). The account in *The Futurist* is in turn based on Henry Winthrop, 'Existentialism and Phenomenological Frontiers: III. Science, Technology and Existentialism', *Journal of Existentialism*, 7, No. 24, 1966.]

106. Kurt Baier and Nicholas Rescher (eds), *Values and the Future*, New York: The Free Press, 1969. [The first contributor referred to is Alvin Toffler, 'Value Impact Forecaster—A Profession of the Future', pp. 1–30; the second, Nicholas Rescher, 'What Is Value Change? A Framework for Research', pp. 68–109; the quotations on Southern California and intelligence are from page 84.]

range of its application, and so on. He thinks that personal independence may be less valued in the future ('we may consider the Southern California of today as setting the pattern for the America of the future'[107]), that 'intelligence and inventiveness' will 'probably be in the ascendant for many years ahead', that 'gadgetry' will increase, that nationalism will diminish, that family links will loosen. Professor Galbraith contributes to this volume,[108] and he predicts that the power of trade unions will decline as the numbers of production workers are reduced, and that the 'educational estate', instead of being subordinated to the business community, will be needed to give it leadership and advice. 'The pre-Cambrian entrepreneur who once denounced long-haired and radical professors has been warned about hurting the recruitment program.' It is interesting to compare this with the view of Ruyer quoted on p. 139 above.

In an excellent article, 'Futurology and the problem of values'[109] Dr Irene Taviss raises some sceptical questions. Are not futurologists really commenting on their own times rather than predicting what will come? (One could compare 'instant sex' with the dreams of Ben Jonson's Sir Epicure Mammon.) Are they not unduly optimistic, along the lines of the Liberal Establishment? What are the reasons for supposing that in some cases (e.g. democracy) threats to a value will upgrade it in the future and in other cases (e.g. privacy) threats are likely to downgrade it? Who should do the value

107. Written before the burning down of the Bank of America at Santa Barbara on 26 February 1970. [A branch of the Bank of America was burned down in the course of a disturbance involving students and other young people; see the *New York Times*, 27 February 1970, p. 18.]

108. [John Kenneth Galbraith, 'Technology, Planning, and Organization', pp. 353–67; the quotations are from page 367.]

109. [I. Taviss, 'Futurology and the Problem of Values', *International Social Science Journal* 21, no. 4, 1969, pp. 574–84. This issue of the journal was devoted to futurology.]

forecasting? And as the forecasts will inevitably be linked with normative *plans*, should the planning be done by experts, by a plurality of agencies, or by advocates of some particular plan?

The merging of prediction into planning and control is, of course, the most serious aspect of what might otherwise be regarded as a sort of academic *Old Moore's Almanac*. In this same volume an article entitled 'Imagination and the future' by Dr Robert Jungk, founder of the Institut für Zukunftsfragen in Vienna, shows how futurology and centralised planning can be regarded as a sort of romantic 'social titanism', to use a phrase at one time used in Russia. Of man aware of the ubiquity of change Dr Jungk writes:[110]

> Instead of the firmly circumscribed, the ever-changing would be recognized as the condition of his existence. But this would mean a readjustment of man's inner being, which would probably have to go even deeper than the Copernican system, as it would require the abandonment of all firm certainties and the recognition of perpetual change. In such a 'floating world' creative imagination will then become man's prime faculty . . . for he will be logically forecasting the future no longer on the basis of supposedly eternal laws, but conjuring it forth from within himself (p. 562).

The planning prophet regards himself as producing future generations as if they were verses in a poem of his own making. Planning becomes the realisation of kaleidoscopic dreams.

---

110. [Robert Jungk, 'Imagination and the Future', *International Social Science Journal* 21, No. 4, 1969, pp. 557–62.]

CHAPTER 6
SUMMARY AND CONCLUSIONS

Collectivists of various sorts have said that the pursuit of profit by businessmen and firms spreads greed throughout the community. We have argued that economic activities are only a part of what is done in civilised societies. The making of profits need not be the sole concern of those who engage in business, and is sometimes a means of obtaining the wherewithal for enterprises of non-pecuniary and philanthropic importance. Not all the evils in capitalist societies are due to profit-seeking and profit-making. They may be due to a failure in moral education, to deficiencies in public spirit and *individual* morality rather than to the ways in which economic activities are organised. Competitive markets influence the rest of society, but they are themselves affected by moral, religious and aesthetic considerations. It is begging the question to say that the evils of societies in which business is carried on competitively for profit are wholly or mainly due to their economic arrangements. It may well be, as Hayek suggests, that under a competitive system bad men can do least harm.

Those taking part in competitive markets are not consciously devoting themselves to the common weal, nor are they engaged in acts of individual charity. Devotion, friendship, self-sacrifice are found in other circumstances of man's life, in their personal relationships and family concerns. In exchanging goods and services we may hope for honesty and diligence and perhaps forbearance but, just as the players in a game try to win and expect their opponents to play to win also, so in competitive markets the participants, from large producing firms to individual purchasers, are trying to do as well for themselves as possible.

Carlyle, Ruskin and Tawney considered that businessmen are inferior to such professional men as doctors, lawyers and soldiers, because the latter, they held, put service before profit, and would sacrifice their lives if need be, and were in honour bound to do their very best work. I have suggested that such moral differences as there are between businessmen and professional men are due to the differences in their work and circumstances. An important difference is that the businessman finances his productions and gains a profit or incurs a loss at the end of this operation, whereas many professional men work for fees or salaries. Hence the latter contract with their clients or employer for what they receive, whereas the businessman's profit is not something for which he has any contractual entitlement. To call for the assimilation of profits to professional fees or salaries is, therefore, to call for the abolition of the competitive market system. This connection is not generally noticed by those who are impressed by Ruskin's and Tawney's rhetoric.

J. A. Hobson was discussed as a representative of those who regard trading as wicked in that it requires individuals and firms to threaten rivals or employees with starvation, and is hence fundamentally coercive. I suggested that in competitive markets coercion is at a minimum and that bargaining with threats is more characteristic of political behaviour. When employees are organised in trade unions the threats often come from them. The moral condemnation of employers that is widespread today is based on arguments which were not overwhelmingly strong when first put forward and are irrelevant in present circumstances.

Collectivists believe that competition is a state of strife, discord, antagonism and unseemly rivalry, and hence that it is morally noxious. But it is necessary to distinguish different types of competition. Competition for a prize, for example, need not be striving *against* one another, but only *for* the prize. Competitors in industry and commerce are frequently in this non-antagonistic relation towards one another. There is also *impersonal* competition, in which individual animals, species, firms and whole industries are injured or eliminated if they fail to adapt to changing circumstances. The phrase 'law of the jungle' (or more recently, 'free-for-all') is not always apt even when applied to biological competition, and is less so when applied to firms and industries. The growth of trade unions and of similar protective and aggressive organisations has led to some replacement of non-antagonistic peaceful competition by deliberate manœuvring for getting and increasing power. What the newspapers call 'show-downs' between unions and employers' associations result from a breakdown of economic competition and should not be regarded as outcomes or exercises of it. I have suggested that competition, and perhaps rivalry and antagonism between ultimate consumers, is intensified by the spread of the attitude that opposes saving and encourages unlimited consumption. 'The right to be happy' has as its consequence the possibility of struggling to 'keep up with the Joneses'.

At this point we may call attention to a further important consequence of the present forms of trade union organisation in Great Britain. The unions bargain with the employers for a wage that is the same for all members of each category or workmen. This may be added to by overtime (often restricted by the union) or by output bonuses (which, again, are generally limited), but by and large individuals are not allowed to obtain benefits for themselves as a result of individual agreements. The policy of 'one out, all out' leads to the conclusion 'one up, all up'. In consequence, few individuals see any prospect of improving their financial position by means of special *individual* skill or industry, and any incentive to exercise it is therefore diminished if not completely destroyed. Payment in terms reached by bargains that concern only categories of workers depresses individual achievement and personal ambition. Furthermore, it gives rise to a dimly felt hopelessness as individuals are merged in a group controlled by men whose ambition is for power rather than for money. The very men who lead the collective activities of their workmates might, in different circumstances, use their energies and abilities in work that would benefit both themselves and the concern they work for. Perhaps they take on such leadership because they see no other means of utilising their powers or of distinguishing themselves from the mass. Few professional people realise the individual hopelessness on which collective trade union 'militancy' depends. Both the militant leader and his passive followers are in the toils of a system which continuously depresses the hopes that might stimulate individual excellence.[111]

There are some things, such as honour or criminal services, which ought never to be bought and sold, but educa-

111. Incidentally, it would be interesting to estimate the *costs* of industrial bargaining apart from losses due to strikes. What is the cost of the whole trade union organisation and the elements within employing bodies that exist to bargain with the unions? The bill would also include the costs of the relevant parts of the Department of Employment and Productivity and of the officials and lawyers which the Royal Commission on Trade Unions and Employers' Associations think necessary for the future working of industrial relations.

tion, medical care and housing are not among them. When certain basic needs are provided for in proportion to need by governments out of taxation, there must follow a tendency for individuals to attribute more importance to luxury spending than they would or could do if they had to provide for these basic needs out of their own disposable incomes. If the government forces its priorities on everyone, then the priorities of each individual in the disposal of his remaining income are priorities within a less essential range. What began as a humanitarian campaign to help the unfortunate could end as a system of bureaucratic control over a population of irresponsible and endlessly dissatisfied seekers after gratification.[112]

The form of collectivism most favoured in Britain aims to get basic welfare (education, medical care and perhaps housing) distributed in accordance with need rather than by purchase in competitive markets. The complex bureaucracies necessary to carry this out, however, along with their academic and journalistic supporters, would make independent discussion of the social and moral implications increasingly unlikely and practically ineffective. Once, indeed, they are established in their full panoply radical criticism is regarded as 'unrealistic'. Furthermore, in developed societies as many people as possible should have the opportunity of personal choice in these items of welfare, as well as in food, apparel and amusement. Welfare planners wish to force everyone to integrate, but in such a community of

112. The following passage, headed 'The "Conspiracy of Dishonesty" on Psychiatry', appeared in the *Glasgow Herald,* 29 April 1967, p. 5: 'Dr Forrest quotes Professor Galbraith as suggesting that when customers have satisfied their more pressing needs for cars, washing machines, and refrigerators, they tend to wish to purchase happiness, and turn to the psychiatrist as the most appropriate vendor.' Dr Forrest is Consultant Psychiatrist at the Royal Edinburgh Hospital.

forced friends there would still be competition, both to obtain a maximum of the services provided and to obtain special benefits. Plausible leaders, political lobbyists and sea-lawyers might set the tone.

In so far as egalitarian collectivists wish to secure distributive justice throughout society they must require the establishment of a distributor of justice who will from time to time (or even continually if there is inflation) override commutative justice. Even democratic collectivism, therefore, tends to become authoritarian. By claiming moral authority for their schemes democratic socialists come to regard those who oppose them as a sort of moral heretic who must ultimately be treated as criminals if they refuse to admit their errors. In a letter to *The Times*, 5 Sept. 1967, page 9, R. G. Wallace, General Secretary of the Socialist Educational Association, writing about the Appeal Court's decision on the Enfield comprehensive schools,[113] ends his letter as follows: 'We are told that we live in an age of consensus politics. The new Secretary of State may feel that the present law makes the national consensus in favour of comprehensive education difficult to achieve and that the time has come to change the law.' What this means is that the law should be changed so as to *bring about* or *enforce* a consensus. No doubt what Mr Wallace intended it to mean is that there is

113. [British Secondary Schools in the state sector prior to the time when Acton was writing were divided into three different kinds of institutions: academically orientated Grammar Schools, Technical Schools, and Secondary Modern Schools. Pupils were assigned to one of these on the basis of an examination taken after they had reached the age of 11 (the '11-plus'). A policy was then pursued of consolidating schools of these different kinds into larger, non-selective, Comprehensive Schools. There were extensive disputes among officials of local government and central government and parents concerning these changes. The decision of the Court of Appeal, to which Acton refers, was the granting of an injunction forbidding a local council from proceeding with plans to turn eight schools into comprehensives. See *The Times*, 1 September 1967, p. 1.]

already a consensus in favour of comprehensive education and that therefore it should be enforced upon those few who do not want it. A few months before this letter was written the parties in local government who supported comprehensive education had suffered a severe setback at the polls. What it is most important to notice, however, is that 'consensus' is the mid-twentieth-century euphemism for 'orthodoxy'. Antisocialists, too, sometimes seek 'consensus', but should beware lest they find themselves committed to the enforcement of a moral and social orthodoxy.

'Galbraithism' is an elaborate expression of confused despair, not a realistic policy.

Since a comprehensive and rapidly developing technology involves constant movement into the unpredictable, centralised economic planning will always meet with disappointment in societies in which science and technology play a major role. In addition, then, to the many economic objections to a centrally planned economy, there is the further objection that a rapidly advancing technology makes it impossible to obtain the data essential for a centralised economic plan. Competitive markets are likely to do less harm than centralised economic planning and to give more scope for intellectual and moral excellence. A centrally planned economy is bound to monopolise ideas and even to ration them, whereas in a society where competitive markets prevail it is not only trade, but also thoughts and men that are free.

TRADITION AND SOME
OTHER FORMS OF ORDER

[I]

It will be generally agreed, I think, that there is a good deal
of uncertainty in such thinking about political fundamentals
as takes place today. Traditional forms of society—the forms
within which most men have lived hitherto—have been
criticised by two main schools of thought, by liberals on the
one hand and by the various sorts of collectivist on the
other, but the views taken of all three types of order tend to
become blurred as the defenders of one combine with those
of another against the third. The supporters of tradition
have believed in a 'natural' order of society to which men
should piously conform. Liberals advocated a form of society in which the spontaneous efforts of individuals would
lead to constant improvement. Collectivists believe in organising and controlling by state power the social changes
which, in a liberal society, take place haphazardly and pain-
fully. Liberals and collectivists join together against tradition
when there is some 'superstition' to be attacked. It was in
this way that the late Professor Laski's[1] rationalism constantly revived the liberalism in him which no less constantly wilted again in the heat of his collectivist ardour.

1. [Harold Laski (1893–1950). Noted advocate of political pluralism and socialism. Professor at London School of Economics for many years and a leading
member of the Labour Party.]

Collectivists and traditionalists make common cause against liberalism, which they both see as a source of social anarchy and moral nihilism. Thus socialists and Catholics unite in defence of a 'just price', a notion which many liberals find difficult to make sense of. Liberals and traditionalists, however, sometimes combine in opposition to what they both consider the 'tyranny' of collectivists. A traditionalist like Mr. T. S. Eliot,[2] for example, moves towards liberalism when he considers how collectivist planning ignores the rights of family and region. From the liberal side, Professor Hayek expresses admiration for Burke because, like that defender of the traditional European order, he thinks it preferable for society as a whole to grow rather than to be planned.

What I have to say in this paper is concerned with some of the connections between a liberal and a traditionalist view of society which I have been led to examine as the result of reading Professor Hayek's expositions of the liberal philosophy. Before I come to consider these, however, I must give some account of the nature of tradition.

[**II**]

A tradition is a belief or practice transmitted from one generation to another and accepted as authoritative, or deferred to, without argument. An example of a traditional belief is the story of King Alfred's burning of the cakes, which, until fairly recent times, was handed on from one unquestioning generation to the next. Examples of traditional practices are the coronation of the kings of England or the shapes and sizes in which hay is stacked in different counties and countries. When a traditional belief has been questioned, investi-

---

2. [T. S. Eliot (1888–1965). Poet and philosopher. Acton discusses his work in 'Religion, Culture and Class', *Ethics* 60, 1950, pp. 120–30.]

gation of evidence may show it to be true or false. Those who, after such an investigation, accept a traditional belief because there is conclusive evidence for it, are no longer mere adherents of a tradition, for they have considered and overcome the arguments against it. They no longer accept the belief on its own authority, but because of the evidence that supports it. A traditional belief may be rejected on the ground that there is conclusive evidence against it. So too with practices. If, after discussion, it is decided that a traditional practice ought to be continued because it subserves some desirable purpose, then it ceases to be a merely traditional practice, for it is now deliberately pursued as a means to something else. The process of justification presupposes argument and thus cannot fail to undermine the traditional character of the practice that is justified. On the other hand, of course, a traditional practice may be abandoned because it does not lead to the desirable end, and if a new practice is then adopted because it is thought to promote the end in question, this is not a traditional practice at all. However, what began as a non-traditional practice might become a tradition if the end were lost sight of and the practice nevertheless continued from inertia. It is said that at a certain university a notice was posted saying: 'From the first of January it will be a tradition that no one shall walk on the lawn.' We regard this as ludicrous because of the incongruity between the deliberate command to do something on a particular occasion and the idea of doing something because it has been done very often before. Traditions may *result from* knowledge, discoveries, commands or decisions, but cannot themselves be intuited, inferred, commanded or decided. Thus, before it can rightly be called traditional, a belief or practice must have been accepted or performed by several generations. The generations, of course, need not be biological ones; traditions exist, for example, in a school, if a belief or practice extends unquestioned over several successions of student careers. Again, a tradition may change or develop, though if it changes too rapidly or too much it ceases to be a tradition. Professor Oakeshott, surely, exaggerates when, in his interesting articles on *Rationalism in Politics*[3] he says that tradition is 'pre-eminently fluid'. If such a metaphor is to be used, then tradition must be a very viscous fluid.

We may summarise this by saying that a belief or practice becomes a tradition when (a) it persists over several generations, (b) if it changes at all, it changes only slightly and gradually, and (c) it is not questioned by its adherents nor thought by them to need justification. More briefly still, we may say that traditions are chronic, continuous and authoritative.[4]

The opposite of a tradition would be a belief or practice that was (1) short-lived, (2) discontinuous with the past, and (3) the result of argument or rational decision. For example, in some societies there is a traditional style of dress. This means that in that society the same styles of dress are worn from one generation to another and change, if at all, slowly and slightly, without being considered critically with a view to novelty or improvement. The opposite of this may be seen in societies where the style of dress changes often and radi-

3. *Cambridge Journal* 1, 1947–8. p. 153. See also Michael Oakeshott, *Rationalism in politics and other essays*, Indianapolis: Liberty Fund, 1991, p. 36.

4. In Christian theology there has been a use of 'tradition' according to which it consists of beliefs and practices handed on by word of mouth or practical example as opposed to what was written down and preserved in the Scriptures. This, however, is a limited and technical use. In the ordinary sense that I am considering traditions do not cease to be traditions by being written down. A song or dance, for example, does not cease to be traditional because those who receive it take notes to aid their memory. Indeed, writing may, on occasions, *fix* a tradition, as has happened with laws.

cally as the result of deliberate designing and re-designing. In the society that is traditional as regards dress there are dressmakers and tailors. In the society that is anti-traditional as regards dress there are fashion houses as well. In a society like our own where men's dress is traditional and women's dress is not, there are fashion houses for the women, but none, or only insignificant ones, for the men. Or we may take an example from the intellectual sphere. What philosophers call 'the traditional logic' retained its main features over a very long period, evolved very slowly and, it is said, on points of detail only, and was accepted as a whole without radical questioning of its fundamentals. But in the last few generations logic has been changing rapidly and radically as the result of fundamental critical scrutiny, and is undoubtedly an anti-traditional element in modern thought.

A traditional story is told by parents and teachers to the young. A traditional practice is taught by the old hands to the newcomers. Each telling of the story, each performance of the practice, is said to *follow* the tradition. The believers and performers tend to be deferential, modest, malleable, even lazy. A tradition continues in its original state by a sort of inertia. We may talk of obeying traditions, or of submitting to them, but there need be no question of obedience or submission in any sense in which they involve commands or threats, as Lord Acton saw when he spoke of self-government proceeding 'not from a code, but from custom'. There is, on the contrary, a not unwilling conformity. When there is a tradition, the recipient or learner makes himself responsible for its transmission to others in the course of time. It becomes incorporated in him to such an extent that he would regard criticism of it as somehow criticism of himself. Thus, the follower of a tradition does not regard himself as being coerced. It is as though the tradition has become a part of his conscience, so that in conforming to it he is acting in accordance with his own nature.

We may now consider the relative importance of the three chief marks of a tradition, viz., (a) its chronic character, (b) its continuity, and (c) its authoritativeness. Clearly (c) is the most important feature. There is a tradition only when the belief or practice is handed on unquestioned. When there is criticism and counter-criticism, what survives or emerges is no longer purely traditional but has in it an element of triumphant argument or rational decision. When criticism is brought to bear, either it is ignored or suppressed, or else some sort of answer is made to it and reasons are given for preferring the tradition to any proposed alteration. Rote and imitation are characteristic of tradition, and reason runs counter to them both. When reason is employed, beliefs are not merely handed on, but argued for, and practices not merely taught, but justified. Beliefs and practices that are supported by cogent argument are often called rational, and there is a certain opposition between tradition and reason, just as there is between authority and criticism. There may be good reasons for a tradition, but if those who uphold it have recourse to reason, they have detracted from the authority of the tradition by so defending it, for to lend support is to admit the possibility of collapse.

However, a good deal of reasoning can be carried on by defenders of traditions without danger to them. One tradition may be supported by another, as happens when one political practice is supported by reference to another or by reference to religious dogmas. When traditional practices are justified, appeal is made to other traditional practices or beliefs, to ultimate principles of conduct, or to desired ends. Justification would lose all point if there were no fairly fixed principles or ends in terms of which it could proceed.

If there were reason to believe that the principles or ends would themselves soon cease to command acceptance, the process of justification would not be taken very seriously. The anti-traditionalist, therefore, has to justify his proposals in terms of long-lived ultimate principles of conduct or in terms of fairly permanent ends. It would seem, therefore, that those who attack traditional practices and seek to justify new ones must nevertheless accept traditional moral standards or traditional ends of conduct.

Let us see whether this must be so. A proposed new practice may be justified in terms of a new moral standard which is to be accepted by the parties in the discussion for the future. The anti-traditionalist says: 'Do you not see that this new principle of conduct is *right*? And do you not see that if it is, then our behaviour should be modified thus and thus?' It is possible that the traditionalist will accept this. Justification is then in terms of a principle that was not in fact a tradition when it was first adduced in the discussion. But I suggest that, if it were to be effective in 'justifying', it would have to be regarded by the parties concerned as likely to *start* a tradition. Indeed, if it were accepted by the parties concerned as right, they would expect its rightness to be accepted by others who reflected on it too, so that it became itself a traditional standard of conduct. Justification may also be in terms of moral principles that are held to be *ultimate*. 'Ultimate', in such a context, means 'neither capable of further justification nor in need of it'. Ultimate moral principles are therefore somewhat like traditions, though we do not often given them that name. They are thought to be impervious to rational criticism. Their adherents instil them into the next generation who, in submitting to them, regard themselves not as oppressed but as fulfilling their own natures.

Justification may also be in terms of ends. The form of justification most opposed to tradition would be in terms of a single end, such as happiness has been supposed to be, for this would be to reduce the chronic and authoritative to one thing only. If this were the sole end in fact pursued, then it could be argued that everyone must desire the most effective means to secure it, and that what are the most effective means at one time are not the most effective means at another time, so that frequent changes of policy are needed if happiness is to be obtained. On the other hand it is possible that there are certain means that make for happiness at all times. If this were so, some traditional modes of life could be justified in terms of utility, as Hume seems to have believed. The least anti-traditional mode of justification for any traditional practice, I suppose, would be to claim that the practice is self-justifying, and that is how many traditions are regarded by their adherents. There is thus some kinship between traditionalists and Ethical Intuitionists.

We speak not only of particular traditions, but also of traditional societies. A traditional society would be one in which there was a large proportion of traditional beliefs and practices. All societies have, and indeed must have, a great many traditional elements in them, such as the established ways of building houses or of eating and drinking, and to compare them in respect of the *number* of these is likely to be difficult and inconclusive. So perhaps it is better to say that a traditional society is one in which the fundamental organisation is traditional, i.e., has lasted a long time, has changed slowly and continuously, if at all, and has not been questioned, and so is not the object of enquiry and radical reform. In a society that is traditional in this sense, the modes of government, forms of property, methods of education and objects of worship are accepted as if they were parts of the natural order like hills, streams, beasts, plants and climate. The members of such a society seldom realise how much changed their natural surroundings are from their original state, and do not think there is much they can do to modify them—hardly, indeed, think of modifying them at all. In the same way they pursue their individual, rationally purposeful lives within a social framework that they take for granted and treat as independent of their wills. For example, in a society where kingship is traditional, there may be disputes about who is the rightful king, but that there should be a king is not brought into question at all.[5] In traditional societies, again, people do not study which is the best way to bring up children, but just bring them up in the way they find in use around them. The opposite of a traditional society would be one which was consciously organised as a whole, and was continuously re-organised so as to be kept in conformity with the conscious aims of the organisers. It would be the least natural and most contrived society possible. Fundamental beliefs would be continuously under scrutiny, and the justification for fundamental practices would be continuously demanded. An artificially contrived social order would be under continuous and conscious adjustment and re-construction. In such a society, to take the example we have just made use of, there would be a conscious readiness to exchange kingship for something else, and constant experimenting with the modes of education. It is the condition which has been called 'permanent

5. 'When resistance occurs, it is directed against the person of the chief or of a member of his staff. The accusation is that he has failed to observe the traditional limits of his authority. Opposition is not directed against the system as such. It is impossible in the pure type of traditional authority for law or administrative rules to be deliberately created by legislation.' Max Weber, *The Theory of Social and Economic Organization*; English translation, New York: Oxford University Press, 1947, p. 314. The revolution of 1688 comes to mind.

revolution'. The major institutions are always under sentence of death and escape the executioner, when they do, only as the result of a reprieve.

I suppose it is clear that tradition and custom are closely connected, if not identical, notions, though we tend, perhaps, to use the word 'tradition' for the more elaborate and civilised forms of custom. A fuller treatment of them both would lead to the examination of such conceptions as those of habit and skill. Professor Oakeshott, if I understand him, regards 'skill' as most important among these conceptions.

[**III**]

We have now very briefly considered how traditions are manifested in beliefs, practices, standards, and the social order as a whole. Particular traditional practices we are not here concerned with, but our next task is to discuss how liberalism is related to the other three. 'Liberal', of course, is, in this country, still a predominently eulogistic epithet, and is therefore applied by their members to all sorts of different social movements. What I wish to discuss, however, is liberalism in the sense of that social philosophy in which reasons are advanced for preferring the spontaneous action of individuals or of fairly small groups to the large-scale planning of social life through state agencies. Briefly, it is the philosophy according to which the burden of proof, by a principle of moral inertia, is always on those who wish to force people from their own chosen path rather than on those who wish to be left alone and to leave others alone. It is stated by Professor Hayek as 'The fundamental principle that in the ordering of our affairs we should make as much use as possible of the spontaneous forces of society, and resort as little as possible to coercion. . . . '[6]

The coercion of beliefs is something that takes place when traditional beliefs have been questioned. When a belief is accepted as a tradition there is no need for force, for the method of transmission makes it a part of each individual's store of habits and hence a part of each individual's second nature. The individual holder of a traditional belief, therefore, feels himself thwarted, not when the belief is accepted, but when it is criticised. Criticism of the belief is to some extent criticism of him. The liberal, on the other hand, upholds freedom of thought against those who attempt to impose beliefs by force, i.e., by threats of violence. In so far as what the liberal wants is truth, then he is right to oppose both the traditional acceptance of beliefs and their forceful imposition. If, however, he merely wanted freedom from coercion, then tradition would be as good a way of getting what he wanted as free discussion. It is thus clear that an interest in truth is an important element in the liberal philosophy. The liberal opposes coercion in intellectual matters not only because he is opposed to coercion generally, but also because he attaches value to avoiding error and to finding out what is true, and knows that he can best do this when beliefs are freely criticised. There are differences, however, among those who have argued for intellectual freedom, about the nature of their ultimate aim. Some have regarded truth as a means, either to human happiness or to other human achievements. Others have regarded it as worth having for its own sake. Indeed, W. K. Clifford, with his famous dictum, 'It is wrong

6. F. A. Hayek, *The Road to Serfdom*, London: Routledge, 1944, p. 14.

always, everywhere, for any one, to believe anything upon insufficient evidence',[7] seems to suggest that truth ought to be the chief, if not the sole end of mankind. Broadly speaking we may say that those who regard science as a self-justifying activity will be opposed to interference with it on principle, while those who regard it as subserving other ends will be opposed only to the sorts of interference that conflict with the ends that they wish to promote. However this may be, the pursuit of scientific truth, whether for its own sake or for some other end, is bound to be an anti-traditional activity, for criticism, which is essential to science, is the antithesis of tradition. It is apt, also, to be anti-traditional in its effects on society, since changes in beliefs about how things are often lead to rapid changes in the ways in which things are done.

[**IV**]

We now pass on to consider the traditional organisation of a society as a whole. Our object is to see how such traditions are related to the liberal philosophy. A traditional society, we have said, is one in which the fundamental organisation has lasted a long time, has changed slowly and continuously, if at all, and has not been questioned, and so is not the object of enquiry and reform. 'It has been the misfortune . . . of this age', wrote Burke, 'that everything is to be discussed, as if the constitution of our country were to be always a subject rather of altercation than enjoyment.' Now according to the liberal philosophy I have in mind the whole en-

7. W. K. Clifford, 'The Ethics of Belief', in *Lectures and Essays*, ed. Leslie Stephen and Frederick Pollock, London: Macmillan, 1886, p. 346. Clifford's point is not quite clear, since he stresses the dangers to society of believing on insufficient evidence. But he writes of our *conscience* asking, not 'Is it comfortable or pleasant?' but 'Is it true?' (p. 351).

terprise of deliberately designing a whole social order is a perverted one. It is held, on the contrary, 'that the spontaneous collaboration of free men often creates things which are greater than their individual minds can ever fully comprehend.'[8] Professor Hayek, in his exposition of this view, speaks of 'an acute consciousness of the limitations of the individual mind which induces an attitude of humility toward the impersonal and anonymous social processes by which individuals help to create things greater than they know'. A contrast is drawn between 'a social order resting on the general recognition of certain principles', which is approved, and 'a system in which order is created by direct commands', which is not approved. Again, the contrast is between the view that all discoverable order in human affairs is due to 'deliberate design', and the view that 'most of the order which we find in human affairs is the unforeseen result of individual actions.' A passage from Burke's *Reflections on the Revolution in France* is quoted in which Burke is held to have feared that the theories of Rousseau would rapidly dissolve the commonwealth 'into the dust and powder of individuality'. The approval that Professor Hayek gives to this passage is most significant, for the passage in question occurs in the course of a discussion in which Burke contemplates 'the evils of inconstancy and versatility,' and argues that without religion and traditional order society will be 'at length dispersed to all the winds of heaven'. Immediately afterwards comes the famous passage commencing 'Society

8. F. A. Hayek, *Individualism and Economic Order*, London: Routledge, 1949, p. 7. The subsequent quotations from this important essay are from pages 8, 1 and 8, in that order. Hayek's references to Burke are on pages 4, 5 and 7. All the quotations from Burke in the present paragraph are from the *Reflections on the Revolution in France*. Compare Edmund Burke, *Reflections on the Revolution in France, 1790*, in *The Works of the Right Honourable Edmund Burke*, intro. F. W. Raffety, volume iv, London: Oxford University Press, 1907. The quotations in this paragraph are from pages: 100, 105, 105, 105, 106, 106, 104 and 105.

is indeed a contract' and going on to talk of 'the great pri-
meval contract of eternal society'. In leading up to all this
Burke had said that in the absence of tradition 'No one generation could link with the other. Men would become little
better than the flies of a summer.' 'No principles', he had
continued, 'would be early worked into the habits. As soon
as the most able instructor had completed his laborious
course of institution, instead of sending forth his pupil, ac-
complished in a virtuous discipline, fitted to procure him
attention and respect, in his place in society, he would find
everything altered; and that he had turned out a poor crea-
ture to the contempt and derision of the world, ignorant of
the true grounds of estimation.' I do not suggest that an author is committed to all that surrounds a sentence that he
quotes, but it is at first sight surprising that an upholder of
liberalism should appear to give his approval to propositions
extracted from this milieu. This is why it seems to me worth
while to attempt to compare liberalism and traditionalism
rather more closely than has, perhaps, been done hitherto.

I have already suggested that the members of a traditional
society tend to be modest and deferential towards their traditions. But it now appears that Professor Hayek,[9] speaking
in defence of liberalism, thinks there is value in 'an attitude
of humility towards the impersonal and anonymous social
processes'. Individuals are not to suppose that they can devise social arrangements that are superior to these. On the
contrary, the suggestion is that at any rate some of these
'impersonal and anonymous social processes' are 'greater'
than anything that an individual or limited group of individual minds could 'fully comprehend'. There seems to be
something about them that calls for reverence. To be rever-

9. [The quotations that follow are from Hayek, *Individualism and Economic
Order*, pp. 8 and 7.]

ent or humble towards unplanned social processes which are superior to anything that could have been designed by individual men—could anything that is not traditional be more traditional than this?

The fundamental difference, of course, is in respect of liberty. The liberty of the traditionalist consists in not being forced; he goes on as his forefathers did and is at one with himself in doing so. The liberty of the liberal, too—any liberty indeed—consists in not being forced. But the force that would conflict with traditionalism would be force that drove men from their habitual lines of action, whereas the force that would conflict with liberalism would also be force that prevented men from departing from their habitual lines of action. The traditionalist wants to be left alone to follow the ancient paths. The liberal wants to be left alone to follow new ones also. In a liberal society, all sorts of talking, thinking, manufacturing, trading, inventing, promoting good causes, would be going on, but all of it would be initiated by individuals or by relatively small groups. If a traditional society became liberal, the change would be a change towards more change. There would be more types of goods, more books, more reformers. There would even be men advocating deliberate reform of the fundamentals of society, though, as long as the society remained liberal, they would not get many followers. For liberals are agreed that the fundamental institutions of a liberal society must be sacrosanct, like those of a traditional society. These sacrosanct fundamentals are: a government the chief function of which is to use force to stop force and fraud; a rule of law; private property. These are institutions that have existed in some traditional societies, but in a liberal society they cannot exist *as* traditions, but must become objects of criticism. If they are to work so as to support a liberal society, they must become part of the conscience of the members of that society. But once something has become a part of anyone's conscience, criticism of it is taken as criticism of the person in whose conscience it is, and may thus be regarded as an affront rather than as an exercise of rationality. Liberals, by the very nature of their philosophy, tend to be sceptical and self-critical. In consequence they are reluctant to accord to the practical principles essential to a liberal society the degree of authority that would ensure that they are generally followed. In their zeal for spontaneity they tend towards the extreme of an anti-traditional social order where nothing is sacrosanct, where there are no principles, and where there is no conscience. I do not here use 'principles' and 'conscience' in a eulogistic sense, since, of course, all sorts of behaviours can become accepted in this way. But it is clear, as Burke pointed out, that where there is permanent revolution, there can be few loyalties and only short-lived ones at that. That is why governments aiming at the reconstruction of a whole society cannot allow freedom of speech. Propaganda that is constantly adjusted to each new requirement of policy is essential as a substitute for the traditions that normally prevent the commonwealth from dissolving 'into the dust and powder of individuality'.

However, though a government with limited functions, a rule of law, and private property, would have to be fundamental institutions of a liberal society, they might well come into existence as the result of deliberate endeavour. They are, indeed, advocated by liberals as objects of policy. It is not towards them that an 'attitude of humility' is regarded as appropriate, but rather towards social processes that are 'anonymous' and 'impersonal', and may be 'greater' than individual minds 'can ever fully comprehend'. These anonymous and impersonal forces, again, are closely connected with, if they are not the same as, 'the unforeseen results of individual actions'. We must now attempt to get a clearer view of what this amounts to.

Obviously there is a lot of difference between something that happens in a society because someone has intended it to happen, and something that happens though no one intended that it should happen. If something is to happen as I intend it to happen, I must (a) have a clear view of what I want to bring about, (b) know how to bring it about, i.e., know what are the means that will bring it about, and (c) have the means within my control. I may intend to do something and nevertheless do something that I had not intended because I was not clear what I intended, or because I did not know how to bring it about, or because, although I knew clearly what I wanted and knew what would bring it about, I was prevented by other people from bringing the means to bear. Thus my actions have unintended results when I *fail* in my intentions as the result of my own muddleheadness or lack of skill or because of other people's opposition. This sort of unintended result is seldom welcomed by anyone, though there are sometimes lucky failures as was the case with Columbus. When someone has done what he intended, then what he had thought would happen has happened, and to that extent he has foreseen what would happen. An unintended result, on the other hand, is something unforeseen, that turns out differently from what was planned, a failure, though possibly a lucky failure.

Now I do not think we need spend time on the thesis that we should be humble before unforeseen results in the sense of failures of intention such as these. At any rate one sort of unforeseen or unintended result that liberal philosophers have in mind is something that happens when individuals *succeed* in carrying out their intentions. The idea is that each of a number of individuals aims at a particular object and each of them succeeds in his aim, but that the result of their individual successes in carrying out their individual intentions is something that none of them had intended. This sort of result, it is further held, is frequently, and by no means accidentally, something very good. Thus Adam Smith argued that if each owner of capital succeeds in laying it out to his own best advantage, he promotes the advantage of the whole society, though that is not his intention. 'He generally, indeed, neither intends to promote the public interest, nor knows how much he is promoting it. By preferring the support of domestic to that of foreign industry, he intends only his own security; and by directing that industry in such a manner as its produce may be of the greatest value, he intends only his own gain, and he is in this, as in many other cases, led by an invisible hand to promote an end which was no part of his intention.'[10] An unintended result of action is thus something that is not specifically aimed at by any member of a group of agents but that arises as a result of each agent's successful pursuit of his particular aim. According to Adam Smith, if each man with capital to invest invests it so as to give him the maximum return, the return on all the capital in that society will be the greatest possible also. By this he does not mean the tautology that if, in a society consisting of A, B and C, if A aims to get, say, 2 units and gets them, B aims to get 3 units and gets them, and C aims to get 4 units and gets them, then A is intentionally getting 2 units but unintentionally contributing to the production of 9, and so for B and C. He has in mind a contrast between what would be produced if some fourth party, X, was able to force A, B and C to invest their capital in the way he thought best,

10. Adam Smith, *The Wealth of Nations*, IV.ii.10, Glasgow edition, Indianapolis: Liberty Fund, 1981, p. 456. The second quotation is from the same page.

and what would be produced if each individual invested according to his own view and interest. 'The statesman, who should attempt to direct private people in what manner they ought to employ their capitals, would not only load himself with a most unnecessary attention, but assume an authority which could safely be trusted, not only to no single person, but to no council or senate whatever, and which would nowhere be so dangerous as in the hands of a man who had folly and presumption enough to fancy himself fit to exercise it.' It is assumed that there is some best employment of the capital of a society, and then argued that this best employment is more likely to ensue if individuals invest as they wish than if a government deliberately influences their investments by tariffs or other similar means.

It will have been noticed that, in the case that Adam Smith puts before us, the results that were unintended and unforeseen by the particular agents may nevertheless have been intended and foreseen by some other party such as the government. A government may regard the free venturing of capital as the best means of obtaining the capital equipment of the society for which it is responsible, and therefore, in allowing freedom to invest, it would be adopting the most effective means of carrying out its intentions. Such a government, by not interfering, is carrying out its intentions more effectively than if it had interfered. Things are happening as it intends them to happen because (*a*) it has a clear view of what it wants, (*b*) knows how to achieve what it wants—in this case by relying on the knowledge and endeavours of investors, and (*c*) has the means of achievement within its power—in this case, the ability to refrain from interfering. A government intending a result in this way, would be intending much as a gardener intends who, wishing to have a certain fruit, provides the conditions in which the seed can grow. This, of course, is the aspect of *laissez-faire* that attracted Burke, whose view that society was a natural growth led him to think that statesmen should not conceive themselves as constructors but—he does not, to my knowledge, actually use this comparison himself—as a kind of silviculturist, for forests are composite and long-lived like peoples. Nevertheless, deliberate contrivance may be at work here, though the trees always, and the investors sometimes, are not aware of it.

Another, more complex, example of unintended results of individual actions given by Adam Smith is that of the division of labour in society as a whole. A Red Indian, for example, confines his work to the production of bows and arrows, thus becoming 'a sort of armourer'.[11] He then exchanges the bows and arrows he does not need for his own use, for the meat that some other member of the tribe, who has specialised in hunting, does not need for his use, and in this way occupations are specialised and the output of society is increased. 'This division of labour, from which so many advantages are derived, is not originally the effect of any human wisdom, which foresees and intends that general opulence to which it gives occasion. It is the necessary, though very slow and gradual consequence of a certain propensity in human nature which has in view no such extensive utility; the propensity to truck, barter, and exchange one thing for another.' Adam Smith goes on to point out that mutual exchange is characteristic of human beings—'Nobody ever saw one dog make a fair and deliberate exchange of one bone for another with another dog'—and enables them to get benefits from one another without relying on each other's benevolence, and without having to waste time

11. Adam Smith, *The Wealth of Nations*, I.ii.3, Glasgow edition, p. 27. The subsequent quotations are from I.ii.1–2 (pp. 25–6).

and energy in 'servile and fawning attention'. Each party to the exchange intends his own benefit and gets it by providing the other party with a benefit too. The benefit of both, and of the whole society, emerges in a situation in which each intends his own.

What each individual does is to specialise (e.g., to make bows and arrows only) and exchange (e.g., give bows and arrows to men who give meat and hides in return). When individuals do this there emerges a highly complex society in which there are so many bakers, so many butchers, so many weavers, and so many philosophers, but no one has decreed how many members of each of these occupations there should be. As Mandeville had put it in the *Fable of the Bees*, 'This proportion as to Numbers in every Trade finds it self, and is never better kept than when no body meddles or interferes with it.'[12] It may be said, then, that from the spontaneous trafficking of individuals there emerges a complex civilisation which no individual could have organised or even thought of. It is towards such a result, perhaps, rather than towards a successful capital investment policy, that an attitude of humility is appropriate. There can here be no question of a definite, individually conceived end, to the realisation of which effective, even though non-interfering, means have been employed. Adam Smith admits the *possibility* that a group of men might plan a national investment policy, however badly they might do it, but not the possibility that mortals might invent the arts and allocate the specific tasks of mankind. Thus the fundamental structure of the society may be looked at as if it were a particularly impressive natural phenomenon, in much the same way as members of a traditional society regard their traditional

12. Bernard Mandeville, *The Fable of the Bees*, ed. F. B. Kaye, Indianapolis: Liberty Fund, 1988, volume 1, pp. 299–300.

order. Indeed, traditional orders have themselves grown in this very way. It is interesting to note that in the title to Book I of the *Wealth of Nations*, Adam Smith says he is writing of 'the order' according to which the products of labour are 'naturally distributed among the different ranks of the people'.[13]

However, there is another part of this view which takes us a long way from tradition. This is the part in which the notion of exchange is developed. Men 'truck, barter, and exchange' because each individual wants a great many things and sees he can get more of them by exchanging what he is good at producing for what others are good at producing than by trying to make everything for himself. Here is a man trying to satisfy as many of his wants as possible. Might he not also get many things from other people by entreating them to *give* him what he wants? But this could only be successful with the few people who are likely to have a special sympathy for him, and in any case would waste a lot of time as he endeavoured to put them into the right frame of mind. If we relied for the satisfaction of our wants on the sympathy of other people, we could be satisfied from only a few sources. Exchange, however, enables us to extend the range of people from whom we may hope to receive benefits far beyond those who love us or feel sorry for us or dislike us so much that they will give us things in order that we may go away from them. Reliance on their love or dislike is not the only way, besides exchange, by which an individual may get his wants satisfied by others. Adam Smith does not mention it in the passage I am discussing, but obviously, forceful expropriation—called 'spoliation' by Bastiat—may serve the same purpose. It is

13. 'Order' was a word much used by the Physiocrats. For the quotation from Smith, see *Wealth of Nations*, Glasgow edition, p. 3

the liberal view that exchange is generally a more effective means than the other two, but I imagine that most liberals have thought it morally superior also. At any rate they would point out that those who wish only to enjoy the fruits of love and neighbourliness should also be willing to satisfy only those wants that a pretty small society can satisfy. I cannot, at this stage, enter into such arguments, but must call attention to the sense in which exchange in a market may be regarded as *impersonal*. It is impersonal in the sense that it is consistent with all sorts of personal attitude of the parties towards one another. It cuts across differences of status and nationality. Through market prices it always diminishes and sometimes eliminates even that element of personal conflict that is aroused in the process of bargaining.[14] It makes a way between family, friendship and rank on the one hand, and command or obedience, force or submission on the other. It is therefore pretty clear that the impersonality of free exchange is something that runs counter to traditional orderings of things. In a liberal society the claims of family and rank have to be made and met in an environment that must necessarily diminish their influence within the whole. Thus, whereas the 'natural' character of its structure links liberal society with tradition, the impersonal character of its market dealings tends to draw it away from tradition.

It is interesting to notice that some philosophers of liberalism have sought for impersonality elsewhere than in the market. Rousseau is a thinker whom Professor Hayek, for reasons that I do not accept, stigmatises as a 'false individual-

---

14. 'The Economic man neither competes nor higgles—nor does he co-operate, psychologically speaking; he treats other human beings as if they were slot machines.' Frank H. Knight, *Freedom and Reform*, Indianapolis: Liberty Fund, 1982, p. 66.

ist'. But in the *Social Contract* (I.VI.) Rousseau argues that the individual's subordination to his society is not a loss of liberty because it is not a personal subordination.[15] 'Thus each one', he writes, 'since he gives himself to all does not give himself to anyone, and since there is no member against whom he does not obtain the same right that he has been allowed to obtain against oneself, each individual gains the equivalent of what he has lost, and, in addition, more strength to preserve what he has.' Commenting approvingly on this passage Halbwachs writes: 'There is a big difference between giving oneself to one or to several individuals, and giving oneself to a collectivity (of which all form a part, oneself equally with others). In the first case, one is obeying particular individuals, which is opposed to freedom; in the second case, one is obeying an impersonal being, which is guided, not by passion but by reason, and which is like the impersonal forces of physical nature, and this is not opposed to freedom. In this sense, in the second case one does not give oneself to anyone.'[16] On the Rousseau-Halbwachs view it is subjection by and to particular persons that renders slavery objectionable, whereas subjection to something that is not a particular person, whether this be nature or society, does not involve the indignity that is the moral evil of slavery. Adam Smith and Rousseau thus both seem to be in search of a state of affairs in which no one is subservient to anyone else, and in which, when people are thwarted, it is by something that does not thwart them for its particular

15. [Jean-Jacques Rousseau, *The Social Contract and Discourses*, tr. G. D. Cole, revised by J. Brumfitt and J. Hall, London: Dent, 1973, p. 174. The Hayek reference is to his 'Individualism: True and False' in *Individualism and Economic Order*, Chicago: University of Chicago Press, 1948, p. 4.]

16. J. J. Rousseau, *Du contrat social*, ed. Maurice Halbwachs, Paris: Aubier, Éditions Montaigne, 1943. The quotations from Rousseau and from the commentary are from page 120.

satisfaction and does not, therefore, injure their moral dignity. This much the market and the general will have in common, though they differ widely in other respects. The market, the general will, and nature are alike in not being respectors of persons, but the general will, according to Rousseau, is a moral, though not a personal being.[17]

We must now return for a moment to the general conception of a social structure that is designed by no one but is the unintended and unforeseen result of the actions of individuals. As is well known, Marx, in his *Critique of Political Economy*, wrote of men entering into 'definite necessary relations independent of their will'.[18] He thought that men were often as it were imprisoned and depressed by such anonymous creations. Thus he deplored the very thing that Mandeville and Adam Smith admired, and believed that the anonymous creations would be replaced by 'human' arrangements corresponding to men's conscious desires. The implications are (1) that the unintended and unforeseen institutional results of individual actions are sometimes, if not always, bad, and (2) that an improvement may be obtained by replacing them by institutions that are deliberately contrived. Both of these are very wide topics, and I must content myself with a few brief comments on each of them.

As to (1), we are confronted with the problem of distinguishing the different *sorts* of unintended, unplanned, institutions that result from individual actions. So far we have considered (a) the capital equipment of a society, and (b) the structure of a society in so far as this is shown in the division of labour arising from the exchange of commodities. Marx,

17. Rousseau says that all the parties to the social contract gain from it, so that the utilities that they exchange are also multiplied. I do not know whether this idea had any influence on the theories of later economists such as Condillac.

18. [Karl Marx, *A Contribution to the Critique of Political Economy*, London: Lawrence & Wishart, 1971, Preface, p. 20.]

as I understand him, would have regarded (b) as good by comparison with what went before it, but bad by comparison with what could and would happen in the future as the result of social planning. It is not my purpose in this paper to consider the merits of different sorts of organisation, but only to say something about their likenesses and differences, and most liberals, I imagine, would themselves admit that there are serous defects in the sort of society they advocate. What they claim is that it is superior to the alternatives, which are small-scale, slow-moving, traditional societies on the one hand, and consciously planned, centrally controlled, collectivist societies on the other. I suggest that there is also an element of aesthetic admiration in the liberal's attitude towards the spontaneous adjustments of a free society, not unlike the theologian's admiration for 'design in nature'. But there is, of course, no necessary connection between what is interestingly complex and what is morally desirable. Again, wars and slumps may be mentioned as deplorable instances of unintended results of individual actions. I suggest, however, that they are rather different sorts of entity from what I have so far been discussing. They are, indeed, rather different from one another, and those who are interested in that sort of consideration could point out that whereas wars are *declared,* we do not talk about declaring a slump. Similarly, whereas the Continental System[19] was built up as an instrument of British policy, it was, in 1805, though not perhaps now, absurd to talk about 'the economic system' in similar terms. If we take the example of a war, we see that in some circumstances it may have been the aim of all the interested governments to avoid it even though it ultimately broke out.

19. [The Continental System was the name given to the closure of Europe to British trade announced by Napoleon in the Berlin Decree of 1806. We think Acton may have had in mind the naval blockade that was the British response.]

It may have been unintended in the sense that A aimed at peace, B aimed at peace, and C and D also, but nevertheless war broke out between them. But some, at any rate, of the governments concerned must have regarded the making of war as something they would deliberately engage in if certain circumstances arose. It is fighting that makes the war, and fighting is deliberate. There is no war unless troops fight under orders from governments or from would-be governments. In any case, 'a war' may be regarded as standing for a particular instance of the working of an institution. 'War', on the other hand, may be regarded as standing for an institution that resembles a tradition.[20] It is obvious that slumps are a very different sort of entity again, but I hope I may be excused here from discussing them, though it is clear that their analysis is particularly important for philosophers of liberalism. Natural languages and science are other (very different) instances of unplanned social growths that can be compared with traditions on the one hand and with spontaneous economic growths on the other. Mr. Stalin, the Pope of planning, has recently stressed the spontaneous and gradual character of the growth of language.[21]

As to (2), the question arises whether men could ever be in

20. A point discussed by Professor Popper in 'Towards a Rational Theory of Tradition', *Rationalist Annual*, 1948; see pp. 52–3. Compare K. R. Popper, *Conjectures and Refutations*, London: Routledge & Kegan Paul, 1963, pp. 120–35.

21. 'Marxism holds that the transition of a language from an old quality to a new does not take place by way of an explosion, or of the destruction of an existing language and the creation of a new one, but by the gradual accumulation of the elements of a new quality, and hence by the gradual dying away of the elements of the old quality. It should be said in general for the benefit of comrades who have an infatuation for explosions that the law of transition from an old quality to a new by means of an explosion is inapplicable not only to the history of the development of languages; it is not always applicable to other social phenomena of a basis or superstructural character.' J. V. Stalin, *Concerning Marxism in Linguistics*, 1950; cf. B. Franklin (ed.), *The Essential Stalin: Major Theoretical Writings 1905–52*, London: Croom Helm, 1973, p. 425.

control of their social life to such an extent that all the fundamental institutions of their society were results of deliberate
contrivance. This is a very complex question, and here I
have only time to make one suggestion. There are two factors, it seems to me, viz., error and conflict of wills, which
make it certain that unintended results of actions will
be constantly occurring in all human societies. That error
should have this effect is quite obvious, for even if everyone
in a given society were agreed that such and such a thing
should be done in order to bring about an end that they all
desired, something that none of them had intended would
result if they were all wrong about what would produce the
end and had all acted accordingly. If, furthermore, there are
differences of view about what will produce the end they all
desire, and if there is freedom for the different courses of
conduct to be undertaken, then a further sort of unforeseen
result is likely to ensue. For if some men think that one sort
of conduct will lead to some common end, and others that
quite another sort is required to bring about that same end,
then they may come into conflict with one another at least
to the extent of unwittingly interfering with one another's
policies of action. If two groups of politicians each want
their country to keep out of a war, and if one group thinks
that friendship with X is the best means and the other that
friendship with Y is the best means, the result may well be
something not foreseen by either. The occurrence of the
unintended is even more apparent when there are differences of end. If, in a given society, some men are aiming at
one sort of public end and others at another, then they compromise or they oppose one another. If they compromise,
then they have changed their intentions and, if the compromise policy is well devised, but not if it rests upon error, the
result will be something intended though not what was orig-

inally intended by most of them. The man who is persuaded to a compromise policy is in between two extremes, one of which is the securing of his own primary aims, and the other of which is 'being at the mercy of social forces over which he has no control'. Generally, compromises come after struggles, so that what the compromisers have to work with is already different from what they had in mind before they came to the point of compromising. Should there by no compromise, then one party may overcome the wills of the others and impose his. Here again, however, the struggle will in most cases have changed the situation in a way that no one had intended. If no single will is imposed, then what happens continues to be the unintended resultant of them all. I think it is clear from this that without omniscience and complete unanimity of aim, things will be happening that no one had intended to happen. To that extent, the social world will seem independent of men's wills, like the natural world of hills, rivers and climate. We may thus say that in any human society there must be a sort of unintended social detritus. But whereas intending involves foreseeing, it does not follow that the unintended cannot be foreseen in some measure also. There is something of a paradox here, since foreseeing the unintended leads to the possibility of its becoming in some sense intended, as I have explained above.

[**V**]

In conclusion, I must say something about how traditional *standards* of morality appear in the light of the liberal philosophy. In the first place we may note that a minimum morality which prohibits murder, assault, theft and lying may be accepted by liberals and traditionalists alike. I suggested earlier that the rule of law and private property are fundamental elements in the liberal code. They may also be found in traditional societies. This common moral basis has generally been called Natural Law, and may be accepted without question in traditional societies and as reasonable in liberal societies. In accepting the principles of Natural Law, the liberal also, in a sense, *adopts* them. According to the liberal, to accept a traditional moral standard unreflectively is to fall short in human dignity, which is only fully achieved by individuals who accept only those standards that they consciously approve of for themselves and others. The member of a traditional society is brought up to conform to certain rules and expects his children to conform to them also. In acting in accordance with his conscience, he will be acting in accordance with rules that he feels somehow identified with. But the liberal appears to require more than this, and to suppose that men should act in accordance with a conscience that they have not only received from their predecessors but have also in some measure themselves helped to frame. If we say that a certain inertia is characteristic of the traditionalist conscience, then spontaneity is characteristic of the liberal conscience. One thing that liberals mean by freedom is acting in this rationally spontaneous manner.

To say that the liberal not only receives but in some measure adopts the principles of Natural Law may give rise to the ludicrous notion that people are to patronise immutable morality. The idea, however, is that these principles are, in a liberal society, not only followed, but followed because they are seen to be reasonable. The liberal, I think, must suppose that the principles of Natural Law will appear reasonable to all sane persons who reflect on them, that, for example, all sane persons will see that the pacific mutual exchange of goods and services is better than their acquisition by force, fraud and appeals to sympathy. This is a fundamental principle of organisation which, on the liberal view, should guide *all* social behaviour. He, therefore, will regard the principles of Natural Law as of absolute authority, and will submit them to scrutiny only because he is quite sure that they will stand up to it. A liberal who begins to doubt Natural Law is on the way to becoming something else.

Natural Law, however, relates to minimum moral standards. No one is thought to have done anything at all remarkable by way of moral performance if he has merely refrained from murder, theft and perjury. Models are held before us of men and women whose lives were not only free from crime but also had in them elements of positive moral achievement. St Francis, William Wilberforce, Florence Nightingale, Cecil Rhodes, Mahatma Ghandi, are instances of such moral exemplars. It is hoped that when the young learn about such people, they will be fired to attempt analogous feats of moral prowess so far as their station in life allows. In this way ideals are presented of equanimity, benevolence, friendship, patriotism and the like. No one could combine the virtues of St Francis and of Cecil Rhodes, and therefore chance or choice determines which model will most influence any given individual. There is thus a variety of ideals by which moral endeavour may be inspired. The examples I have given show different types of achievement and are drawn from different centuries and different sorts of society. Knowledge of this variety is available to us because in our society the attempt has been made to understand leading figures in other societies as well as in our own. An isolated and ignorant society must draw its ideals from within itself. An isolated and ignorant society in which there is little division of labour will have few types of life in terms of which its moral virtues may be exhibited. In such a society there may perhaps be only a single pattern of human virtue. All the virtues known to a complex society might be included in it, but they would be shown in a much smaller range of circumstance. Its conception of courage, for example, might be of a single form only, and therefore limited much as a people's conception of red would be limited if they had only had experience of one shade of that colour.

Now liberal societies are societies in which scientific enquiry is highly valued and in which the free exchange of commodities promotes new divisions of labour. It follows that liberal societies are also societies in which new circumstances and ways of life must constantly emerge. Traditional societies, on the other hand, are less given to critical scientific enquiry, and tend to remain in whatever division of labour they have reached. Their moral patterns will therefore be limited in variety. The differentiation of the liberal society will multiply its moral patterns. A marked characteristic of it will be the 'variety of lives' that Plato noted in the commercial democracy known to him. The more traditional the society, the more simple its virtues, the more liberal the society, the more complex they become. Again, since the imagination requires the aid of experience, to extend experience is to extend the range of the imagination. It therefore follows that in a liberal society the moral imagination will run more freely. We may compare, in this respect, the limited perfection aimed at by the artists of a traditional society, with the variety of styles that are created and cause confusion in a liberal society. Whereas Natural Law may be equally respected in traditional and in liberal societies, the ideals of traditional societies tend to be conserved whereas those of liberal societies tend to be multiplied. Herbert Spen-

cer's account of progress in terms of increasing 'heterogene-
ity' and 'differentiation' is no misapplication of superseded
biological theories, but expresses the central idea of the liberal philosophy.

OBJECTIVES:
AN ESSAY ON HAYEK'S
CONSTITUTION OF LIBERTY

The Good Society

During the last thirty years there has been little to encourage serious thought about the fundamentals of politics. The increasing specialisation of university studies has been against it, and a code of academic manners has grown up which sanctions no more than an ironical profession of ignorance in the face of manifest absurdities in some other person's specialism. The crisis of self-criticism and abnegation within philosophy has been against it, and philosophers have sought respectability in specialism too. But chiefly, perhaps, the course of events has been against it, since so many of the societies and institutions set up in response to the idealism of former times are foundering, and social policy is more often approached in an attitude of disillusioned pragmatism than considered in the light of principles.

Professor Hayek, in his *The Constitution of Liberty*,[1] goes against all these tendencies. He appeals deliberately to first principles. Although entitled as few others to do so, he lays no claim to specialist expertise, and does not allow oppo-

1. [F. A. Hayek, *The Constitution of Liberty*, London: Routledge & Kegan Paul, 1960.]

nents to escape criticism by that device. He attempts to work out a comprehensive and closely reasoned political philosophy on the scale that our more confident predecessors found acceptable. His account of the task of the political philosopher reveals what Hayek is aiming at. It is the duty of the political philosopher, he says,

> to show possibilities and consequences of common action, to offer comprehensive aims of policy as a whole which the majority have not yet thought of. It is only after such a comprehensive picture of the possible results of different policies has been presented that democracy can decide what it wants (p. 114).

The political philosopher, he goes on, should not confine himself to pointing out possibilities, but should be 'prepared to defend values which seem right to him' (p. 115), and to be critical of prevailing or majority views. Indeed, it follows from what Hayek says that the formulation of comprehensive political philosophies is essential to the functioning of a liberal-democratic society, and its absence is a sign that liberal democracy is in danger or in decline.

Aims of Policy

Let us first consider, then, the comprehensive aims of policy that Hayek recommends. There is at any rate a superficial paradox in this very enterprise. For on the one hand the type of liberalism which Hayek supports is opposed to the manufacture of detailed blueprints as guides to deliberate social reconstruction, and yet on the other hand he advocates, as we have seen, the formulation of comprehensive aims of policy. But there is no real contradiction here, since Hayek rejects what he calls the rationalistic method of consciously reconstructing society, in favour of the spontaneous adjustment of free activities to one another through market processes. His view is that the arrangements and institutions that arise in this way are generally superior to those which are planned by powerful individuals or groups, however wise they may be. Various reasons are offered, but the most important is that any man or group of men must be ignorant of many of the circumstances and consequences of their policies, whereas the adjustments of a multitude of individuals to one another frequently achieve a harmony too complicated for individual comprehension. In this connection Hayek writes of 'that higher, superindividual wisdom which, in a certain sense, the products of spontaneous social growth may possess' (p. 110). This is in the tradition of Bastiat, whose *Harmonies Économiques* has on its title-page the motto 'mens agitat molem'.[2] For Hayek, as for Bastiat, the mind which works through the whole ('unites and mingles with the mighty mass', as Dryden translates it) achieves an impersonal and natural, rather than an artificial form of organisation.

Hayek contrasts his conception of a society which develops in unforeseeable ways by means of the progressive adaptation of free activities one to another, with that of a society in which an overall system of priorities is maintained by the threat of force. The latter type is most favoured today, although some of its supporters fail to realise the extent to which coercion is essential to it. In his role of critical political philosopher, therefore, Hayek reveals the bludgeon hidden behind the backs of many of those who call for social justice, fair shares, abolition of inequalities, and the like. From his criticism it emerges that in the society he would

2. [Frederick Bastiat, *Harmonies of Political Economy*, tr. P. J. Sterling, London: J. Murray, 1860–70; or *Economic Harmonies*, tr. W. Hayden Boyers, Princeton: Van Nostrand, 1964. The quotation is from Vergil's *Aeneid*.]

like to see, individual freedom, in the sense of freedom from coercion by the will of other men, would be taken as the guiding aim. This, however, is the least exclusive absolute that there could be, since adherence to it is the means of allowing the pursuit of many varying and conflicting ideals. The objective is, so to speak, that no objective should crowd out others, but that the way should always be left open for new ones to be invented and pursued. Hayek conceives progress not in terms of the degree of approach towards some already understood ideal, but in terms of the possibility of ideals not yet conceived. Progress, understood in this way, is a consequence of freedom.

The Conditions of Freedom

A free and progressive society, therefore, cannot be confined within the range of moral vision of any single man or group or class or generation. Its policies and institutions will develop and adapt themselves in unforeseeable ways. Nevertheless, there are, Hayek believes, a number of institutions and rules which, as far as can be seen at present, are essential for the preservation of any free society. Among these, private property and the rule of law are the most important. An individual is free, according to Hayek, to the extent that he is not coerced by others.[3] To be coerced by others is to have one's actions controlled by the will of someone else under threat of some penalty if one disobeys. The only sure way of being free is to have a private sphere into which no

3. Discussion of Hayek's definition of freedom is not part of my assignment in this volume. I should say, however, that I agree with him that freedom, in the social and political context, is best regarded as the absence of deliberate coercion. Deliberate coercion can operate, however, indirectly as well as directly, and be exerted both by governments and by economic organisations.

one else can penetrate without permission. Private property is the chief though not the sole means by which this independence is secured. It has to be maintained, of course, by the threat of governmental coercion against thieves and cheats, but the coercion is for upholding rules, not for furthering the particular aims of the property owners. A system of private property established in the interests of specific persons, and varied to suit their demands, would infringe individual freedom, since those not so benefited would be coerced in the interests of the favoured owners and hence would not be free. Governmental coercion should always be in order to uphold rules. A law should not relate to specific individuals or interests, but should leave citizens free to decide which among them are to come within its scope. In this way, the coercion that is inseparable from legal enactment is kept to a minimum, and each individual can decide upon his own course of action without fear of unforeseen irruptions from the public authorities. He has quite enough to do in coping with the unpredictable effects of free activities.

The Role of Independence

In the society that Professor Hayek would like to see there would be a considerable proportion of people able to support themselves otherwise than by earning wages and salaries. For employed men generally are not in a position to understand the conditions in which inventiveness can flourish, so that a democracy of wage-earners will tend to favour a rather unimaginative social order. Furthermore, if there is to be freedom and progress, there must not only be opportunities but also individuals who will make opportunities for themselves and exploit them to the full. Claims to opportunities as of right are claims that people should be placed in positions guaranteed by the state, and the state can only guarantee these positions if it maintains them by force. No doubt there is a place in Hayek's vision for unambitious public service, but he makes much more of the need for active enterprise and resourcefulness. In so far as we try to find scope for our abilities, we are 'all', he remarks, 'entrepreneurs' (p. 81). No free society, Hayek argues, can make distributive justice its aim, that is distribution of incomes in accordance with merit, without putting the distribution under the control of public authorities and losing freedom thereby. The pursuit of distributive justice must, he holds, lead to an hierarchical society in which the rule of law is constantly flouted in the vain attempt to make each reward fit each individual degree of merit.[4]

Other contributors to this volume will discuss the application of this view of society to specific problems. There are three main topics, however, which need to be considered on a fairly abstract level. The first of these is Hayek's view about the relevance of knowledge and ignorance to social reform. His views on this matter run counter to the widely held opinion that the accumulation of knowledge and the application of scientific methods may be expected to bring social processes under conscious control for the general good.[5] The second main topic is that of progress. Hayek's appeal on behalf of individual freedom differs from the fashionable Existentialist protests against regimentation in that it is associated with a belief in progress rather than with a

4. I state the argument in more detail on pp. 204 ff. below.

5. John Dewey was the ablest modern supporter of this view, which, of course, goes back to Francis Bacon.

denial of its possibility.[6] The third topic which I propose to discuss is that of distributive justice. This is the central objective of democratic socialism, and although Hayek may be right in his view that this form of socialism is in decline, the ideal that inspires it continues to influence both popular beliefs and public policy. Discussion of it, therefore, is of practical as well as theoretical interest.

Freedom, Knowledge and Ignorance

Hayek holds that the fact of necessary or inevitable ignorance (he uses both adjectives) provides the chief reason for allowing the fullest possible scope to individual freedom. It is because of this ignorance that it is better to allow society to develop by spontaneous adjustment than to control it all by some central agency. Those who recognise the inevitability of ignorance will not pin their hopes on plans for society as a whole, but will want there to be scope for everyone to gain from the impersonal beneficence of transactions that are imperfectly understood. What is this inevitable ignorance, then, how does it tell in favour of limiting governmental activity, and how does it come about that a spontaneously developing society is better than one that is regulated from above?

Hayek calls attention to various types of inevitable ignorance. It is obvious how limited the knowledge of each more or less specialised individual must be. Even of the knowledge he has a considerable part is not apparent to him, since it is in the form of skills, traditions and institutions which he takes for granted. The man of science is ignorant, not only of other specialisms, but also of the unforeseeable new

6. For an Existentialist view see Karl Jaspers, *The Origin and Goal of History*, New Haven: Yale University Press, 1953.

problems to which every scientific advance will give rise. Hayek appears to hold that these new problems are both theoretical (i.e., within the particular science) and practical (i.e., relative to its social effects), and that they accumulate at a faster rate than new knowledge does. If this is so, then the hope, entertained by so many since the time of the Enlightenment, of a gradual diminution in the field of ignorance, is seen to be illusory. Again, people do not know what they really want until specimen opportunities have come to their notice. Still less, therefore, can anyone know what future generations will want. From all this it follows, in Hayek's view, that the men who would be called upon to devise and implement a comprehensive social plan cannot possibly know enough for their project to be a reasonable one. The likelihood is that it will misfire, prove unsatisfactory to those for whom it is devised, give rise to all sorts of unforeseen reactions, and ultimately appear pointless in the light of future systems of valuation.

This view raises philosophical questions of great interest which we must reluctantly ignore. I confess that I do not follow Hayek's argument for the view that growth in scientific knowledge constantly extends the field of ignorance. It is rather misleading, I suggest, to call the opening up of new and unsolved problems a growth of the realm of ignorance. It is rather the replacing of mere ignorance or nescience, i.e., complete unawareness that there is anything to be known, by a set of unanswered questions hitherto not conceived of. Blank nescience becomes specific ignorance with more blank nescience beyond it. Although this renders untenable the idea that knowledge can ever be completed, it does not appear in itself to provide a reason against comprehensive social plans based on whatever scientific knowledge is available.

However, the main element in the argument from ignorance is that no one can know enough about how men's
wants can be satisfied, and about what men's future wants
will be, to justify embarking on comprehensive governmental plans for their satisfaction. Hayek does not discuss the
point, but it would appear that governments have means of
collecting and collating knowledge which private individuals do not have. It must be his view, then, that the advantage
that governments have in this respect is not enough to justify their claiming to have the knowledge necessary for their
plans. Such knowledge would have to be so vast as to be
outside the comprehension of any man or group or organisation. But how can we be so sure that this is the case? I do
not think that Hayek's thesis is based on any calculation of
more or less. It is rather an implication of some propositions
about predictability. Certain actions and certain wants, on
this view, are unpredictable. It is not known how other people will react except in so far as they follow routines. Resourcefulness and inventiveness can, in general, be expected
from some people, but the forms which they will take are
so various that they cannot be anticipated in any central
plan. Furthermore, people do not in general know what
they want until they get it. New wants are frequently the
result of some accidental encounter, and no one can predict
what will arouse them. The planner's task is impossible
because if he is to succeed he must foresee the unforeseeable.

I am myself convinced that the argument from unpredictability is a strong one. Its force, nevertheless, would be
somewhat lessened in a society where ingenuity was rare,
science stagnant and wants stereotyped. If it were possible
to utilise electronic computers in planning for such societies,
then the range of predictability could be extended. A society

can for a time, perhaps for a long time, be rendered *more* predictable by being strait-jacketed. It is in the free and progressive societies that Hayek so eloquently depicts that unpredictability is, so to say, endemic. On this matter he speaks, I think, with two voices in the space of one page. On the one hand he suggests that if there were omniscient men 'there would be little case for liberty' (p. 29). On the other hand he holds that 'Liberty is essential in order to leave room for the unforeseeable and unpredictable' and to allow scope for 'the emergence of what we shall want when we see it' (p. 29). It might be argued that there is no conflict here, that Hayek, in saying there would be little case for liberty if there were omniscient men, is not weakening his argument at all since it is, as he says, 'the main contention' (p. 29) of his view that there are not and could not be omniscient men. But when he argues that liberty serves the purpose of leaving room for the unforeseeable and unpredictable, he is resting his case, not on the *impossibility* of there being knowledge that leads to successful social planning, but on the *undesirability* of a society in which coercively imposed planning prevents the development of the unexpected. If the unexpected and unpredictable are necessary anyway, why is freedom required in order to leave room for them? Hayek thinks, and I agree with him, that a society in which room is kept open for novelty and invention is better than one of enforced routines.

Free societies deliberately lay themselves open to the inspirations provided by the new and unexpected. Hence they will, by their variety and inventiveness, actively prevent the possibility of anything approaching social omniscience. Omniscient men are only conceivable, if at all, in societies where routine prevails, in the sort of society favoured by Mr. Khrushchev, in which 'every minute is calculated, a life built on calculation.'[7] It is not that liberty would be unnecessary if there were omniscient men, but that men who prize liberty will develop their knowledge, their aims and their skills so that social omniscience is rendered impossible.

The spontaneously developing society that Hayek advocates is one in which individuals and associations make arrangements with one another within a framework of criminal and civil law. Each individual and each group will act in the light of the knowledge relevant to its own concerns—and these need not, of course, be selfish. If A and B come to a certain agreement, this will have repercussions for C and D who, in their turn, will adapt themselves in the ways that seem best to them. In this way an interlocking system of adjustments will arise of enormous extent and complexity. The whole that emerges from this is not the best conceivable, for there is no comprehensive view of it. But it will be more free than the alternative form of order because fewer possibilities of action will be forcibly excluded or kept from being thought of.

Progress

Progress may be regarded as advance towards some definitely determined goal, or as a movement in which new goals are constantly emerging. Professor Hayek is mainly concerned with progress of this second sort. From what has already been said, it will be seen that according to Hayek progress of this sort is a consequence of freedom, on the ground that when scope is given to spontaneous activity, chance and experiment elicit hitherto unconceived aims and

7. [Khrushchev is quoted from E. Goldhagen, 'The Glorious Future—Realities and Chimeras', *Problems of Communism*, IX, No. 6, p. 10, who in turn refers to the *New York Times*, 2 March 1960.]

preferences. The growth of the sciences is progressive in this way, as application to one set of problems opens the road to further problems only conceivable on the basis of the solutions found to the first. Comparable developments take place in the growth of technique, of tastes and perhaps of institutions. Hayek is particularly impressed by the progressive development of wants, since this means that future generations will have other scales of preference than our own. He extends this idea to moral codes. Moral rules are not deliberately framed, and a new system of them could never be constructed all at once. Nevertheless, he speaks of their being modified and improved under the impulsion of experience (p. 63). But this idea, I think, needs very careful examination if liberalism (or, as Hayek prefers to call it, 'libertarianism') is not to collapse into moral nihilism. Indeed, this, in my view, is the danger to which liberalism, in the twentieth century, is most liable to succumb—the danger of indiscriminate tolerance.

In order to bring out its weakness we need to distinguish, I think, between primary and secondary moral rules. A primary moral rule is universal and irremovable. Once acknowledged as part of the corpus of morality, its exclusion, although theoretically conceivable, is morally unthinkable. For example, the rules prohibiting cruelty and false witness are just not subjects for moral reform. On the other hand, there are more specific moral rules such as some of those relating to property or to sexual behaviour, which can be modified without affecting the primary ones. It is these secondary ones that permit of moral innovation, experimentation and development, whereas the primary ones are not of a type that allows this. (The principle enunciated by Aquinas that the primary principles allow additions but no removals is in my view correct.) What I have called primary moral principles coincide with what was formerly called the natural law. This doctrine, in its earlier formulations, cannot be easily accommodated to present-day modes of thought, but without it liberalism would not have been created and would not long survive. There is an essential conservatism about morals which is lacking from natural science, where no principles (apart perhaps from principles of method) are irremovable. It was at one time a task of liberalism to secure freedom for the pursuit of natural science, but liberalism commits suicide if it takes the sort of progress characteristic of natural science as generally operative. If we compare the additive progress of the moral law with the transformative progress of the natural sciences we see that within the various departments of human life there are different sorts of progress. Thus the progress of society as a whole must remain an elusive idea, if, indeed, it has any meaning at all.

I am suggesting, then, that the development of morality should not be assimilated to the progress of science, that there are aspects of morality that, once appreciated, permit of specification but not of abolition. I suggest, furthermore, that it is a defect of contemporary liberalism that it does not unambiguously recognise this. A consequence of not recognising it is to introduce into the liberal outlook a form of moral scepticism which could well prove fatal. By comparison with the systems opposed to it, liberalism is, of course, critical and undogmatic, but no outlook can survive at all if it regards *all* rules of behaviour as merely provisional. There is nothing self-stultifying in holding that the science and art of the distant future may take forms that are now unimaginable to us, but seriously to suppose that this could hold for morality (or for logic) opens the way to nihilism.

Hayek is far from being a nihilist, for it is a leading feature of his book that in it liberalism is defended, as Constant put it, as the 'system of principles'.[8] Nevertheless, I do not think that he altogether avoids the difficulties inherent in regarding progress as a single concept. He appears to think that if progress is towards what is not yet known it cannot be justified in terms of its end. In one passage he therefore seems to justify it in terms of movement. 'Progress', he writes, 'is movement for movement's sake' (p. 41). If this stood alone it would be most unconvincing, for why should some people not prefer to stand still? Hayek also says, however, that human intelligence 'proves itself' by 'living in and for the future' (p. 41), and that 'it is in the process of learning, and in the effects of having learned something new, that man enjoys the gift of his intelligence' (p. 41). These phrases imply that the movement that is for movement's sake is the exercise of intelligence in invention and discovery—an exercise, he points out, from which the less intelligent get benefits (pp. 41–2). It would seem that scientific discovery and technological invention are being put forward as intrinsically valuable for those who engage in them and as means to the happiness of those who do not. If this is what Hayek means, then he is regarding the advance of science as the aim and justification of progress.

Distributive Justice

According to Hayek, 'distributive justice is irreconcilable with freedom in the choice of one's activities: it is the justice of a hierarchic organisation, not of a free society' (p. 440). By 'distributive justice' he means distribution of rewards in ac-

8. [B. Constant, 'De l'arbitraire', in *Oeuvres politiques de Benjamin Constant*, ed. C. Louandre, Paris, 1974, pp. 91–2; as quoted by Hayek in *The Constitution of Liberty*, Chicago: University of Chicago Press, 1960, pp. 68 and 437.]

cordance with merit, and by 'merit' he means 'the attributes of conduct that make it deserving of praise, that is, the moral character of the action and not the value of the achievement' (p. 94). By 'value of the achievement' he means, I think, what the beneficiaries of the achievement are prepared freely to pay for it. He objects to distribution in accordance with merit in the first place because there is no objective means of assessing it. When the attempt is made, distribution can be decided only in accordance with what other people decide it is. When the reward is determined in terms of the work or product offered the transaction is between two willing parties, whereas when it is determined by assessing the merit of the producer, this can only be decided by some public body. Distribution in accordance with value needs no authority to determine it, but only to keep the parties from coercing one another. Distribution in accordance with merit can only be secured by a public assessment and enforcement of who merits how much. Furthermore, once this sort of distribution is established in respect of one type of income, it will be demanded in respect of more and more until all incomes are decided on the basis of a publicly established scale of merit. Hayek contrasts this system, which assumes a single set of moral priorities, with the system he prefers, in which people's dealings by way of service and exchange are largely independent of the moral outlooks of the parties involved.

My first comment is that it would have been better if Hayek had written of distribution in accordance with *desert* rather than in accordance with merit. When desert is taken as the measure, it becomes obvious that it is associated with demerit as well as with merit, with punishment as well as with reward. Hence to call for distribution in these moral terms is to call for a society in which, under official auspices, men are constantly rehearsing a travesty of the Day of Judgment. This would certainly require a respect for the authorities and a degree of regimentation greater even than was found in Calvin's Geneva.

But distributive justice is seldom conceived in such strict terms. More often the argument is that remuneration should be justified in terms of the skill, training and moral qualities required for the job. It seems to me that remuneration in accordance with such qualities may be influenced by custom, which is impersonal like the market, and like market prices is not ordained. If this is so, then a customary but uncoercive hierarchy is a third possibility between a coercive hierarchy (Herbert Spencer's 'militant type of society') on the one hand and a society based on uncoerced agreements (Spencer's 'industrial type of society') on the other.[9] Hayek's most powerful objection to distribution in accordance with merit is not, then, that it requires force to maintain it (it often does, of course), but that it ignores commutative justice. For distribution in accordance with merit is from the point of view of the worker and ignores the requirements of the user of his product. The producer's moral claims must be met before there is any question of the consumer's wishes. This can lead to demands for payment for work that is not required on the ground that skill and effort have been put into it. On moral grounds someone would be having to pay for what he does not get. One sort of justice would be driving out the other.

It is clear that an equal distribution of incomes would conflict with a distribution in accordance with desert, and in fact few have advocated it. Nevertheless, over the past one

9. [Compare Herbert Spencer, *The Principles of Sociology*, volume 2, New York: D. Appleton and Company, 1887, pp. 658–730.]

hundred years there has been an increasing pressure *to-wards* equality. Hayek is not averse to this in principle.

> 'One may well feel attracted' [he writes], 'to a community in which there are no extreme contrasts between rich and poor and may welcome the fact that the general increase in wealth seems gradually to reduce those differences. I fully share these feelings and certainly regard the degree of social equality that the United States has achieved as wholly admirable' (pp. 87–88).

His objection to egalitarianism is (briefly) that it requires the granting of excessive power to men who cannot know enough to use it properly. Furthermore, equal distribution would hinder the development of capacities which are of advantage in the first place to the individuals who profit by them, but in the long run to all the other members of the community.

Hayek does not, however, directly consider an aspect of egalitarianism which is widely accepted today, the view that justice requires any distribution to be equal unless there are reasons to the contrary. If it is accepted that the presumption is in favour of equality and that the burden of proof is on those who would depart from it, then existing unequal states of affairs are put on the defensive as against an ideal equality. It is necessary, therefore, to comment briefly on this fundamentally radical view.

Support for it, I believe, is partly due to the fact that equality is a feature of any distribution in accordance with rules.[10] It is of the essence of a rule that similar cases are dealt with in a similar way. For example, if there is a rule of distribution such that payment is in proportion to output, then the rule is violated if men whose output is the same do not get the same reward. What has been called 'formal jus-

10. Sir Isaiah Berlin, 'Equality', *Proceedings of the Aristotelian Society*, 1955–6, pp. 301–26; see p. 305.

tice' is achieved when all the members of a given category are treated in the same way.[11] If the rule of distribution were in proportion to height or weight formal justice would be secured so long as men of the same height or weight obtained the same reward. A distribution that was not in accordance with formal justice would be whimsical, arbitrary or irregular.

Upholders of the view I am considering, however, would want substantial as well as mere formal equality. One line of argument is that everyone has an equal right to consideration or respect and that any departure from equal treatment would violate this right unless there were adequate reasons for it. It seems to me, however, that the right to consideration or respect is absolute and that no violation of it would be justified by any reason whatsoever. Is a man not being treated with respect if he receives less than someone else who is in like case with himself? I think he is not if he is in this position as a result of deliberate arrangements, as he would be, for example, if he were employed by the same employer on the same work. To employ several people for similar work, and to pay less to some than to others, and yet to have no justification for this on grounds of time or effort or output or seniority or exhaustion of funds or some other reason, leaves lack of respect or downright contempt as the only alternatives. (In a free market, of course, the aggrieved man could go elsewhere.) But differences of reward that are not deliberately contrived are quite different. For A is not failing to respect B merely because R is paying S more than A is paying B. If this is denied, then the assumption is being

11. Chaim Perelman, *De la justice*, Bruxelles: Université Libre de Bruxelles, Institut de Sociologie Solvay, Office de la publicité, 1945, p. 27. An English version, 'Concerning Justice' is in Chaim Perelman, *The Idea of Justice and the Problem of Argument*, London: Routledge & Kegan Paul, 1963; see p. 16.

made that it is wrong to *allow* different systems of reward to exist side by side. This, in its turn, implies that the attempt should be made to bring all systems of reward under deliberate and co-ordinated control. These steps, I believe, give support to Hayek's view that the pursuit of distributive justice tends to become *total*, and does this not only in practice, but as a matter of logic.

Another aim of those who strive for distributive justice (or social justice, as they more often call it) is to break down the divisions between classes. The argument here, I think, is not merely that the class structure prevents the distribution of incomes from being equal or in accordance with merit, but also that in the absence of class distinctions men would associate with one another more easily and with greater friendliness than they do now.[12] Briefly, the point is that if greater social equality is brought about by governmental measures, the result will be an increase in fraternity. It is, of course, most hazardous to prophesy the moral effects of political changes, and it is open to doubt whether a spread of friendly feeling could be secured in such a way. But Professor Hayek, I think, is less perturbed by the absence of universal brotherhood than some socialists would think he ought to be. At any rate he calls attention to the fact that the workings of the market enable men freely to benefit one another even though they do not share the same tastes or moral outlook. I think he regards it as an advantage that business arrangements are separable from personal attachments. In a society where men are free to choose their friends, there are bound to be groups which disapprove of one another. This should not prevent their respecting one another's rights, but they are not required to seek for friend-

12. C. A. R. Crosland, *The Future of Socialism*, London: Jonathan Cape, 1956, p. 169.

ship with those they find uncongenial. Absurd class distinctions are better dealt with by ridicule than by legislation.

Conclusion

Professor Hayek's main theses depend on the distinction between the essential features of free association on the one hand and enforced hierarchy on the other. Free association requires the maintenance by force of private property and the rule of law. A society where free association predominates will be complex, morally variegated and unpredictably progressive. Those who seek to bring society under centralised control necessarily extend the area of coercion, impose a single moral scheme, and diminish the possibilities of progress. Furthermore, when their plan is devised to secure distributive justice, incomes are settled and enforced so as to maintain an hierarchical order in which little attention is given to a man's right to pay for what he wants; what he has to pay for is the cost of upholding the status of the suppliers.

The contrast between free association and coercive hierarchy is, of course, a contrast of ideal types, and in actual societies the two elements are found in varying proportions. But Hayek is doing an important service in calling attention once more to the enormous difference between being assigned a place and making an agreement. Contract has certain moral advantages over status which at present tend to be lost sight of. Perhaps I have stressed more than Hayek has done the moral difference between these types of social order. I have in mind particularly two observations by Adam Smith in *The Wealth of Nations*.[13] The first is that 'It is not

13. Compare Adam Smith, *The Wealth of Nations*, Glasgow edition, I.ii. 2, Indianapolis: Liberty Fund, 1982, pp. 26–7.

from the benevolence of the butcher, the brewer, or the baker that we expect our dinner . . . ', and the second is that 'when an animal wants to obtain something either of a man or of another animal, it has no other means of persuasion but to gain the favour of those whose services it requires', and that some men too who want things from their fellows endeavour 'by every servile and fawning attention to obtain their good will'. Adam Smith contrasts with this the method of offering something in exchange for what is desired. This is the method of independent men who can co-operate without servility and without more than a minimum of moral agreement. This type of arrangement allows moral differences to co-exist with social cohesion. If men will only do business with those whose ideals they share, society is faced with the alternatives of uniformity or disruption. The boycott is not necessarily a sign of enhanced moral sensibility.

At this point I must mention a possible objection to Hayek's view which should not be allowed to pass unnoticed. He argues on the one hand that, because of their inevitable ignorance, planners are bound to fail in their attempts to build a society that conforms to their ideals. On the other hand he argues that the future of free societies is likewise unpredictable. Now an objector may well ask what reason there can be for preferring one unpredictability to another. The answer must be that the unpredictability of the coercive social order is linked with the failure of coercion and hence with the likelihood of social breakdown and civil strife, whereas the unpredictability of the (relatively) non-coercive social order relates to the positive discoveries and arrangements by which men adjust their relations to one another. The unforeseen consequences of coercion, it would seem, are more likely to be bad than are the unforeseen possibilities left open in a free society. A further point is that the failure of coercive plans is not completely unforeseen, although the planners themselves do not foresee it. On the other hand, many of the future achievements of a free society are absolutely unpredictable, for the reasons which have already been given.

As I see it, then, Professor Hayek's main theme is the contrast between the form of organisation that arises out of agreements freely entered into and the form that is forcibly imposed by some central authority. I agree that this is a most important distinction, though I do not think that Hayek pays sufficient attention to the fact that hierarchy and status can arise without being forcibly imposed by anyone. He goes on to argue that those who value freedom will prefer the first form of order, and will try to confine the second form to the work of upholding the first. With this, which was Locke's view, no liberal, it seems to me, can disagree. Hayek justifies his preference for the first form of order by the argument that no one can know enough to make the predictions necessary for operating the second sort effectively, and by the argument that freedom is best secured by leaving room for the unforeseeable. I find it logically disconcerting when social predictions are regarded both as impossible and as undesirable, for there would be no point in urging the prevention of the impossible. I have therefore suggested that social predictions are likely to be more successful in straitjacketed societies than in societies where invention is encouraged. I have also suggested that Hayek, in regarding freedom as the basis for progress considered as single and total, inadvertently encourages the nihilism that is the Achilles' heel of liberalism. In my view Hayek succeeds in showing that when distributive justice is made the object of public policy a forcibly imposed hierarchy has to be set up.

But I do not think that he considers all, or even the most important, of the arguments for the general establishment of a system of distributive justice. I believe, however, that they can be dealt with within the framework of his view, in which commutative justice—which is logically linked with the first form of order—receives its rightful emphasis. That there is indeed a logical link between free association and distributive justice, and a certain incompatibility between free association and a universally imposed distributive justice, is one of the most interesting conclusions of this most penetrating book.

DISTRIBUTIVE JUSTICE, THE INVISIBLE HAND AND THE CUNNING OF REASON

[I]

Distributive justice is an end sought by various socialist movements; the invisible hand is appealed to by some non-socialists for guidance towards national prosperity; by the cunning of reason, it has been supposed, justice will be established here on earth as it was once thought it would be established by Divine Providence in Heaven. By distributive justice an artificial distribution is to be effected which would not come about if the invisible hand were left to its own devices, since it is not directly concerned with justice at all. Believers in the cunning of reason, however, expect that from war, turmoil and greed all the capacities of mankind will eventually fulfil themselves. As Hegel put it in his *Lectures on the Philosophy of History*: 'That the History of the World, with all the changing scenes which its annals present, is this process of development and the realisation of Spirit—this is the true *Theodicaea*, the justification of God in History. Only *this* insight can reconcile Spirit with the History of the World—viz., that what has happened, and is happening every day, is not only not "without God", but is essentially His Work.'[1]

1. The last paragraph of J. Sibree's translation, which refers to the text of the version selected and edited by Karl Hegel, the philosopher's historian son.

In what follows I shall first try to interpret some of the original texts in which these three ideas were put forward. I shall also try to draw out their logical structure and some of their connections and ethical implications. It is not possible in a single paper to do this in detail, but one of the pleasures of Political Philosophy is the opportunity it offers, as Lucretius says of philosophy in general, of observing from 'the serene fortified sanctuaries built from the teachings of the wise' the 'mental strife, the struggle for eminence, men working night and day to reach the pinnacle of riches and the summit of power'.[2] This opportunity I now propose to take, and in so doing to make some remarks about justice which eschew any form of the social contract theory without adopting the holism which has hitherto been its main alternative.

[**II**]

The expression 'distributive justice' came into general currency from Book V of Aristotle's *Nicomachean Ethics*, and although the discussion there gives rise to problems it is as good a starting-point as any for an examination of the theme.

(*i*) Aristotle distinguishes between distributive justice and rectificatory justice. The latter is the righting of *in*justices between individual men, as when they dispute about the terms or fulfilment of a contract or claim that they have received an injury. Distributive justice is concerned with the distribution of divisible goods, such as 'honour, wealth, and the other divisible assets of the community' (*N.E.* V,ii). The

---

Compare G. W. F. Hegel, *Lectures on the Philosophy of History*, tr. J. Sibree, London: Bohn, 1861; the quotation is from page 477.

2. [Lucretius, *De rerum natura*, Book 2, lines 7–13. See W. H. D. Rouse, ed, *De rerum natura*, Loeb Classical Library, London: William Heinemann, volume 1, 1937, pp. 84–5.]

sort of distribution of wealth that Aristotle is thinking of is not the distribution of the social capital or income of the whole society, but the distribution of public property such as 'gifts of corn from foreign potentates, or goods escheated to the State'.[3] Aristotle also writes of distributive justice in the distribution of 'common funds' such as those of a benefit-club from which members receive in accordance with their contributions (*N.E.* V,iii). Distributive justice, then, can be exercised whenever there is some divisible good or evil that can be distributed among individuals with claims to participate in it. An example of a divisible evil is danger in battle, and this can cover military service itself as well as what happens to those already enlisted. According to Aristotle there are some goods that are not divisible, so that an individual can have them and at the same time augment the share of other individuals. A virtuous or wise man adds to the common good in the very process of augmenting his own virtue or wisdom (*N.E.* IX,viii).

(*ii*) (*a*) When they think of distribution most people think primarily of the distribution of property, although, like Aristotle, they may also have in mind such things as honours, offices, military service and, today, medical attention and education. What is it, then, about knowledge and virtue which makes them non-divisible goods? Aristotle's phrase about the effects of virtuous activity is: ' . . . the common welfare would be fully realised, while individuals would enjoy the greatest of goods'. It is clear that in endeavouring to be honest, friendly, gracious and generous an individual is necessarily trying to do what is beneficial to others and will often or generally succeed in doing so. In *Utilitarianism*, Chapter IV, Mill argues that aiming at virtue can harm no

3. H. H. Joachim, *The Nicomachean Ethics, a Commentary,* Oxford: Clarendon Press, 1951, p. 139.

one, whereas aiming at power or fame can do so.[4] Of course, in being honest or generous a man *may* inadvertently harm someone, but essentially honesty and generosity are not harmful and it is not purely contingent that they are not so.

(*b*) Knowledge is of so many different kinds that its divisibility or indivisibility is less easily settled. Nowadays there is property in intellectual productions in the form of copyright, but copyright in a book is not copyright in the knowledge or views contained in it, and the reader can pass on its contents by word of mouth to as many as will listen. Particular secrets can be kept and books can be censored, but most of what is known or discovered finds its way into the common stock of knowledge. Since, however, some secrets might be kept for ever and all the stocks of a book destroyed along with its author, it can hardly be said that *all* knowledge is essentially public. Indeed, as Spinoza showed in his account of *Imaginatio,* or the First Kind of Knowledge (*Ethics,* Book II),[5] there is a sort of knowledge based on each individual's personal experience and the emotions associated with it which differs from one person to another and contains what we may call an irreducible element of personal nuance or nostalgia. This is particularly prominent in Romantic literature but plays a part in practically all poetry. Even personal styles and cadences can be copied, however, and exert their influence on literature as a whole. Even so, Spinoza contrasted *Imaginatio* with *Ratio,* the scientific knowledge that forms an objective common possession. This

4. [John Stuart Mill, *Utilitarianism, Liberty, Representative Government and Selections from Auguste Comte and Positivism,* ed. H. B. Acton, London: Dent, 1972, p. 35.]

5. [Benedict de Spinoza, *Ethics,* Part II, Proposition 40, Scholium II. Cf. E. Curley (ed.), *The Collected Works of Spinoza,* Princeton: Princeton University Press, 1985, pp. 477–8.]

is added to and borrowed from by scientific men of different generations, and 'borrowing' here does not imply any private ownership. Is a plagiarist a thief? He is if he uses without acknowledgement what by law he should have paid for, but if he draws without acknowledgement from some earlier author whose work is out of copyright he is not a thief but an egotistical deceiver. We should also include in the common stock of knowledge the skills and institutional devices which, as we say, are inherited (a property word) by one generation from the previous ones. These forms of knowing how, of expertise and tradition, are *res publicae* just as much as are the institutions of government themselves.

(*c*) Is education a divisible form of knowledge and a form of wealth or property in consequence? Fundamentally it is the system of initiating the young into the skills and traditions, the institutions and knowledge of society, and is therefore subject to all the risks and disappointments that life in society gives rise to. It cannot be bought and sold and provided in the way that food or clothes can be, since what is received depends so very much on the activity and response of the 'recipient'. Nor is what is called 'education' as separable from what is not so called as food and clothing are from what is not food and clothing. This is partly a consequence of the greater element of response and activity in being educated, but also a result of the pervasive intrusion of society into the activities of the growing individual. Whatever system obtains, all education is public education. It can be neither bought nor given.

(*iii*) Plato had criticized democratic societies for giving equality 'to equals and unequals alike' (*Republic*, 557c). Aristotle appears to make this comment the basis of his own account of distributive justice which, he thinks, consists in securing that each recipient receives in accordance with his rank if what is being distributed is some windfall of public money, and in accordance with his contribution if what is being distributed is the surplus of a benefit-club. In the *Politics*, Book III, Aristotle considers the distribution of offices in a state, and says, as he had argued in the *Ethics*: 'Justice is relative to persons; and a just distribution is one in which the relative values of the things given correspond to those of the persons receiving.'[6] This means that in oligarchic states persons are considered equal if they are equal in wealth, unequal if they have unequal wealth; and in a democracy all who are not slaves but free men are thereby held to be equal. Aristotle's comment is that persons can be equal in wealth or as free men, and yet unequal in all sorts of other respects, even though the oligarchic or democratic devotees each regard their sort of justice or equality as 'absolute and complete'. According to Aristotle supporters of oligarchic justice regard the state as a sort of commercial enterprise in which citizens have shares; but it is much more than this, much more than a mere trading alliance,[7] much more, indeed, than a system of associated living. From this Aristotle concludes that both the oligarchic and the democratic conceptions of distributive justice 'speak of a part of it only'. The suggestion is, however, that he thought it possible that honours and offices in the state could be distributed in proportion to the services that each individual had performed,

6. Aristotle, *Politics*, III, chapter ix, paragraph 3; see Sir Ernest Barker, *The Politics of Aristotle*, Oxford: Clarendon Press, 1946, p. 117.

7. Burke takes this up in his *Reflections on the Revolution in France*: ' . . . but the state ought not to be considered nothing better than a partnership agreement in a trade of pepper and coffee, calico or tobacco, or some other such low concern, to be taken up for a little temporary interest, and to be dissolved by the fancy of the parties.' Compare Edmund Burke, *Reflections on the Revolution in France, 1790*, in *The Works of the Right Honourable Edmund Burke*, intro. F. W. Raffety, volume iv, London: Oxford University Press, 1907, pp. 105–6.

and that these services would be made up of subordinate, more limited ones.

(*iv*) Aristotle is quite clear that a distributor is necessary in order to make the just distribution. He must know what the law or principle of distribution is, and he commits injustice if he departs from it. In his translation of the *Politics* Barker inserts a linking, explanatory sentence not in Aristotle's original but intended to fill in a gap in the argument: 'It follows that a just distribution of offices among a number of different persons will involve a consideration of the personal values, or merits, of each of those persons.'[8] It is interesting to notice that the English word 'merit' is indirectly derived from the Greek verb *meiromai* which means to receive as one's portion or share, and is connected with the Greek noun *meros*, a part. An individual's merit is that which entitles him to receive a definite part of what is being distributed. An individual merits such and such a payment or reward by relation to what he is or has done, or he might not merit or deserve anything, or might have demerits which deserve criticism or punishment. In such cases as that of a share-out of profits, all that counts is the share of the capital contributed by each individual, and this is easy enough to allow of computation. But as Aristotle saw, when an individual's contribution to the good of the state is in question, all sorts of different merits have to be considered and somehow added together.[9] Aristotle considered that this is difficult; Mr. J. R. Lucas that it is impossible.[10] No distributor can allocate if there is no worka-

8. Barker, *The Politics of Aristotle*, p. 117.

9. Aristotle, *Politics*, III, chapter 12.

10. J. R. Lucas, *The Principles of Politics*, Oxford: Clarendon Press, 1966, p. 261. 'The criteria of apportionment are too diverse: and the compromises required for the sake of Freedom, Humanity (in some respects), and other ideals preclude our ever achieving an absolute Justice in the distribution of goods.' The insertion of 'absolute' here leads, in my opinion, to an understatement of the position.

ble rule of apportionment. The achievement of what is called 'social justice' in modern societies is not only a question of honours and offices, but of opportunities, types of education, privileges, incomes, tax-burdens, and much else besides. Each of these distributable goods and evils presents its own problems. Should incomes, for example, be distributed according to work done, effort made, individual or family need, or in accordance with some contrived combination of them? I do not think we know how such a points system for the construction of a just society could be formed. We all now recognize the fraudulence of wage tribunals.

(v) It may well be that, once this is recognized, there would be less encouragement for those who would like to occupy the judgement seat of universal distribution. Particular *in*justices might then be examined with a view to a better distribution in particular areas, but society as a whole would be allowed, as it is now, and perhaps as it must be, to take its own mysterious course. This would need an extension to those politicians with a taste for 'social Titanism' of that resignation which has hitherto been the attitude of the population at large.

(vi) 'Distribution' in the sense of a given arrangement of portions or shares or even of locations, as when we speak of the distribution of trees or factories in a district, has to be distinguished from 'distribution' in the sense of deliberately giving to or allocating among a group of individuals, as when the headmaster distributes the school prizes. The distribution in distributive justice appears to be of this second type, but this does not answer the question whether a distribution in the first sense can be regarded as just or unjust. The headmaster, we say, is just if he gives the prize for mathematics to the pupil who got most marks, unjust if he gives it to someone else, and the second and third prizes should go to those who have the next highest marks in that order. We can imagine the names of the prizewinners written in the books and the prizewinners taking each his own prize from a pile of them outside the headmaster's study. Would this be a case of distributive justice without a distributor? It would not be, since the allocation would already have been made on the authority of whoever required the names to be written in the books. A computer may settle how much each shareholder in a company is to have, but it is the secretary acting for the directors who gave the computer its task and is just or unjust. Suppose the books and the shares miraculously transferred themselves in the just proportions to their proper recipients, would this be a case of just distribution without a distributor? Hardly, for the acceptability of the miracle would still remain to be allowed or disallowed by the headmaster or firm. An objector may go on to question whether the sanctioning authority need be the distributor himself. Might it not be an outside umpire or the democratic will of the whole community? It might be the former, but only if appeal to an umpire is legally provided for. If it is not, the sanctioning has no authority whatever, and is nothing but the opinion of someone with no standing in the matter. As to the latter, if the whole community can decide what it likes, the rule of distributive justice has been abandoned. If the whole community's decision is limited by some rule, then it is acting as an umpire or distributor. From this I conclude that a distribution that has not been made by anyone is neither just nor unjust. Those who condemn the injustice of such distributions must really mean that they want to substitute for the given distribution another one controlled by a distributor acting according to a rule of apportionment which they can specify.

(*vii*) (*a*) As we have seen, Aristotle contrasts distributive justice with rectificatory justice, the latter being decided by a judge in a dispute about property or a suit for assault. But Aristotle adds to his analysis of rectificatory justice an analysis of justice in exchange. This has proved puzzling to commentators. In the *Summa Theologica* St Thomas Aquinas contrasts with Aristotle's Distributive Justice what he calls Commutative Justice, by which he means justice in exchange: ' . . . in commutation', he writes 'something is paid to an individual on account of something that has been received, as may be seen chiefly in selling and buying, where the notion of commutation is found primarily.'[11] In this way the distinction between justice in distribution and what in effect was justice in restitution and retribution, became transformed into a distinction between justice in distribution and justice in exchange. Aristotle's account of the latter in the *Nicomachean Ethics* is in terms of proportion, the number of shoes exchanged for a house being proportional to the shoemaker's value by relation to that of the builder.[12] Aristotle introduces into the discussion the concepts of needs and demand (*chreia*), of money, and the idea that exchange can only get started when each party lacks something that the other possesses. He points out that this

11. St Thomas Aquinas, *Summa Theologica*, IIaIIae Q61, Art. 2. Compare St Thomas Aquinas, *Summa Theologica, Complete English Edition*, tr. Fathers of the English Dominican Province, Westminster, MD: Christian Classics, 1981, volume 3, p. 1447.

12. *Nicomachean Ethics*, V.v. (1133a 20–25). 'As therefore a builder is to a shoemaker, so must such and such a number of shoes be to a house . . . .' Joachim writes: 'How exactly the values of the producers are to be determined, and what the ratio between them can mean is, I must confess, in the end unintelligible to me.' *The Nicomachean Ethics, a Commentary*, p. 150. W. F. R. Hardie writes: 'He does not make explicitly the point that, since prices are fixed by the market, the value of the producer is only a disguised form of the demand for his product.' *Aristotle's Ethical Theory*, Oxford: Clarendon Press, 1968, pp. 196–97.

can take place between countries as well as within them,[13] and that it is made possible by a readiness to exchange kindnesses which are not legally enforced. Joachim, after pointing out that according to Aristotle exchange value is determined by demand, and exchange is possible when two demands coincide, concludes: 'The reference to justice in exchange has disappeared. Aristotle is determining what is essential to exchange: not what exchange ought to be, i.e., not what an ideal exchange would be.'[14]

(b) In working out, then, the implications of rectificatory justice, Aristotle came to ask what is a just exchange, and answered this question by analogy with the proportionate equality of distributive justice, in terms of 'proportionate re-quital' (*hē antidosis hē kat' analogian*—this is closest to rectificatory justice and then 'proportionate reciprocation' (*to antipeponthos kat' analogian*).[15] He then went on to analyse the nature of exchange and the conditions under which a price is determined. Why does he refer to a readiness to exchange kindnesses, underlined by a reference to the

13. *Nicomachean Ethics*, 1133b. The reference is to states which export wine and import corn.

14. *The Nicomachean Ethics, a Commentary*, p. 151.

15. The meaning of *to antipeponthos* (lit. 'acting in return') has been much discussed. See W. F. R. Hardie: *Aristotle's Ethical Theory*, pp. 198–201. But less has been said about *hē antidosis* (lit. 'giving back in return'). It may be worth mentioning, however, that the system of 'liturgies' (*leitourgiai*), by which a rich man called upon to perform some public duty at his own expense, was allowed to offer some other rich man who was not being asked to contribute, the alternatives of exchanging his property with him or performing the duty in question at his own expense. This was called the *antidosis*. Here the relative wealth of the two men, which would determine the distributive justice of which of them was to perform the public duty, is, so to say, revealed in the response of the one man to the challenge of the other. Presumably it was regarded as distributively just for the richer man to bear the expenses of the public duty and was believed that his attitude towards the proposed exchange would show whether he was or considered himself to be richer or poorer.

statue to the Graces? Perhaps he means that the Graces preside over the process of endeavouring to reach an exchange-bargain. The law comes in if there is dispute about whether a bargain was actually made or about its terms if it was. But in the majority of cases the buyer and seller are satisfied, and this is possible because they recognize a common interest. The idea perhaps is that a friendly readiness to give and take is a presupposition of economic exchange, without which every bargain would be a matter of legal dispute. We might take the idea a little further and say that economic exchange as a continuing institution presupposes trust between the parties.

(*viii*) Having, in the *Nicomachean Ethics*, worked out an only partially ethical theory of exchange from what began as an account of rectificatory justice, in the *Politics* (Book I, Chapters viii–xi) Aristotle sketched the outlines of a special science of wealth, the art of acquisition or 'chrematistic'. He distinguished between (*a*) producing, without the mediation of money, goods for consumption in the household; (*b*) producing goods for consumption but with the mediation of money; and (*c*) producing goods for the purpose of making as much money as possible. He recognizes the necessity for (*b*), which he calls 'the natural art of acquisition', (I, viii, §15) but deplores (*c*), which, he says, 'is not natural, but the product of a certain sort of experience or skill' (1257a). (*c*) is unnatural because the articles produced are not produced for use but for the making of money. Production for use has a limit, which is the satisfaction of the demand of the users, but the search for money has no limit, 'and all who are engaged in acquisition increase their fund of currency without any limit or pause' (1257b), and act as if 'to make money were the one aim and everything else must contribute to that aim' (1258a). The most unnatural use of money is to lend it at interest (1258b). In this way ethics came back into Aristotle's account of exchange, and was kept there by later adherents of his theory. According to St Thomas (Part II-II, Q. 78. Art. 1) the purpose of money is to facilitate the exchange of goods; if, therefore, it is lent at interest, it is not being used for its proper and natural purpose of buying and selling goods, and hence it is being used 'unlawfully'. Marx, in his *Critique of Political Economy*, I, ch. 2 (3) (1859) and *Capital*, vol. I, Part II, ch. 4 (1867) expressly takes over from Aristotle the view that money is being used unnaturally when production is for the purpose of obtaining and accumulating it. If M stands for money and C for commodities, the right sequence of economic operations, according to Marx, is C-M-C, and the wrong or unnatural sequence is M-C-M. It should be noticed, however, that this criticism of a money-oriented economy is not that it is unjust but that it is unnatural (perverted) and based on greed.

(ix) The Roman Catholic theory of a Just Price is another development of Aristotle's account of money. St Thomas held that to seek for immoderate profit is wrong, but that if profit is sought for some legal end, or for an end that is good for the community, it may be just. Thus, a seller of goods may have it in mind that they are needed by the community at large and make them available for sale; then his profit may be regarded as 'the remuneration for his work'.[16] It was later argued that when buyer and seller agreed on a price in an orderly market where the mode of life of seller and buyer were traditionally fixed in a reasonable way, the price that emerged would be a just one.[17] A. San-

16. *Summa Theologica*, IIaIIae Q.LXXVII, Art. 4, volume 3, page 1511 of English translation.
17. A. Dauphin-Meunier, *La Doctrine Économique de l'Église*, Paris: Nouvelles éditions latines, 1959, pp. 146–50.

doz, utilising ideas of sixteenth century moral theologians
such as Cajetan, argued later that in effect a just price is the
market price established in a free market for the goods in
question.[18] Catholic critics of this view, however, have argued that markets are never perfectly free, are always affected by the activities of the state, and are often unjustly
'managed' by the governments of democratic countries. To
be just, prices should reflect the common valuation reached
by expert collective estimates so as to cover costs with a just
profit and enable customers to satisfy their legitimate
needs.[19] The view, it will be seen, has vacillated between
support for a free market in which moral requirements exert their influence through demand, and a sort of corpora-
tive system in which the various interests make agreements
with one another. It should be noticed, too, that St Thomas's
idea that profit is remuneration for work done would be the
death of capitalist enterprise in which profit is the residue
kept by the entrepreneur after he has taken the risks of
making the goods available. Profits therefore, are 'unlimited', in the sense that they might be anything or might not
be forthcoming at all. They are 'unlimited' because they are
problematic and because the hopes of energetic and imagi-
native men tend to run high.

[**III**]

(*i*) The phrase 'invisible hand' is, of course, Adam Smith's.
He uses it in *The Theory of Moral Sentiments* (1759) and then

---

18. A. Sandoz, 'La notion de juste prix', *Revue Thomiste*, XLV, 1939, pp. 285–
305. Sandoz's article is quoted and discussed in the work of Dauphin-Meunier.
19. Dauphin-Meunier, *La Doctrine Économique de l'Église* pp. 168–71.

in *The Wealth of Nations* (1776). Let us consider what he means by it in these passages.[20]

Part IV, Chapter I of *The Theory of Moral Sentiments* is headed: 'Of the Beauty which the appearance of utility bestows upon all the productions of art, and of the extensive influence of this species of Beauty.' Smith here makes a contrast between the sanguine view a man takes of wealth and luxury when he first thinks of going in pursuit of it, and the toil he undertakes in pursuing it and the disappointments and inconveniences he suffers even when he has obtained it. 'He is enchanted', Smith writes 'with the distant idea of this felicity', but 'if in the extremity of old age he should at last attain to it, he will find [it] to be in no respect preferable to that humble security and contentment which he had abandoned for it.' 'Power and riches', he goes on 'appear then to be, what they are, enormous and operose[21] machines contrived to produce a few trifling conveniences to the body, consisting of springs the most nice and delicate, which must be kept in order with the most anxious attention, and which in spite of all our care are ready every moment to burst into pieces, and to crush in their ruins their unfortunate possessor.' But, he continues, 'It is this deception which rouses and keeps in continual motion the industry of mankind.' It is this deception, too, which has 'changed the whole face of the globe'; and there follows a passage

20. [Adam Smith, *The Theory of Moral Sentiments*, Glasgow edition, Indianapolis: Liberty Fund, 1984. The quotations in the text are from pages: 179, 181, 181, 182–3, 183, 183, 183, 184, 184, and 184–5.]

21. Bernard Mandeville, *The Fable of the Bees, or Private Vices Publick Benefits*, uses the phrase 'operose contrivances' in remark (L) on the lines:

'whilst Luxury
Employ'd a Million of the Poor.'

Compare *The Fable of the Bees*, ed. Kaye, Indianapolis: Liberty Fund, 1988, p. 119.

translated almost verbatim from Rousseau's *Discours sur l'Origine de l'Inegalité parmi les Hommes* (1755) about turning forests into 'agreeable and fertile plains'.[22] The owner of all these fields of wheat, Smith continues, cannot consume them all himself, even though he would like to. 'The capacity of his stomach bears no proportion to the immensity of his desires, and will receive no more than that of the meanest peasant.' Apart from what the landowner eats himself, the rest of the crop is sold to pay those who fit up his palace and supply his other luxuries.[23] These tradesmen, therefore, benefit from his 'luxury and caprice' and would have obtained less 'from his humanity or his justice'. Agricultural production keeps alive the population it can support. 'The rich only select from the heap[24] what is most precious and agreeable. They consume little more than the poor, and in spite of their natural selfishness and rapacity, though they mean only their own conveniency, though the sole end which they propose from the labours of all the thousands whom they employ, be the gratification of their own vain and insatiable desires, they divide with the poor the produce of all their improvements. They are led by an invisible

22. [Jean-Jacques Rousseau, *A Discourse on the Origin of Inequality*, in *The Social Contract and Discourses*, tr. and intro. G. D. H. Cole, revised and augmented by J. H. Brumfit and John C. Hall, London: Dent, 1973, p. 83. For discussion of this suggestion of Acton's, see the editorial note on pp. 183–4 of *The Theory of Moral Sentiments*, Glasgow edition.]

23. Mandeville, op. cit., Remark K, on 'Prodigality, that noble sin', which he describes as 'that agreeable good nature'd Vice that makes the Chimney smoke and all the Tradesmen smile'. Compare Kaye edition, p. 103.

24. William Paley, too, in *The Principles of Moral and Political Philosophy*, 1785, uses the simile of a heap and compares men with pigeons pecking from it. But his attitude is very different from Smith's. 'If you should see a flock of pigeons in a field of corn . . . you should see ninety-nine of them gathering all they got, into a heap; reserving nothing for themselves, but the chaff and the refuse; keeping this heap for one, and that the weakest, perhaps worst, pigeon of the flock . . . ' (III,I.1). Compare *The Works of William Paley D.D.*, Edinburgh: University Press for Thomas Nelson and Peter Brown, 1828, pp. 22–3.

hand to make nearly the same distribution of the necessaries of life, which would have been made, had the earth been divided into equal portions among all its inhabitants, and thus without intending it, without knowing it, advance the interest of the society, and afford means to the multiplication of the species. When Providence divided the earth among a few lordly masters, it neither forgot nor abandoned those who seemed to have been left out in the partition. These last too enjoy their share of all that it produces. In what constitutes the real happiness of human life, they are in no respect inferior to those who would seem so much above them. In ease of body and peace of mind, all the different ranks of life are nearly upon a level, and the beggar, who suns himself by the side of the highway, possesses that security which kings are fighting for.' Although roads, trade, manufacture, Smith goes on, and 'the great system of government', are means towards the happiness of individuals, which is 'their sole use and end', many of those who engage in attempts to improve them do so 'from a certain love of art and contrivance', from 'a view to perfect and improve a certain beautiful and orderly system', rather than from love or sympathy for mankind. Peter the Great, for example, had little 'humanity' but great 'public spirit'. A public-spirited man is concerned to remove the hindrances to his country and its constitution, 'to put into motion so beautiful and so orderly a machine', rather than to augment the happiness of the subjects.

(*ii*) There are a number of distinct strands in this argument. (*a*) First and foremost Smith is drawing a contrast between what moves people to action and what they 'intend' on the one hand, and what they succeed in obtaining for themselves, for other men, or for society as a whole, on the other. A man who pursues wealth as a means to happiness

finds it a great burden to keep and maintain when he has
it. A greedy landowner would like to eat all the produce of
his estates himself, but cannot possibly do so, and most of it
is consumed by his labourers. Some public-spirited men are
not concerned for the happiness of their fellows but pursue
a certain sort of aesthetic tidiness.

(*b*) The deceptions of avarice, then, lead ambitious men to
clear forests, launch ships, and augment the products of
industry, and as an unintended result a larger population
can enjoy some of the good things of life. Clearing the forests
was intended, other peoples' enjoyments were not. But a
further achievement of the invisible hand, indeed, the
achievement actually mentioned in the sentence in which
the expression 'invisible hand' occurs, is that it brings about
a nearly equal distribution of 'the necessaries of life' or perhaps of 'the earth'. Rich men in pursuit of their own enjoyment produce a result close to what a distributor trying to
secure equality would deliberately bring about. Nature left
to itself, we may add in elaboration of what Smith says, will
bring about a large measure of equality. Quesnay's *Tableau
Économique* had appeared in 1758 and his article *Grains* in
the *Encyclopédie* the year before that, and Smith's discussion may show their influence at this point.[25] In the article
Grains Quesnay writes: 'It is the source of the subsistence
of men [i.e., agriculture] which is the basis of wealth. It is
industry which prepares it for the use of men. In order
to enjoy [i.e., consume] it the landowners pay for the work
industry has done; in this way their incomes become com-

---

25. Professor D. D. Raphael has given me reasons for toning down what I
said about the influence of Quesnay in the paper as read, and Professor A.
Mcfie has made it clear in correspondence that Smith at this time probably got
his idea of the spread of wealth from Mandeville rather than from Quesnay.

mon to all men—*leurs revenus deviennent communs à tous les hommes.*'[26]

(*c*) Another strand in Smith's argument is the idea that unambitious plain living is a hindrance to the economic development of society. Here Mandeville seems to have led the way with the following passage from *The Fable of the Bees*:

> Still Peace and Plenty reign,
> And every Thing is cheap, tho' plain:
> Kind Nature, free from Gard'ners Force,
> Allows all Fruits in her own Course.
> But Rarities cannot be had,
> Where pains to get 'em are not paid.[27]

(*d*) In II (ii)(a) above it was said that virtuous actions tend to have good effects on others, and that this tendency 'is not purely contingent', since honesty, generosity, etc. entail doing good to others or at least refraining from harming them. Now, however, we have the suggestion that 'selfishness and rapacity', which are vices, can have good results, not merely on some few unusual occasions, but quite widely. How, we may ask, can vices lead to good results in a way in which virtues cannot except rarely lead to bad ones? In answer to this I suggest that Mandeville, with his 'Private Vices', and Smith, with his 'selfishness and rapacity', have used misleadingly paradoxical language. The virtues opposed to 'selfishness and rapacity' are, I suggest, benevolence and generosity, and the possessor of them necessarily helps others. Selfishness and rapacity may be understood as vices

26. [Compare F. Quesnay, *Oeuvres économiques et philosophiques de F. Quesnay*, ed. A. Oncken, Frankfurt S. M.: J. Baer, and Paris: J. Peelman, 1888; see p. 234.]

27. [Mandeville, *Fable of the Bees*, Kaye edition, p. 34.]

which necessarily injure others, and that is the ordinary usage. On the other hand, a regard for one's own interests and a desire to provide and extend them further do not necessarily injure others, and the former might be described as selfishness and the latter as rapacity. The idea that greed can help mankind is somewhat paradoxical, the idea that prudence and honest ambition can do so is not.

(*iii*) The other passage in which the 'invisible hand' is mentioned is Book IV, Chapter II of *The Wealth of Nations*, entitled 'Of Restraints upon the Importation from foreign Countries of such Goods as can be produced at Home'. Smith's general argument is that tariffs and prohibitions on the export of capital are detrimental to the growth of the national wealth. Entrepreneurs will generally prefer to invest at home and know better than governments what is likely to be profitable.[28] 'By preferring the support of domestic to that of foreign industry, he intends only his own security; and by directing that industry in such manner as its produce may be of the greatest value, he intends only his own gain, and he is in this, as in many other cases, led by an invisible hand to promote an end which was no part of his intention. . . . By pursuing his own interest he frequently promotes that of the society more effectually than when he really intends to promote it.'

(*a*) The man who is 'led' here by the invisible hand is not the same man as in *The Theory of Moral Sentiments*. In the earlier book there are really two men: first the man who is deceived into becoming rich by false ideas of the happiness of rich men; this man promotes trade and industry. Then there is the rich man, probably a landowner, who

28. [Adam Smith, *The Wealth of Nations*, Glasgow edition, IV.ii, Indianapolis: Liberty Fund, 1982, pp. 452, 456, and 456.]

through his extravagant expenditures, divides out the 'necessaries of life' much as they would have been distributed by someone seeking to establish equality. The influence of Quesnay's views on the circulation of wealth may be present here. In *The Wealth of Nations*, however, there is an entrepreneur, who may be neither rich nor extravagant, considering how to invest his money. If he invests it as he thinks fit, with a view to his own maximum profit, he will do more for the national wealth than if he were told what to do with it by the government. He is not aiming to add to the national wealth, but will do so if left alone.

(*b*) According to Adam Smith 'every individual necessarily labours to render the annual revenue of the society as high as he can'. We need not suppose that he uses the word 'necessarily' precisely as a logician of our own day would, but it does appear that he is making the arithmetical point that the profit he makes and seeks is part of the national income. It is a necessary truth, therefore, that an individual who makes a profit which he aimed to make augments the national wealth which he did not aim to augment.

(*c*) Adam Smith also argues that the national wealth will gain more from allowing individual entrepreneurs to invest as they please than from a system of tariffs and prohibitions. His argument, as I understand it, rests upon the proposition that entrepreneurs know more about the market than government officials do. If this were not so, the argument would fail, so that there is at any rate an important element of contingency in it.

(*d*) A follower of Quesnay, Le Mercier de la Rivière,[29] gives

29. Le Mercier de la Rivière, *L'ordre naturel et essential des sociétés politiques,* 1767, volume 2, p. 447–8. Compare the edition by E. Depitre, Paris: P. Geuthner, 1910, p. 338.

an example of a fundamental relationship in the economic system which is necessary. He argues that the entrepreneur, in endeavouring to sell more goods is at the same time endeavouring 'to enlarge the mass of enjoyments which he can provide for other men'. This is so because what for him is something sold for profit, for the other party is something he buys because he wants it and finds the price acceptable. The necessity here results from an identity. Around this necessity, however, contingencies may cluster. In conditions of scarcity, for example, a seller may sell to the buyer what the buyer doesn't very much want but has to take *faute de mieux*. Sellers, too, can conceal from buyers defects which they would not wish to buy. Sellers who are intent on profits, however, *must* to some extent provide what the buyers want. Sellers selling what they think is good for the buyers do not have to do so.

(*iv*) At this point something must be said about the concept of 'unintended consequences'. If consequences are regarded as effects, the connection between them and their causes is contingent to the extent that causal connections are. Sir Karl Popper introduced the idea of unintended consequences in his *The Poverty of Historicism*, where, in discussing the dangers of 'Utopian Engineering', he wrote that the 'piecemeal' reformer must be 'always on the look-out for the unavoidable unwanted consequences of any reform'. He also here refers to 'their unintended and largely unexpected repercussions', and he uses this word in *The Open Society*, viz., 'unintended social repercussions'. In both books he also writes of 'indirect' consequences, and of 'by-products'. In *Conjectures and Refutations* he explains that '*nothing ever comes off exactly as intended*' and says that the main task of the theoretical social sciences is '*to trace the unintended social repercussions of international human actions*'.[30] Use of such words as repercussions and 'by-products' indicates that Popper has in mind unintended *effects* of what people aim at, as when they start a war by something intended to prevent it. 'Unintended consequences' prevent the Utopian from carrying through his schemes, and we are reminded of Plato's lament that 'nothing is ever done as it is spoken'. I suggest that there is bound to be an element of the unintended in a society where there are individuals and groups seeking different ends and coming into conflict with one another. In cases of total victory of one party over another something must happen which one of the parties had not intended, and something must happen which no one had intended if there are compromises and accidents. All this fits in with the concept of 'by-products' (what I have elsewhere called 'social detritus'). The word 'repercussions' may mean this too, if we consider sound waves or the waves caused by a stone in a pond. But I wonder whether there are not what we could call *logical* repercussions or logical consequences as well. If, for example, legal polygamy were introduced into a hitherto legally monogamous society, the new law, even if permissive only, would have effects on human behaviour. Some of these would be intended, as when people began to contract polygamous marriages; others would be unintended, if, for example, monogamous marriages ceased altogether. But if some wives are to become one among several, income tax law and the law of inheritance would be 'affected', as would be said. But what does 'affected' mean

30. Karl Popper, *The Poverty of Historicism*, London: Routledge & Kegan Paul, 1957, pp. 67–8; *The Open Society and Its Enemies*, London: Routledge & Kegan Paul, fourth edition, 1962, volume 2, pp. 93 and 323, where Popper refers to conversations with K. Polanyi in 1924. *Conjectures and Refutations*, London: Routledge & Kegan Paul, 1963, pp. 124, 342.

here? If already existing legislation were to be left just as it had been, it would become enigmatic at the very least, since in it 'wife' would occur where it would now be appropriate to have 'wife or wives'. *Because* of this, if nothing were done to amend the other laws, administrative paralysis could result, and if it did, would certainly be a causal consequence. But that because of which the administrative paralysis would ensue is not a causal but a logical consequence of the new legislation. Such measures again, as extensions of the franchise have effects, some intended others unintended, upon the behaviour of the voters, but apart from and prior to these effects, they have made alterations in logical connections too. Changes in legislation present people with alternatives which were not there previously; which they take is contingent, that they had to take them is not. The phrase 'the logic of history' can be misleading but has some point as well.

[**IV**]

(*i*) Hegel's phrase 'the cunning of reason' appears at first to refer to something rather like Adam Smith's 'invisible hand'. Hegel uses this phrase in his *Lectures on the Philosophy of History*[31] in the course of a discussion of 'world-historical' individuals, men such as Caesar and Napoleon who broke through from a form of society which had exhausted itself to a new form which will develop in its turn. 'Caesar', Hegel writes 'knew that the Roman Republic was a lie and that

31. G. W. F. Hegel, *Die Vernunft der Geschichte*, ed. J. Hoffmeister, Hamburg, 1955, pp. 105ff. Compare Hegel, *Lectures on the Philosophy of World History: Introduction: Reason in History*, tr. N. B. Nisbet, Cambridge: Cambridge University Press, 1975, p. 89. The version in Lasson's edition of the *Lectures* appears in *Reason in History*, translated and edited by Robert S. Hartman, New York: The Liberal Arts Press, 1953, pp. 43–4.

Cicero was offering only empty talk and that another form would replace this hollow one, that the form he was bringing forward was necessary . . . it would tread down many innocent flowers and destroy much on its way'. Hegel goes on to say that out of the interests and passions of this particular individual a universal would be brought into activity. 'It is just in the struggle, the decline, of the particular that the universal results. This universal is not disturbed. It is not the universal Idea that is endangered; it remains in the background untouched and unharmed and sends the particular passionate being into battle (*schickt das Besondere der Leidenschaft in den Kampf*) to grind itself down. One can call it *the cunning of reason*, in that reason lets the passions work for it, and that through which it brings itself into existence suffers loss and harm. This it is which is a mere appearance of which part is mere negation, part an affirmation.' Hegel goes on to ask whether this devalues human beings by placing them under the category of means to an end, and his answer is that insofar as they share in morality (*Moralität*), moral life (*Sittlichkeit*) and religion, they are ends in themselves because reason, the divine, is then in them. A little further on Hegel says that the universal law is not designed to carry out the purposes of individuals, and that poets like Schiller have depicted, with melancholy, ideals which individuals have failed to realize. According to Hegel, however, the universal reason *does* actualize itself in history.

(*ii*) One element in this view is like one element in Smith's account of the 'invisible hand', viz. that an individual acting from personal ambition may bring about universal benefit. Hegel's world-historical individual, acting from passion, helps to destroy a form of life which he knows is exhausted (he acts from knowledge on the negative side) and to bring in a new and (presumably) better form of life which he cannot understand in advance of its development. His intention is personal and destructive, his achievement is universal and creative, his clear-sighted destruction is balanced by his blind effort of construction. Even here, however, there is the difference that many men succeed in becoming rich and in helping their fellows thereby, whereas there are only a few world-historical individuals, who appear only at turning-points in the history of the world.

(*iii*) The motivation of Hegel's world-historical individual is more like Adam Smith's ambitious man than like his entrepreneur. The ambitious man, according to Smith, may succeed in life, but he is generally unhappy and does good to others rather than to himself. Hegel's world-historical individual is unhappy too but (presumably) helps towards the establishment of a better society since the society he destroys was in decay. The world-historical individual is, so to say, the tool of reason in its development of world-history. Indeed, in his first sketch of the cunning of reason given in his Jena lectures in 1805–6, Hegel introduces the notion of cunning by the analogy of a tool by means of which, he says, the workman makes use of nature to overcome it, 'nature's own activity, the elasticity of the watch-spring, water, wind, are used in order that in their sensible existence they can do something different from what they wanted to do, that blind action made into something purposive'.[32] There is nothing far-fetched in linking this with Adam Smith's 'invisible hand'. In Hegel's lecture-notes it appears in the course of his discussion of will, impulse and desire, the fulfillment of impulses needing labour, labour requiring tools, and

32. Hegel, *Jenenser Realphilosophie II*, ed. Lasson, Leipzig, 1931, p. 198 (compare Hegel, *Jenaer Realphilosophie*, ed. J. Hoffmeister, Hamburg: Felix Meiner, 1967).

satisfied desire being 'destruction of the object' (i.e., consumption). Hegel's first account of the cunning of reason, therefore, occurs in the course of a discussion of the subjective element in production and consumption. In these notes he discussed exchange under the heading of 'actual mind', later described as 'objective mind'.

(*iv*) Another element in Hegel's concept of the cunning of reason is that material and animal nature is utilized by reason to realize a universal overriding purpose. The contingent is utilized by the necessary so that out of conflict comes justice. This is the 'Theodicaea' mentioned at the beginning of this paper. But Hegel's 'Theodicaea' is not a just outcome secured in a heaven beyond the world. We have seen that in *Die Vernunft in der Geschichte* Hegel refers to 'poets like Schiller' who write in a 'melancholy' way about the failure of unrealized ideals.[33] According to Hegel the 'universal reason' does get realized, and unrealized ideals cannot be fully rational. Hence, as regards human history, 'the history of the world' is 'the world's court of judgment'.[34] This passage in *The Philosophy of Right* (§340) utilizes a line from Schiller's poem *Resignation* (1785), from which Hegel quotes on a number of occasions, showing a prolonged and detailed interest in it. It is too complex to summarise here, but the culminating point is that a man who expects to receive a reward in heaven for his sacrifice of enjoyment here on earth—a widely held eighteenth-century attitude—is told that there is a choice between Hope and Enjoyment and both cannot be had. Let the man who can have Faith refrain from enjoyment.[35] 'The history of the world is the world's

33. [See *Lectures on the Philosophy of World History*, p. 66.]

34. [G. W. F. Hegel, *The Philosophy of Right*, tr. T. M. Knox, Oxford: Clarendon Press, 1942, pp. 215–16.]

35. [*Schillers Sämtliche Schriften*, volume 4, ed. Karl Goedeke, Stuttgart: F. G. Cotta'scher Verlag, 1868, pp. 27–30; and *Schiller's Complete Works*, ed. C. J.

court of judgement. You have had Hope, and hence your reward is settled. Your Faith was your allotted happiness . . . No Eternity gives back what the minute has struck out.' It will be seen that the idea here expressed is that each choice made here on earth has its costs and rewards here on earth, and there is no hope of some further repayment in the hereafter. Justice gets established in the course of human history as a whole. It should also be mentioned that Schiller's Inaugural Lecture as Professor of History at Jena in 1789 was entitled 'What is Universal History, and to what end is it studied?' and in the course of it he uses the word 'world-history' as well.[36] Among other things, the study of universal history, according to Schiller 'preserves us from an exaggerated admiration for the Ancient World and from a childish longing for past times'.

(v) The conclusion I should like to draw is that there is no conception of the achievement of distributive justice for society as a whole. Distributive justice requires a rule of distribution and a distributor, and the rule can only be obtained when the thing to be distributed is clearly distinguished and the distributor knows how to divide it. But even such relatively simple things as incomes or property present the distributor with the insoluble problems that arise from the clash between such different principles as those of need, output or effort. Furthermore, in the absence of a total picture of society as a whole there is no conception of an individual's contribution to it, i.e., of his total merit. The lack of this total picture is like the lack of a conception of history as

---

Hempel, Philadelphia: I. Kohler, 1881, volume 1, pp. 70–1.]

36. F. Schiller, *Was heisst und zu welchen Ende studiert man Universalgeschichte?*; also see *Schillers Sämtliche Schriften*, volume 9, ed. Wilhelm Müldener, Stuttgart: F. C. Cotta'scher Verlag, 1870, p. 99, and *Schiller's Complete Works*, ed. C. J. Hempel, Philadelphia: I. Kohler, 1881, volume 2, p. 352.]

a whole. If Popper is right, history is always the history of some selected topic or aspect, the notion of 'world-history' is incoherent, and hence the notion of the judgement of history is incoherent too. Thus the view that there is no conception of distributive justice in society as a whole goes along with the view that there is no universal history but only particular histories of aspects of society. What Schiller and Hegel called world-history is the history of states at war with one another, of what Popper calls power-politics. There is no way of putting together into a single universal history all the different descriptions and explanations of all the different types of deed, institution and product. The 'just society' is a doubly incoherent conception: there is no way of determining either the nature of the whole nor the nature of the distribution that would be necessary within it.

INDEX

This book was set in ITC Zapf Book, a typeface designed for the International Typeface Corporation by one of the world's foremost typeface designers, Hermann Zapf. The creator of Optima, Palatino, Melior, Aldus, and many other acclaimed typefaces, Hermann Zapf spent more than two years developing ITC Zapf Book as a family of four different weights of type with matching italics. The elegant letterforms are an artful blend of Walbaum, Melior, and Bodoni, distinguished by many subtle refinements. Hermann Zapf was born in 1918 in Nuremberg, Germany. Designer of more than forty typefaces, his first typeface design was marketed in 1940; ten years later, the first of the famous Palatino type family was introduced. All of his typefaces are characterized by exquisite design, quiet distinction, and innovation without eccentricity. Zapf's primary concern is never with single letters, but with their fusion with each other in a working text. To Zapf, "Type is the tie or ligature between author and reader."

Editorial services by BooksCraft, Inc., Indianapolis, Indiana
Book design by Hermann Strohbach, New York, New York
Composition by Shepard Poorman Communications Corporation, Indianapolis, Indiana
Index by Shirley Kessel, Primary Sources Research, Chevy Chase, Maryland
Printed and bound by Edwards Brothers, Inc., Ann Arbor, Michigan